AF585606

AC Targeting Maths

Year 3

Garda Turner

PASCAL
PRESS

Contents

Term 1

Term 2

Term 3

Term 4

New Edition

Targeting Maths Australia's Favourite Maths Program

Australian Curriculum Alignment

This NEW Edition fully aligns each student page with the new Australian Curriculum: Mathematics F-10 version 9.0. The new Australian Curriculum code and content descriptions appear on each student page.

iPad Apps

With an app for each year, from Foundation/Kindergarten to Year 6, the Targeting Maths Apps include all the essential maths content that children need to know in an amazing app that makes learning maths fun, motivating and full of rewards. Look for it in Apple's App Store today! Made especially for the iPad and aligned to each student page in this book.

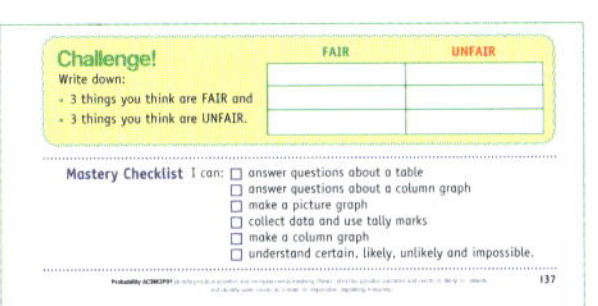

Challenge!
Write down:
- 3 things you think are FAIR and
- 3 things you think are UNFAIR.

FAIR	UNFAIR

Mastery Checklist I can:
- [ ] answer questions about a table
- [ ] answer questions about a column graph
- [ ] make a picture graph
- [ ] collect data and use tally marks
- [ ] make a column graph
- [ ] understand certain, likely, unlikely and impossible.

137

Mastery Checklists

Each unit has a Mastery Checklist. These checklists engage students in visible learning as they recognise and reflect on the specific maths skills learnt in each unit.

Integrated Problem-solving Program

Includes an integrated problem-solving program that actively builds students' problem-solving capabilities.

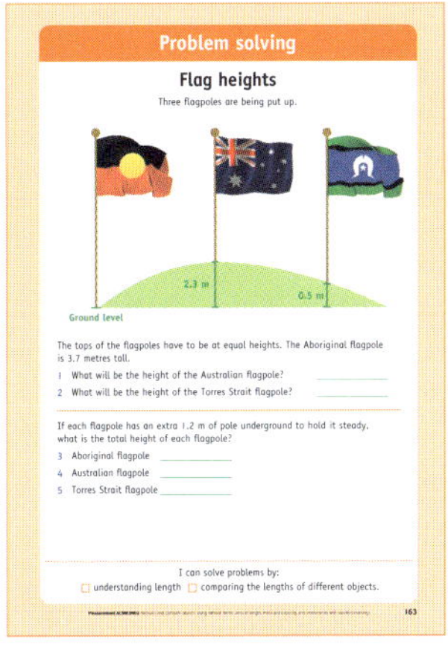

Problem solving

Flag heights

Three flagpoles are being put up.

The tops of the flagpoles have to be at equal heights. The Aboriginal flagpole is 3.7 metres tall.

1 What will be the height of the Australian flagpole?

2 What will be the height of the Torres Strait flagpole?

If each flagpole has an extra 1.2 m of pole underground to hold it steady, what is the total height of each flagpole?

3 Aboriginal flagpole

4 Australian flagpole

5 Torres Strait flagpole

I can solve problems by:
- [ ] understanding length
- [ ] comparing the lengths of different objects.

163

In-stage Topic Alignment for Composite Classes

Great for composite classes too, the contents of each book in one stage, eg Year 3 and Year 4, match topic by topic.

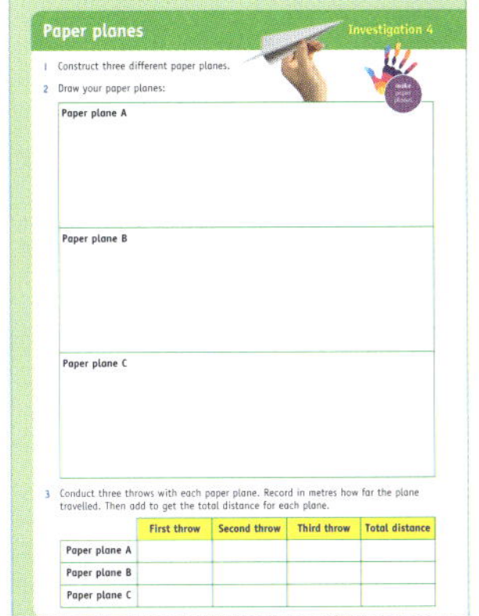

Paper planes — Investigation 4

1 Construct three different paper planes.

2 Draw your paper planes:

Paper plane A

Paper plane B

Paper plane C

3 Conduct three throws with each paper plane. Record in metres how far the plane travelled. Then add to get the total distance for each plane.

	First throw	Second throw	Third throw	Total distance
Paper plane A				
Paper plane B				
Paper plane C				

164

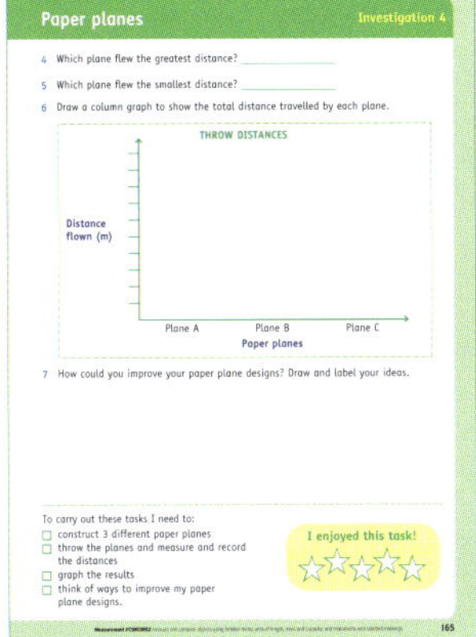

Paper planes — Investigation 4

4 Which plane flew the greatest distance?

5 Which plane flew the smallest distance?

6 Draw a column graph to show the total distance travelled by each plane.

7 How could you improve your paper plane designs? Draw and label your ideas.

To carry out these tasks I need to:
- [ ] construct 3 different paper planes
- [ ] throw the planes and measure and record the distances
- [ ] graph the results
- [ ] think of ways to improve my paper plane designs.

I enjoyed this task!

165

Term Investigations

Each term includes an investigation that will get students planning and working through an extended problem.

Regular Revision

Revision pages appear both at mid term and at the end of each term to revise key concepts.

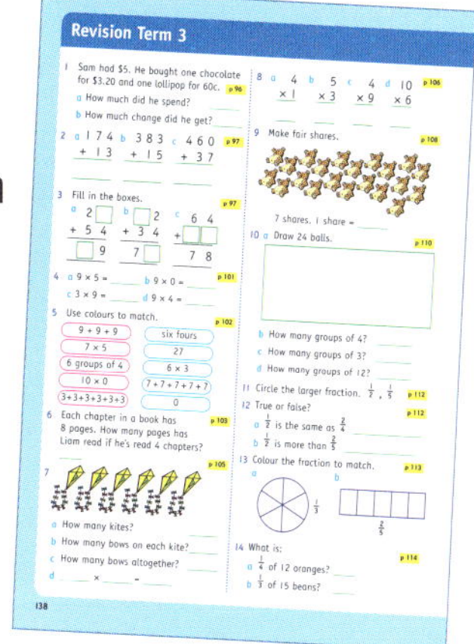

Revision Term 3

1 Sam had $5. He bought one chocolate for $3.20 and one lollipop for 60c.
a How much did he spend?
b How much change did he get?

3 Fill in the boxes.

5 Use colours to match.

6 Each chapter in a book has 8 pages. How many pages has Liam read if he's read 4 chapters?

9 Make four shares.

10 a Draw 24 balls.

11 Circle the larger fraction.

12 True or false?

13 Colour the fraction to match.

14 What is:

138

Hands-on Activities

Various hands-on activities are included in each term, asking students to measure and make, count and compare, using objects from around the classroom or home.

Year 3 Outcomes

	Australian Curriculum Content Descriptions *Students learn to:*	Student pages
NUMBER & ALGEBRA	**Number**	
	AC9M3N01 recognise, represent and order natural numbers using naming and writing conventions for numerals beyond 10 000	2, 3, 4, 5, 6, 7, 8, 10, 15, 57, 58, 59, 140, 143, 144
	AC9M3N02 recognise and represent unit fractions including $\frac{1}{2}$, $\frac{1}{3}$, $\frac{1}{4}$, $\frac{1}{5}$ and $\frac{1}{10}$ and their multiples in different ways; combine fractions with the same denominator to complete the whole	20, 21, 22, 23, 71, 72, 73, 96, 108, 112, 113, 114, 115, 156, 157, 158
	AC9M3N03 add and subtract two- and three-digit numbers using place value to partition, rearrange and regroup numbers to assist in calculations without a calculator	7, 11, 12, 14, 15, 16, 56, 57, 65, 66, 67, 68, 69, 97, 99, 100, 168
	AC9M3N04 multiply and divide one- and two-digit numbers, representing problems using number sentences, diagrams and arrays, and using a variety of calculation strategies	60, 62, 103, 106, 107, 108, 109, 110, 111, 148, 149, 151, 152, 153, 154, 155, 169
	AC9M3N05 estimate the quantity of objects in collections and make estimates when solving problems to determine the reasonableness of calculations	56, 74, 75, 86, 87, 88, 141, 142
	AC9M3N06 use mathematical modelling to solve practical problems involving additive and multiplicative situations including financial contexts; formulate problems using number sentences and choose calculation strategies, using digital tools where appropriate; interpret and communicate solutions in terms of the situation	13, 23, 68, 70, 78, 80, 81, 89, 98, 100, 101, 104, 105, 106, 107, 108, 109, 111, 114, 145, 146, 147, 152, 153, 154, 155
	AC9M3N07 follow and create algorithms involving a sequence of steps and decisions to investigate numbers; describe any emerging patterns	6, 8, 9, 28, 29, 30, 31, 61, 62, 82, 83, 84, 85, 120, 121, 122, 123, 150, 168, 170
	Algebra	
	AC9M3A01 recognise and explain the connection between addition and subtraction as inverse operations, apply to partition numbers and find unknown values in number sentences	14, 63, 64, 69, 70, 123, 169
	AC9M3A02 extend and apply knowledge of addition and subtraction facts to 20 to develop efficient mental strategies for computation with larger numbers without a calculator	9, 10, 16, 17, 63, 64, 65, 66, 67, 84
	AC9M3A03 recall and demonstrate proficiency with multiplication facts for 3, 4, 5 and 10; extend and apply facts to develop the related division facts	60, 61, 62, 85, 101, 102, 103, 104, 105, 145, 146, 147, 148, 149, 150, 151
MEASUREMENT & GEOMETRY	**Measurement**	
	AC9M3M01 identify which metric units are used to measure everyday items; use measurements of familiar items and known units to make estimates	18, 19, 24, 25, 89, 129, 130, 159
	AC9M3M02 measure and compare objects using familiar metric units of length, mass and capacity, and instruments with labelled markings	17, 18, 19, 24, 25, 74, 75, 86, 87, 88, 128, 130, 131, 159, 160, 161, 162, 163, 164, 165
	AC9M3M03 recognise and use the relationship between formal units of time including days, hours, minutes and seconds to estimate and compare the duration of events	90, 91, 133, 174
	AC9M3M04 describe the relationship between the hours and minutes on analogue and digital clocks, and read the time to the nearest minute	32, 33, 34, 35, 91, 132, 133, 174
	AC9M3M05 identify angles as measures of turn and compare angles with right angles in everyday situations	171, 172, 173
	AC9M3M06 recognise the relationships between dollars and cents and represent money values in different ways	11, 79, 80, 81, 96, 99
	Space	
	AC9M3SP01 make, compare and classify objects, identifying key features and explaining why these features make them suited to their uses	36, 37, 38, 39, 40
	AC9M3SP02 interpret and create two-dimensional representations of familiar environments, locating key landmarks and objects relative to each other	124, 125, 126, 127, 175, 176, 177, 178, 179
STATISTICS & PROBABILITY	**Statistics**	
	AC9M3ST01 acquire data for categorical and discrete numerical variables to address a question of interest or purpose by observing, collecting and accessing data sets; record the data using appropriate methods including frequency tables and spreadsheets	41, 42, 92, 93, 116, 117, 134, 136
	AC9M3ST02 create and compare different graphical representations of data sets including using software where appropriate; interpret the data in terms of the context	41, 42, 93, 116, 117, 135, 136
	AC9M3ST03 conduct guided statistical investigations involving the collection, representation and interpretation of data for categorical and discrete numerical variables with respect to questions of interest	43, 116, 117, 135, 136
	Probability	
	AC9M3P01 identify practical activities and everyday events involving chance; describe possible outcomes and events as 'likely' or 'unlikely' and identify some events as 'certain' or 'impossible' explaining reasoning	44, 45, 137, 180, 181
	AC9M3P02 conduct repeated chance experiments; identify and describe possible outcomes, record the results, recognise and discuss the variation	45, 180, 181

How to Solve a Problem

Read • Plan • Work • Check

Read the problem carefully. Underline the question. Circle the facts.

Plan what you will do: +, –, × (multiply) or ÷ (divide).

Work Write or draw a diagram to work it out. Write the answer.

Check your answer! Make sure that your answer makes sense.

Draw a diagram

Draw a simple picture.
Use symbols if you can.

12 – 5 = 7

3 × 4 = 12

Trial and Error

Make a guess and write it down. Check if it is right. If not, work out if your guess should be higher or lower. Make another guess and write it down. Check if it's right. Keep going until you have the correct answer.

Look for patterns

Study the numbers in the problem.
Write them down in a list.
Can you see a pattern?
What comes next in the pattern?
Write it as your answer.

Bundy runs 2 km, then 4 km, then 6 km on 3 days. How far should he run on the 4th day to keep to his pattern?

2, 4, 6, ?　　2, 4, 6, 8

Bundy should run 8 km.

Use a table

Put the information from the problem in columns. Can you see the pattern? The information is clearer in a table.

Use this to work out the answer.

Jerry	5 mins	10 cakes	2 in 1 min.
Cam	4 mins	8 cakes	2 in 1 min.
Tilly	3 mins	9 cakes	3 in 1 min.

Who eats the fastest?

Answer: Tilly eats fastest.

Work backwards

Read the problem all the way through. Find one piece of information. Write it down. Find another piece of information that relates and put them together. Write it down. Keep working backwards until you solve all the pieces of the problem.

Kell has \$2 more than Greg, who has \$3 less than Dee. Dee has \$5. How much do they each have?

Dee = \$5

Greg = \$5 – \$3 = \$2

Kell = \$2 + \$2 = \$4

Dictionary

am (ante meridiem)
The time from midnight to midday

angle
The amount of turning between two lines that meet at a point

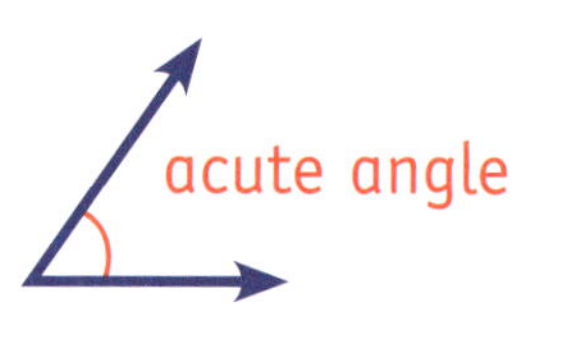

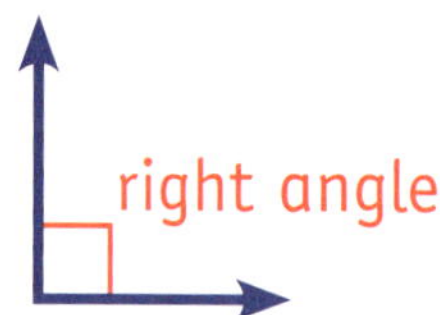

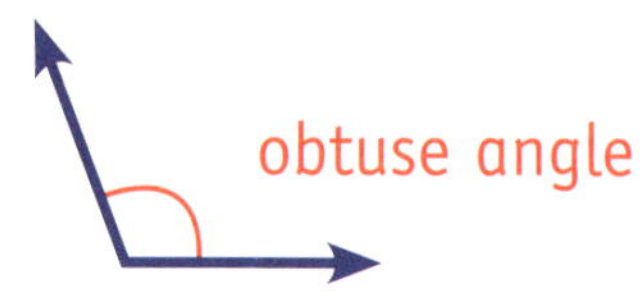

ascending order
In order from smallest to largest

1, 7, 11, 19, 32

capacity
The amount a container can hold

The capacity of this bottle is 1 litre.

centimetre (cm)
A unit of length
10 mm = 1 cm
100 cm = 1 m

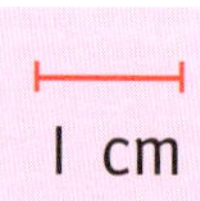

certain
Something that is definite.
It will happen.

cone
A solid shape that tapers to a point and has a circular base

cube
A solid shape which has six square faces

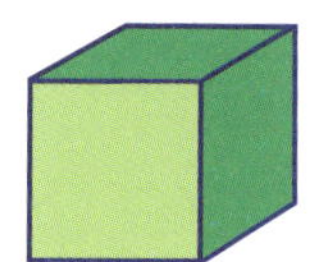

cylinder
A solid shape which has two circular ends and a curved surface

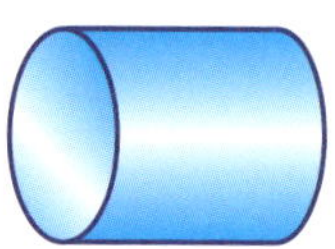

data
A collection of information

Favourite sports		
Sport	**Votes**	**Total**
Soccer		12
Netball		6
Football		8
Chess		11

decimal number
A number that has a decimal point

eg 0·3, 75·16

descending order
In order from largest to smallest

96, 84, 61, 37, 11

diagonal
A line that joins two corners in a polygon but does not make a side

digit
The numerals that are used to write numbers: 0, 1, 2, 3, 4, 5, 6, 7, 8, 9

Dictionary

division (÷)

Sharing into equal groups

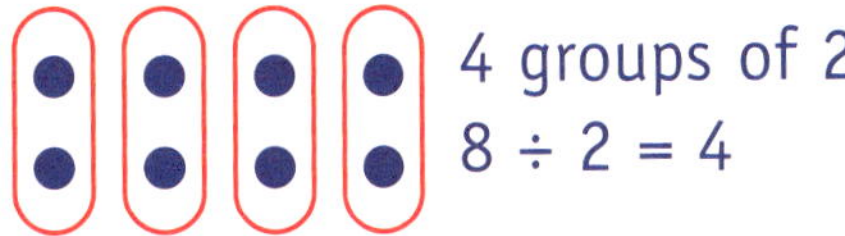

edge

Where two surfaces meet

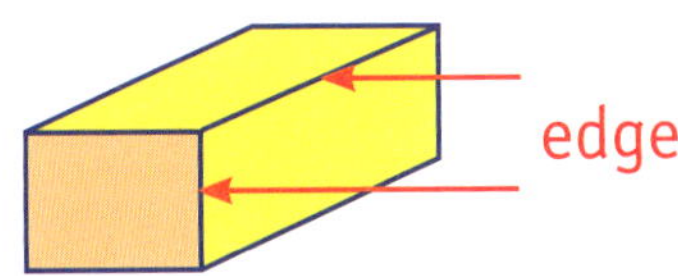

face

A flat surface of a solid shape

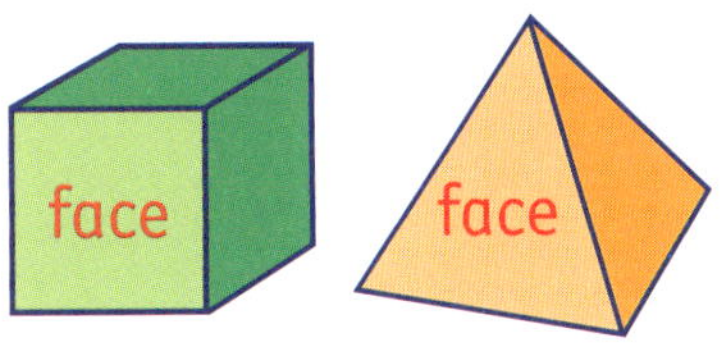

fraction

A part of a whole or a group

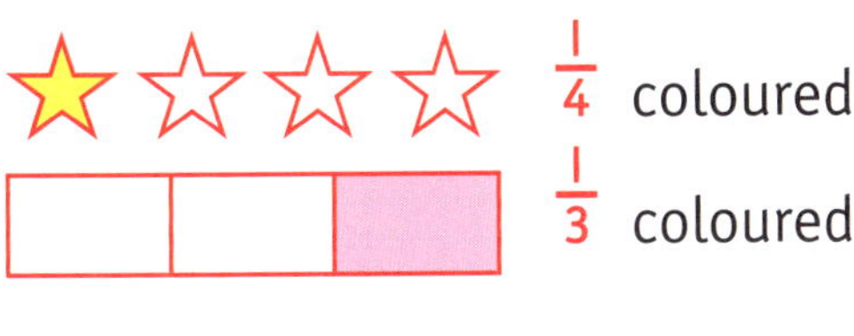

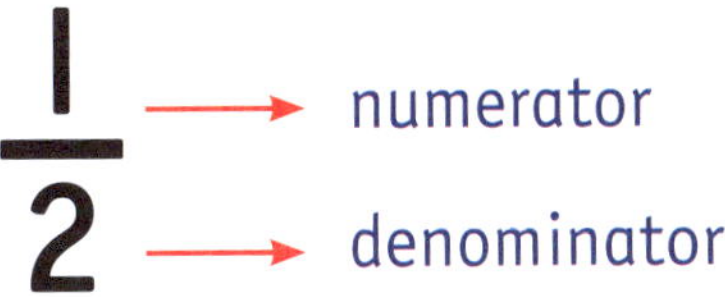

graph

A diagram that shows a collection of data

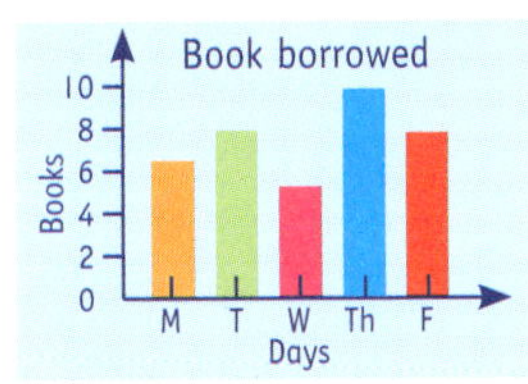

column graph

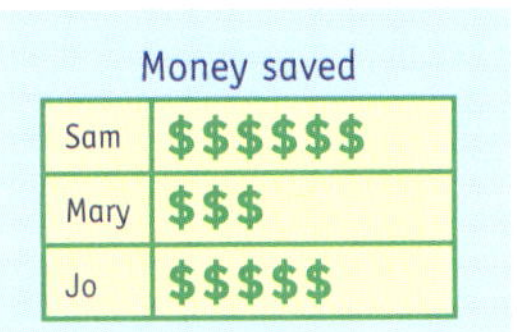

picture graph

hexagon

A 2D shape with 6 straight sides

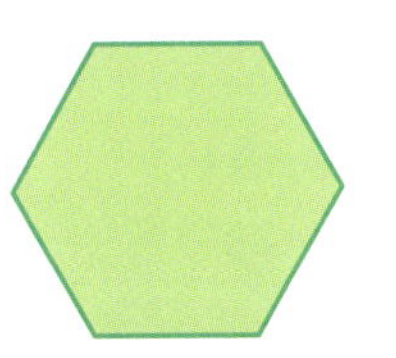

regular hexagon

irregular hexagon

kilogram (kg)

A unit of mass for weighing things

1 kilogram = 1000 grams

1000 kilograms = 1 tonne

line

straight line

parallel lines

curved line

litre (L)

A unit of capacity

1 L = 1000 millilitres (mL)

mass

The amount of material that makes up an object. Measured in grams, kilograms and tonnes.

metre (m)

A unit of length

1 m = 100 cm

1000 m = 1 km

millimetre (mm)

A unit of length

10 mm = 1 cm

Dictionary

multiplication (×)

Find the total of a number of equal groups or equal rows

5 × 4 = 20

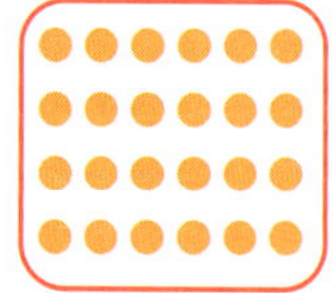

4 × 6 = 24

octagon

A 2D shape with 8 straight sides

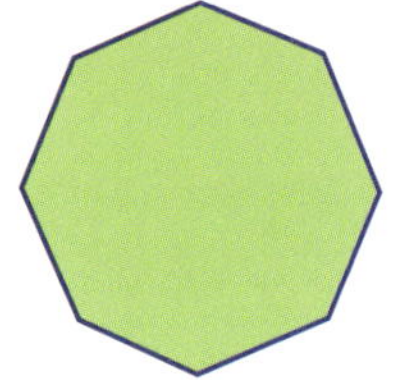

regular octagon

irregular octagon

parallelogram

A quadrilateral with opposite sides parallel

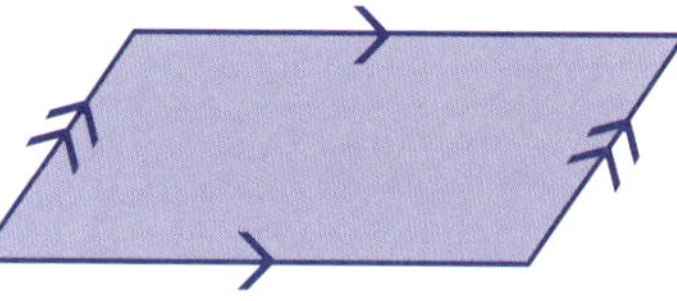

pentagon

A 2D shape with 5 straight sides

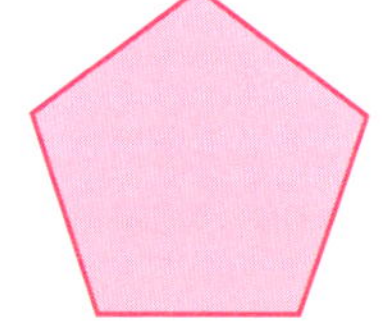

regular pentagon

irregular pentagon

place value

The value of a numeral depending on its position in a number

396 = 300 + 90 + 6

754 = 7 hundreds + 5 tens + 4 ones

8·57 = 8 ones + 5 tenths + 7 hundredths

pm (post meridiem)

The time from midday to midnight

polygon

A shape with 3 or more straight sides

eg

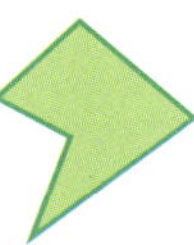

prism

A 3D shape with identical ends. All other faces are rectangles. The ends give a prism its name.

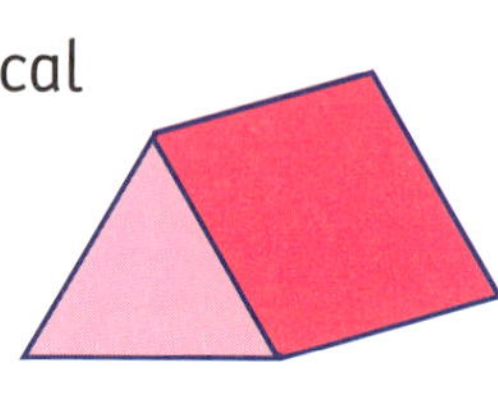

triangular prism

probability

The chance of something happening, eg certain, impossible, likely, unlikely.

product

When numbers are multiplied, the answer is called the product.

pyramid

A 3D object with one flat base. All other faces are triangles coming to a point at the apex. The base shape gives a pyramid its name.

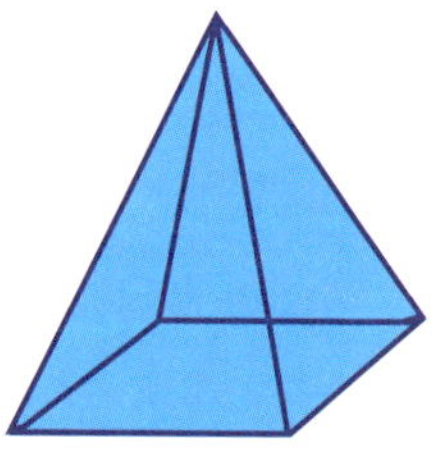

square pyramid

quadrilateral

A 2D shape with 4 straight sides

Dictionary

rhombus

A quadrilateral with all sides equal and opposite sides parallel. It is a special parallelogram.

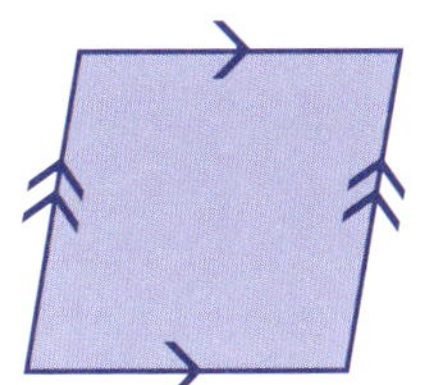

rounding (to nearest 10)

0 Round down ← 1 2 3 4 | 5 6 7 8 9 → Round up 0

eg 675 → 700
(rounded to the nearest 100)
4492 → 4000
(rounded to the nearest 1000)

tally

Count and record in groups of 5

𝍸 = 5 𝍸 𝍸 || = 12

three-dimensional objects (3D)

Solid shapes that have length, width and height

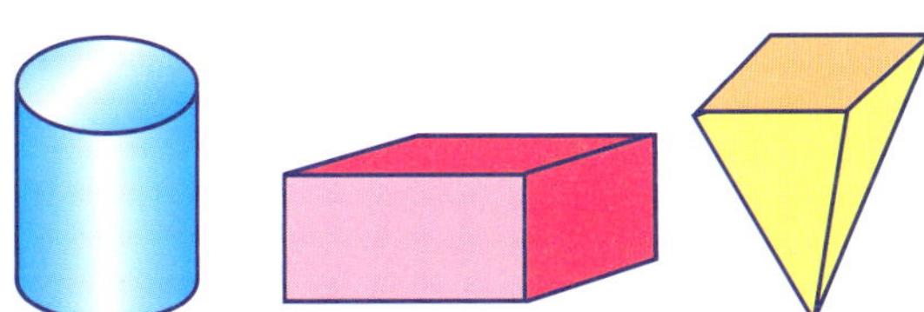

time

1 hour = 60 minutes

1 minute = 60 seconds

trapezium

A quadrilateral that has one pair of parallel sides

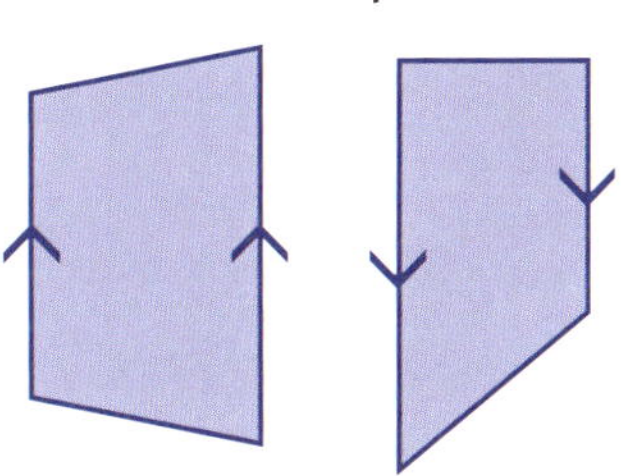

triangle

A 2D shape with 3 straight sides

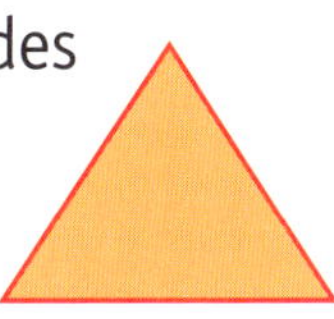

two-dimensional shapes (2D)

Shapes that only have length and width

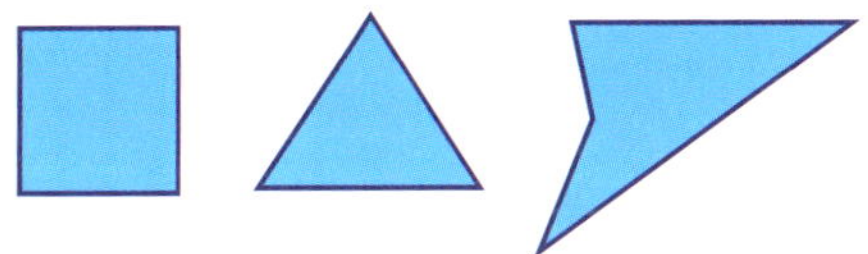

vertex

The point where the arms of an angle meet

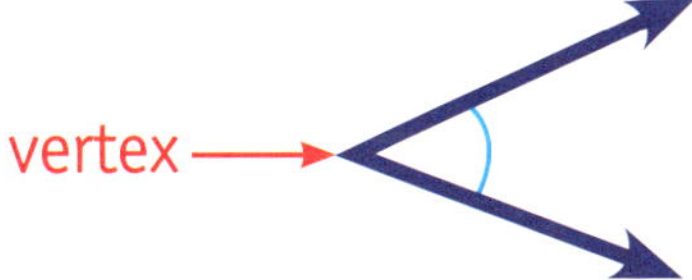

volume

The amount of space a solid object takes up

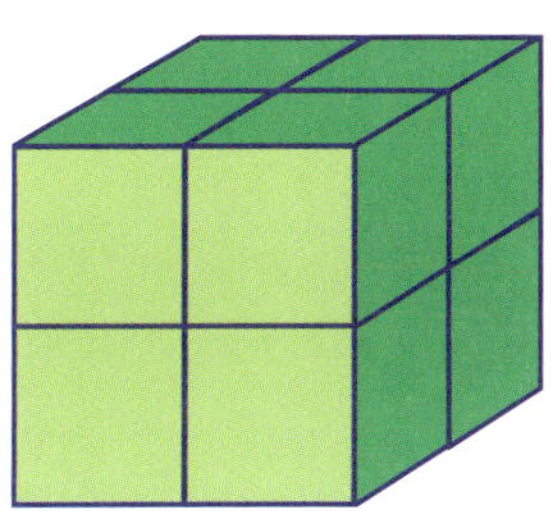

Unit 1 Numbers to 1000

10	20	30	40	50	60	70	80	90	100
110	120	130	140	150	160	170	180	190	200
210	220	230	240	250	260	270	280	290	300
310	320	330	340	350	360	370	380	390	400
410	420	430	440	450	460	470	480	490	500
510	520	530	540	550	560	570	580	590	600
610	620	630		650	660	670	680	690	700
710	720				760	770	780	790	800
810	820	830		850	860	870	880	890	900
910	920	930	940	950	960	970	980	990	1000

1 Write:

a the 5 missing numbers.

b the numbers between 360 and 370. 361, 362 ______

c 10 more than 160. ______ d 10 less than 700. ______

e 100 more than 180. ______ f 100 less than 910. ______

2 Count in 10s from 740 to 800. ______

3 Count in 100s from 440 to 840. ______

4 a Circle the numbers 10 more than 600, 770, 510, 850.

b Circle the numbers 100 less than 600, 770, 510, 850.

Number AC9M3N01 recognise, represent and order natural numbers using naming and writing conventions for numerals beyond 10 000

Unit 1 Counting in tens and hundreds

1 Complete.

a 196 197 198 ___ ___ ___ ___ ___

b 405 406 407 ___ ___ ___ ___ ___

c 770 769 768 ___ ___ ___ ___ ___

2 Complete the table.

Number	1 more	10 more	100 more
a 57			
b 300			
c 690			
d 799			
e 205			

3 Write the number 10 less than:

a 70 ________ b 330 ________ c 500 ________ d 405 ________

4

a 340 $\xrightarrow{+10}$ ☐ $\xrightarrow{+10}$ ☐ $\xrightarrow{+10}$ ☐

b 572 $\xrightarrow{+10}$ ☐ $\xrightarrow{+10}$ ☐ $\xrightarrow{+10}$ ☐

c 870 $\xrightarrow{-10}$ ☐ $\xrightarrow{-10}$ ☐ $\xrightarrow{-10}$ ☐

d 600 $\xrightarrow{-10}$ ☐ $\xrightarrow{-10}$ ☐ $\xrightarrow{-10}$ ☐

Challenge! Who will land on 850? ________

Flea jumps in tens, Grasshopper jumps in 20s, Frog jumps in 50s.

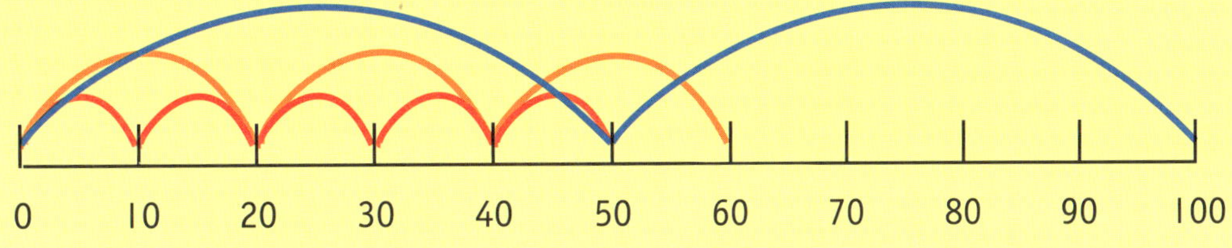

Unit 1 Place value

1 How many?

a

Hundreds	Tens	Ones
100 100 100 100 100	10 10 10 10 10 10	1 1 1

____

b

Hundreds	Tens	Ones
100 100 100 100 100 100		1 1 1 1 1 1 1

____

2 Complete: eg 549 = 5 hundreds, 4 tens and 9 ones

a 362 = ________ hundreds, ________ tens and ________ ones

b 791 = ________ hundreds, ________ tens and ________ ones

c ________ = 6 hundreds, 3 tens and 7 ones

d ________ = 8 hundreds and 4 tens

e 963 = ________ hundreds, ________ tens and ________ ones

f 602 = ________ hundreds, ________ tens and ________ ones

g ________ = 8 hundreds, 4 tens and 7 ones

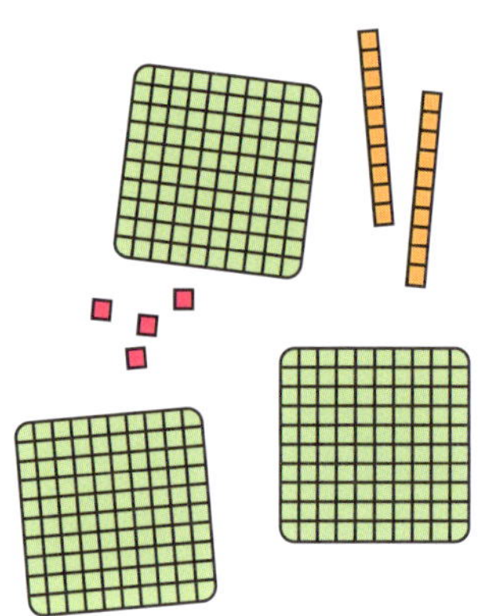

3 Beware! These are not in place value order. Write the number:

a ________ = 2 hundreds, 4 ones and 3 tens

b ________ = 8 ones, 6 tens and 4 hundreds

c ________ = 9 ones and 7 hundreds

d ________ = 1 hundreds and 2 tens

4 Complete.

a 264 = 200 + 60 + ☐

b 670 = ☐ + 70 + 0

c 712 = ☐ + 10 + ☐

d 354 = ☐ + ☐ + ☐

e 617 = 600 + ☐ + ☐

f 409 = ☐ + ☐ + 9

g 555 = ☐ + ☐ + ☐

h 830 = ☐ + ☐ + ☐

Challenge!

About how many marbles would fill the tray?

Number AC9M3N01 recognise, represent and order natural numbers using naming and writing conventions for numerals beyond 10 000

Unit 1 Place value

1 Show the numbers on the numeral expanders.

a 679

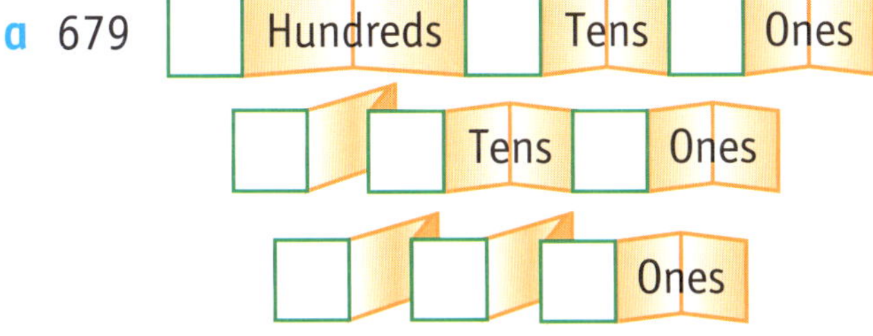

b 107

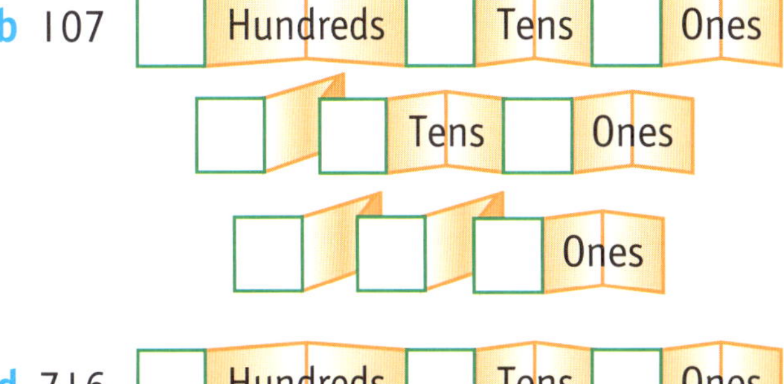

c 820

d 716

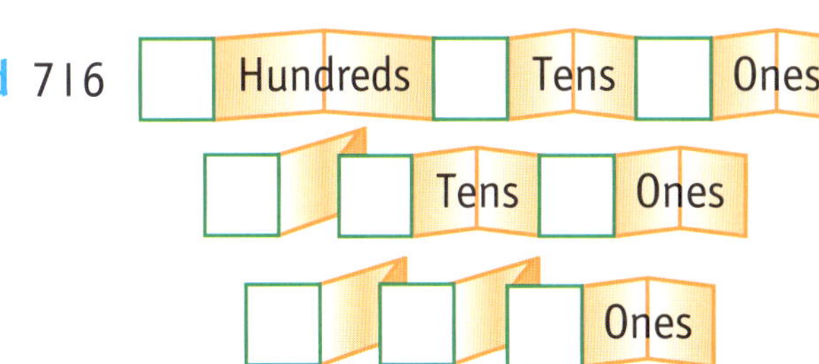

2 Write the hundreds, tens and ones.

a 642

_______ hundreds + _______ tens + _______ ones

_______ tens + _______ ones

_______ ones

b 495

_______ hundreds + _______ tens + _______ ones

_______ tens + _______ ones

_______ ones

c 281

_______ hundreds + _______ tens + _______ ones

_______ tens + _______ ones

_______ ones

d 95

_______ hundreds + _______ tens + _______ ones

_______ tens + _______ ones

_______ ones

Unit 1 Write and order 3-digit numbers

1 Complete each counting pattern.

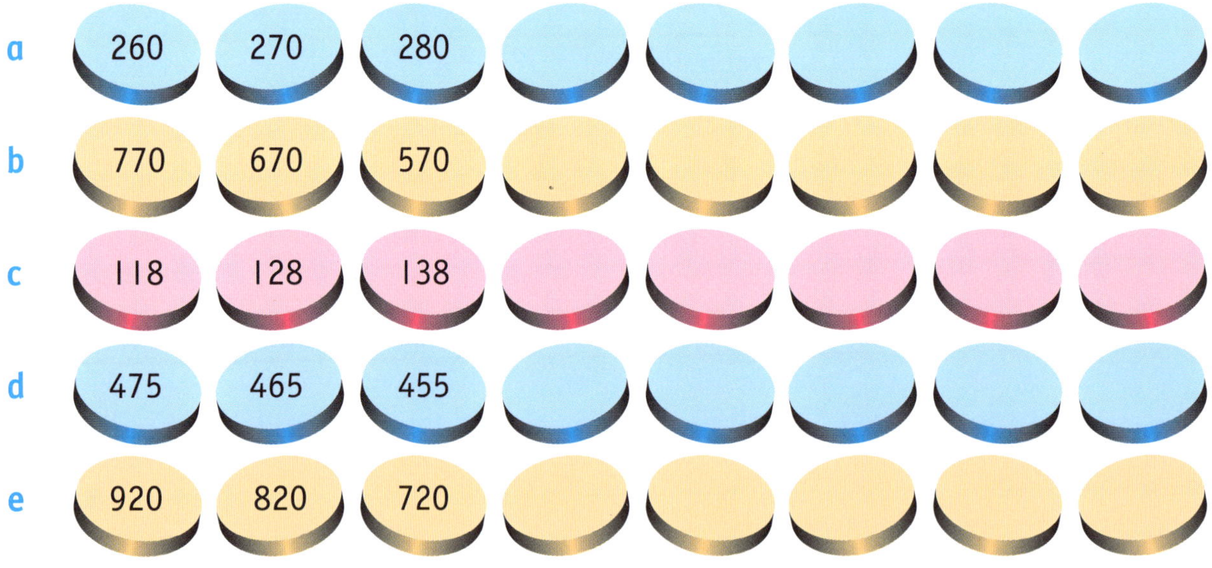

2 Write each number.

a three hundred and forty-two ________ b seven hundred and ten ________

c nine hundred and one ________ d four hundred and fourteen ________

3 Write in words.

a 509 ____

b 213 ____

4 Underline the larger number. Write **is less than** or **is greater than** to compare the two numbers.

a 269 ______________ 312 b 786 ______________ 867 c 499 ______________ 501

d 301 ______________ 199 e 614 ______________ 641 f 221 ______________ 212

Looking for patterns

Make different 3-digit numbers with these numbers.
How many numbers can you make? How many are odd?
How many are even? Repeat with 3 different numbers.
Can you see a pattern?

Mastery Checklist I can:
- ☐ count in 10s and 100s to 1000
- ☐ find 1, 10 and 100 more or less
- ☐ understand place value to hundreds
- ☐ partition numbers into hundreds, tens and ones
- ☐ write and order 3-digit numbers.

Number AC9M3N01 & AC9M3N07 recognise, represent and order natural numbers using naming and writing conventions for numerals beyond 10 000 • follow and create algorithms involving a sequence of steps and decisions to investigate numbers; describe any emerging patterns

Unit 2 Addition

0 10 20 30 40 50 60 70 80 90 100

1 Fill in the boxes.

2 Start at:

a 46 and go forward 8. ____ b 46 and go back 15. ____ c 46 and go forward 23. ____

3 Start at:

a 57 and go back 6. ____ b 57 and go forward 15. ____ c 57 and go forward 29. ____

4 Start at:

a 28 and go forward 2. ____ b 28 and go back 18. ____ c 28 and go forward 26. ____

5 This time keep hopping. Start at 81 and

a go back 5, ____ b now go forward 1, ____ c now go forward 9. ____

6 Start at 6 and

a go forward 14, ____ b now go back 6, ____ c now go forward 20. ____

Unit 2 Counting in 5s and 10s

1 Five more than:

a 20 _____	**b** 40 _____	**c** 75 _____	**d** 25 _____	**e** 10 _____
f 15 _____	**g** 35 _____	**h** 50 _____	**i** 11 _____	**j** 79 _____
k 17 _____	**l** 93 _____	**m** 44 _____	**n** 58 _____	**o** 86 _____

2 Ten less than:

a 60 _____	**b** 85 _____	**c** 30 _____	**d** 45 _____	**e** 95 _____
f 39 _____	**g** 91 _____	**h** 63 _____	**i** 13 _____	**j** 27 _____

3 Fill in the blanks and write a number sentence.

eg I start at 37, go *forward* *30* and stop at 67. [37] [+] [30] = 67

a I start at 48, go ______________ _____ and stop at 88. [ ] [ ] [ ] = 88

b I start at 64, go ______________ _____ and stop at 94. [ ] [ ] [ ] = 94

c I start at 22, go ______________ _____ and stop at 72. [ ] [ ] [ ] = 72

4 Fill in the missing numbers.

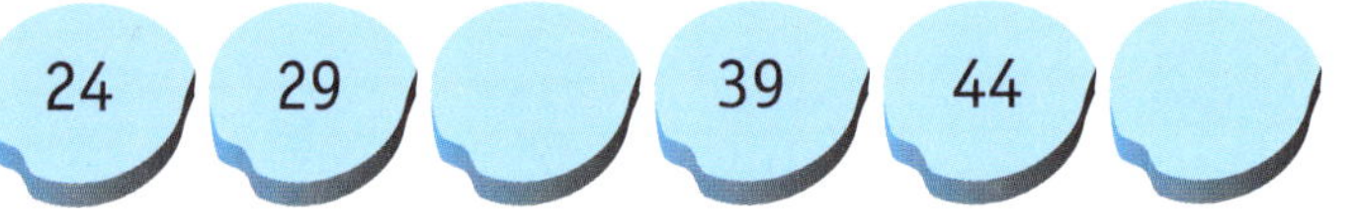

									Rule
a	14		24	29		39	44		+ 5
b	68		88			118			
c	65		55	50			35		
d	32	37		47		57			
e	129			114			99		

Challenge!

A springbok can leap 5 m.

If it travels 50 m, how many leaps does it make? [ ]

A cougar can jump 10 m. If it jumps 7 times, how far does it travel? [ ]

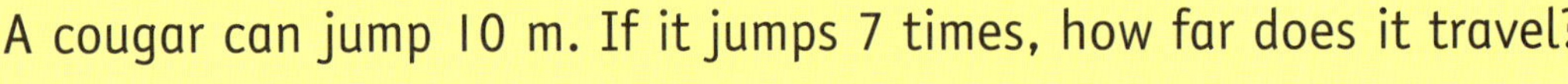

Number AC9M3N01 & AC9M3N07 recognise, represent and order natural numbers using naming and writing conventions for numerals beyond 10 000 • follow and create algorithms involving a sequence of steps and decisions to investigate numbers; describe any emerging patterns

Unit 2 Doubles and near doubles

1 a double 2 ☐ + ☐ = ☐ b double 8 ☐ + ☐ = ☐

c double 5 ☐ + ☐ = ☐ d double 10 ☐ + ☐ = ☐

e double 9 ☐ + ☐ = ☐ f double 16 ☐ + ☐ = ☐

2 a $\begin{array}{r} 4 \\ +\ 4 \\ \hline \end{array}$ b $\begin{array}{r} 7 \\ +\ 7 \\ \hline \end{array}$ c $\begin{array}{r} 11 \\ +\ 11 \\ \hline \end{array}$ d $\begin{array}{r} 13 \\ +\ 13 \\ \hline \end{array}$ e $\begin{array}{r} 0 \\ +\ 0 \\ \hline \end{array}$ f $\begin{array}{r} 9 \\ +\ 9 \\ \hline \end{array}$

Sometimes numbers are near doubles!

3 Show the near double you used.

a 4 + 5 = 4 + 4 + 1 = ______ b 10 + 9 = ______ = ______

c 3 + 2 = ______ = ______ d 8 + 9 = ______ = ______

e 7 + 6 = ______ = ______ f 6 + 5 = ______ = ______

g 12 + 13 = ______ = ______ h 17 + 16 = ______ = ______

i 15 + 14 = ______ = ______ j 19 + 18 = ______ = ______

4 a A cake costs \$9. How much for 2 cakes? ______

b One puppy weighs 5 kg. What is the mass of two puppies? ______

c One bottle of cordial makes 18 drinks.
How many drinks will two bottles make? ______

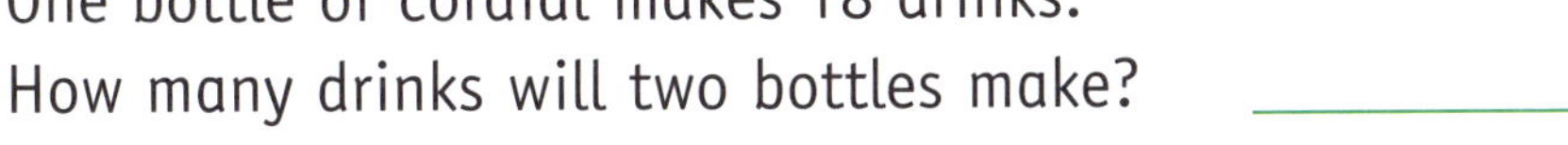

d I bought two books. One book cost \$14 and
the other cost \$13. How much did I spend? ______

5 Keep doubling. a 2 4 8 ______ ______ ______

b 3 ______ ______ ______ ______ ______

c 5 ______ ______ ______ ______ ______

Challenge!

If one box holds 6 watermelons, how many watermelons will 8 boxes hold?

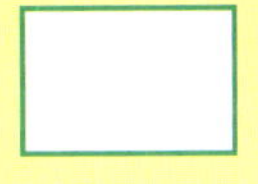

Unit 2 Addition facts to 10 and 20

1 Look for the ten then find the total.

a | 7 | 5 | 3 | = 15 (10 marked over 7 and 3)

b | 5 | 5 | 1 | = ______

c | 9 | 6 | 4 | = ______

d | 6 | 8 | 2 | = ______

e | 1 | 3 | 9 | = ______

f | 9 | 1 | 7 | = ______

g | 4 | 6 | 2 | = ______

h | 2 | 4 | 8 | = ______

i | 3 | 8 | 7 | = ______

2

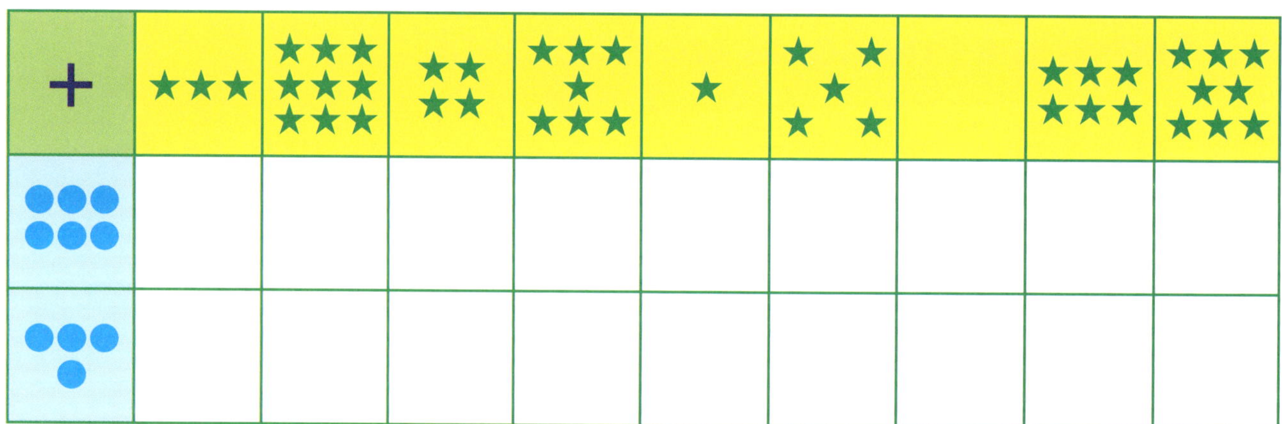

3 a 6 + 7 = ______
16 + 7 = ______
26 + 7 = ______

b 5 + 8 = ______
15 + 8 = ______
25 + 8 = ______

c 9 + 4 = ______
9 + 14 = ______
9 + 24 = ______

d 5 + 6 = ______
25 + 6 = ______
65 + 6 = ______

e 8 + 7 = ______
8 + 37 = ______
8 + 57 = ______

f 3 + 8 = ______
43 + 8 = ______
83 + 8 = ______

= 10

4 Look for tens.

a 6 + 3 + 7 + 4 = ______

b 8 + 5 + 2 + 5 = ______

c 9 + 7 + 1 + 5 = ______

d 4 + 9 + 6 + 9 = ______

e 3 + 8 + 7 + 6 = ______

f 2 + 9 + 7 + 8 = ______

Mastery Checklist I can:
- ☐ count on to add
- ☐ count in 5s and 10s
- ☐ use doubles and near doubles to add
- ☐ make 10 to add
- ☐ use number patterns to add.

Number AC9M3N01 recognise, represent and order natural numbers using naming and writing conventions for numerals beyond 10 000 • **Algebra AC9M3A02** extend and apply knowledge of addition and subtraction facts to 20 to develop efficient mental strategies for computation with larger numbers without a calculator

Unit 3 Subtraction

50c

75c

65c

45c

90c

25c

15c

80c

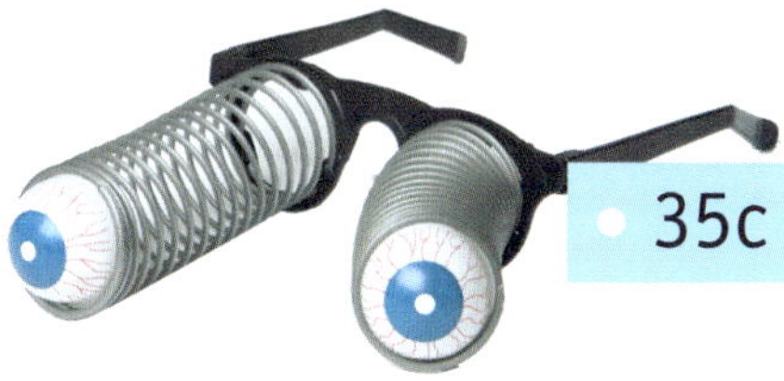

35c

John has $1 to spend at the fair. Draw two different combinations of change John could get if he buys these things.

1

Purchase	Change
a teddy bear	 20c 10c 5c or 10c 10c 10c 5c 
b goggle eyes	
c duck	
d star cookie	
e wand	
f doll	

Unit 3 Use a number line

Look at this subtraction on the number line.

58 – 24 = ☐

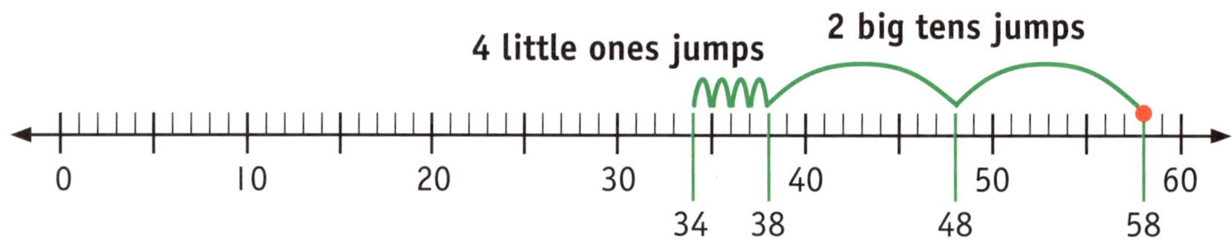

1 Use this number line to help you find the difference.

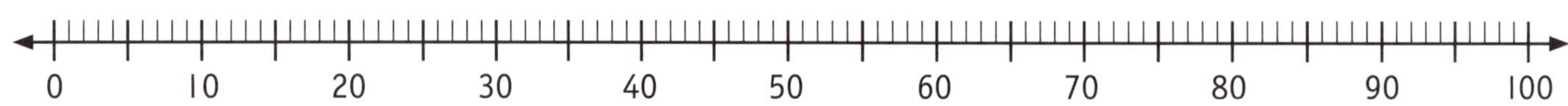

a 12 – 7 = ______	**b** 38 – 11 = ______	**c** 84 – 34 = ______
d 26 – 13 = ______	**e** 47 – 31 = ______	**f** 59 – 37 = ______
g 93 – 56 = ______	**h** 60 – 42 = ______	**i** 19 – 8 = ______
j 75 – 43 = ______	**k** 38 – 24 = ______	**l** 96 – 81 = ______
m 27 – 14 = ______	**n** 85 – 53 = ______	**o** 51 – 37 = ______

2 Write a story for each number line.

a

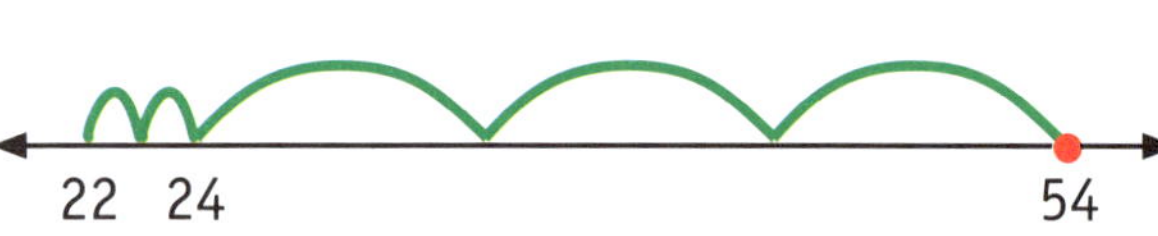

____

____

____

b

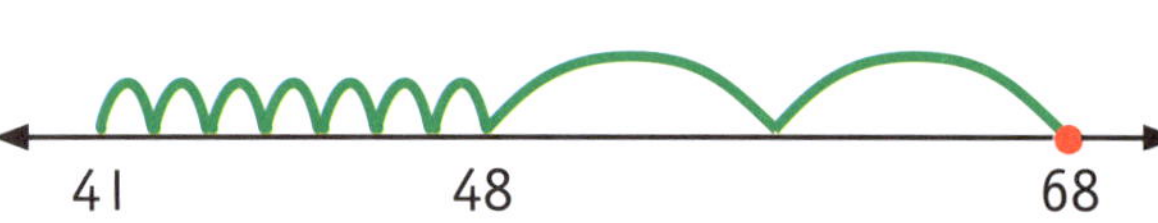

____

____

____

c

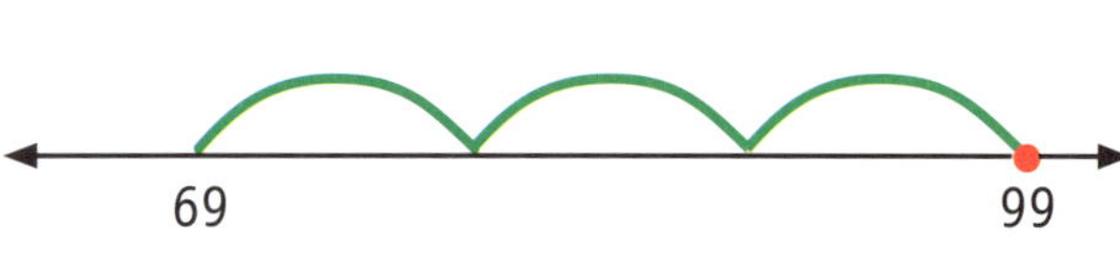

____

____

____

Unit 3 Subtraction on a number line

Word problems

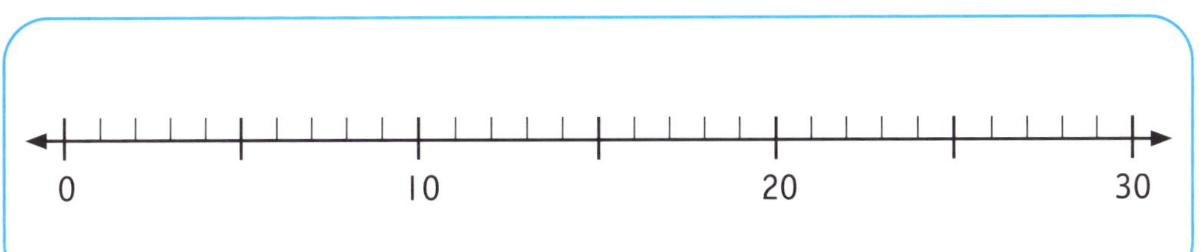

– is the take away sign. It means take away, subtract, difference between, minus or less.

1 Use the number line to find the difference.

a 17 – 9 = ______ b 12 – 4 = ______ c 10 – 3 = ______ d 16 – 7 = ______

e 15 – 8 = ______ f 26 – 9 = ______ g 18 – 12 = ______ h 23 – 5 = ______

i 19 – 7 = ______ j 29 – 17 = ______ k 15 – 9 = ______ l 21 – 7 = ______

2 a 15 pencils, 3 broke. How many not broken? ☐ – ☐ = ☐

b 29 jellybeans, 8 eaten. How many left? ☐ – ☐ = ☐

c 36 books, 5 torn. How many not torn? ☐ – ☐ = ☐

d 22 keys, 0 lost. How many keys? ☐ – ☐ = ☐

e 17 cakes, all eaten. How many left? ☐ – ☐ = ☐

f $48, $12 spent. How much left? ☐ – ☐ = ☐

3 Write a story for each. Then write a number sentence.

a

☐ – ☐ = ☐

b

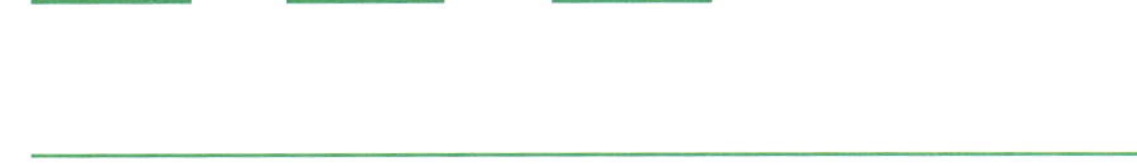

☐ – ☐ = ☐

Challenge! You have 36 lollies.

If you eat 3 every afternoon, how many days will they last? ☐

What if you ate 4 each night? ☐ Or 6 each night? ☐

Number AC9M3N06 use mathematical modelling to solve practical problems involving additive and multiplicative situations including financial contexts; formulate problems using number sentences and choose calculation strategies, using digital tools where appropriate; interpret and communicate solutions in terms of the situation

Unit 3 Subtraction patterns

1

a
9 – 4 = 5
90 – 40 = 50
900 – 400 = 500

b
7 – 3 = ____
70 – 30 = ____
700 – 300 = ____

c
5 – 2 = ____
____ – ____ = ____
____ – ____ = ____

d
8 – 6 = ____
____ – ____ = ____
____ – ____ = ____

e
9 – 8 = ____
____ – ____ = ____
____ – ____ = ____

f
6 – 1 = ____
____ – ____ = ____
____ – ____ = ____

2 One addition fact tells us 4 things.

eg 5 + 3 = 8 3 + 5 = 8 8 – 5 = 3 8 – 3 = 5

a 7 + 2 = ____, ____ + ____ = ____, ____ – ____ = ____, ____ – ____ = ____

b 5 + 6 = ____, ____ + ____ = ____, ____ – ____ = ____, ____ – ____ = ____

c 8 + 5 = ____, ____ + ____ = ____, ____ – ____ = ____, ____ – ____ = ____

d 9 + 7 = ____, ____ + ____ = ____, ____ – ____ = ____, ____ – ____ = ____

e 6 + 7 = ____, ____ + ____ = ____, ____ – ____ = ____, ____ – ____ = ____

f 4 + 9 = ____, ____ + ____ = ____, ____ – ____ = ____, ____ – ____ = ____

3 **a** Cross out some dolls. Write a number story and a number sentence.

____ – ____ = ____

b Write the 3 other number facts.

____ ____ ____

Challenge! Zac had 14 marbles. He gave 2 away and had 16 left.

What is wrong with Zac's story?

How many did Zac give away if he had 2 left?

Number AC9M3N03 add and subtract two- and three-digit numbers using place value to partition, rearrange and regroup numbers • **Algebra AC9M3A01** recognise and explain the connection between addition and subtraction as inverse operations, apply to partition numbers and find unknown values in number sentences

Unit 3 Two-digit subtraction

1 Use a number line.

eg 56 − 24 = 32

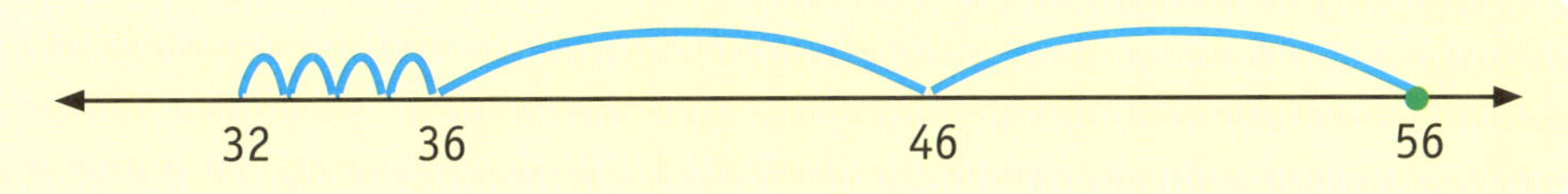

a 75 − 31 = ____

b 89 − 47 = ____

c 38 − 23 = ____

d 64 − 40 = ____

2 a 48 − 21 = ____

$$\begin{array}{r} 48 \\ -\ 21 \\ \hline \end{array}$$

b 66 − 36 = ____

$$\begin{array}{r} 66 \\ -\ 36 \\ \hline \end{array}$$

c 75 − 32 = ____

$$\begin{array}{r} 75 \\ -\ 32 \\ \hline \end{array}$$

d 99 − 61 = ____

$$\begin{array}{r} 99 \\ -\ 61 \\ \hline \end{array}$$

e 57 − 14 = ____

$$\begin{array}{r} 57 \\ -\ 14 \\ \hline \end{array}$$

f 83 − 70 = ____

$$\begin{array}{r} 83 \\ -\ 70 \\ \hline \end{array}$$

3 Jo had 38 baby mice. She sold 15. How many did she have left? ____

4 Ali picked 49 apples. He gave 23 to his friend. How many did he keep? ____

Trial and error

Look at page 11. If you had $3, what toys would you buy?

How much change would you get? ☐

Mastery Checklist I can:
- ☐ subtract money
- ☐ show change
- ☐ use a number line to subtract
- ☐ write subtraction stories
- ☐ write subtraction number sentences
- ☐ make patterns with subtraction
- ☐ use subtraction algorithms.

Problem solving

What's in a name?

Choose two friends and compare your names.

First name	Number of letters	Last name	Number of letters	Total

How many letters in: the longest name? _______ the shortest name? _______

What is the difference between the two totals? _______

Now score each name if you made them with Scrabble tiles.

Working out space

A 1 B 3 C 3 D 2 E 1 F 4
G 2 H 4 I 1 J 8 K 5 L 1
M 3 N 1 O 1 P 3 Q 10 R 1
S 1 T 1 U 1 V 4 W 4 X 8 Y 4 Z 10

First name	Number of letters	Last name	Number of letters	Total

What is the score for: the longest name? _______ the shortest name? _______

What is the difference between the two totals? _______

I can solve problems by:

☐ adding and subtracting numbers ☐ comparing my results with others.

Number AC9M3N03 add and subtract two- and three-digit numbers using place value to partition, rearrange and regroup numbers
• **Algebra AC9M3A02** extend and apply knowledge of addition and subtraction facts to 20 to develop efficient mental strategies for computation with larger numbers without a calculator

Unit 4 Metres

Length 

12
11
10
9
8
7
6
5
4
3
2
1
0
Metres

Elephant Polar Bear Gorilla Giraffe Tom Dog Brachiosaurus

1 Which animal is the tallest? ______________________

2 Which animal is the shortest? ______________________

3 How tall is the giraffe? ______________________

4 How tall is the elephant? ______________________

5 How much taller is the polar bear than Tom? ______________________

6 How much shorter is the gorilla than the elephant? ______________________

7 If Tom stood on the elephant's back how high would he be? ______________________

8 Are all dogs the same height? ______________________

9 Name a tall dog ______________________ and a short dog. ______________________

10 Write the animals in order from shortest to tallest.

____

____

____

Unit 4 Measuring in metres and centimetres

Estimate then measure the length of each item.

measure length in cm and m

	Estimate	Measure
1 a length of your table	about ______ m	______ m
b length of classroom	about ______ m	______ m
c length of school corridor	about ______ m	______ m

	Estimate	Measure
2 a length of this book	about ______ cm	______ cm
b length of your pencil	about ______ cm	______ cm
c length of your desk	about ______ cm	______ cm

3

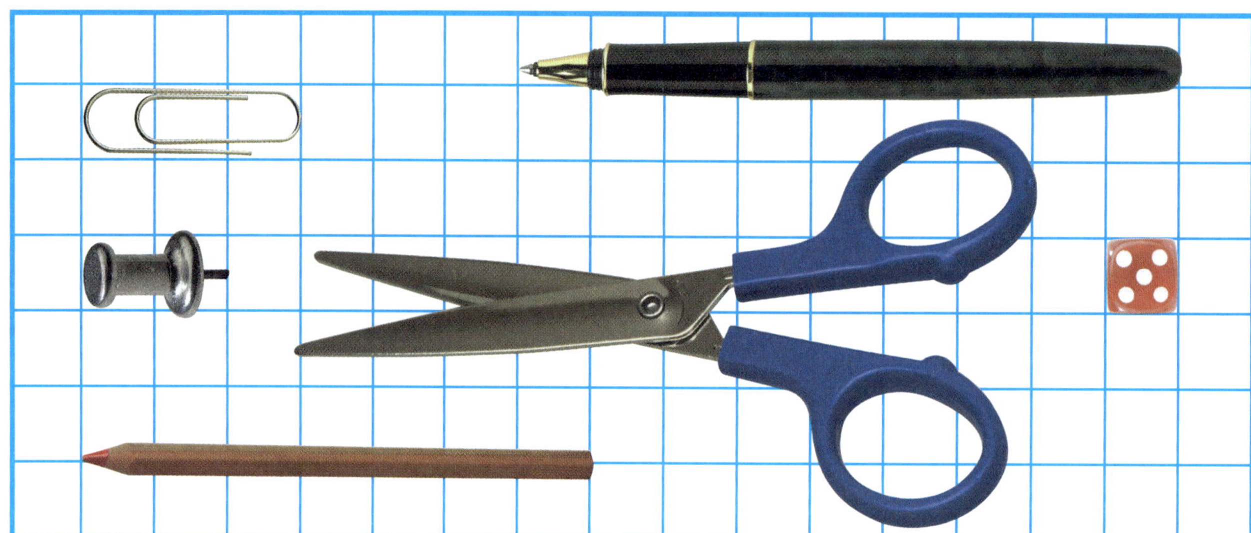

a What is the longest? ______

b What is the shortest? ______

c How long is the pen? ______

d How long is the paperclip? ______

e Which two items together are 5 cm? ______

f The pushpin is ______ cm longer than the die.

g The paperclip is ______ cm shorter than the scissors.

4 Find something in your classroom that is:

a 1 m ______

b 30 cm ______

c 2 m ______

d 10 cm ______

e 50 cm ______

f 80 cm ______

Measurement AC9M3M01 & AC9M3M02 identify which metric units are used to measure everyday items; use measurements of familiar items and known units to make estimates • measure and compare objects using familiar metric units of length, mass and capacity, and instruments with labelled markings

Unit 4 Measuring and estimating length

m = metre
cm = centimetre

1 Use the number bank to complete each sentence.

Number Bank 1 2 4 10 30 180

a The door is ______ m high.

b The globe is ______ cm long.

c The man is ______ cm tall.

d The hen is ______ cm tall.

e The car is ______ m long.

f The wheelbarrow is ______ m long.

2 The bus stop sign is 1 m high.

BUS STOP

a How high is the bus? ____________

b How long is the bus? ____________

3 Use a ruler to measure these lines to the nearest cm.

a

b

c

d

a ☐ b ☐ c ☐ d ☐

measure cm with a ruler

Mastery Checklist I can:
- ☐ compare heights in metres
- ☐ measure lengths in m and cm
- ☐ estimate lengths in m and cm
- ☐ find the difference in lengths.

Unit 5 Fractions

A B  C

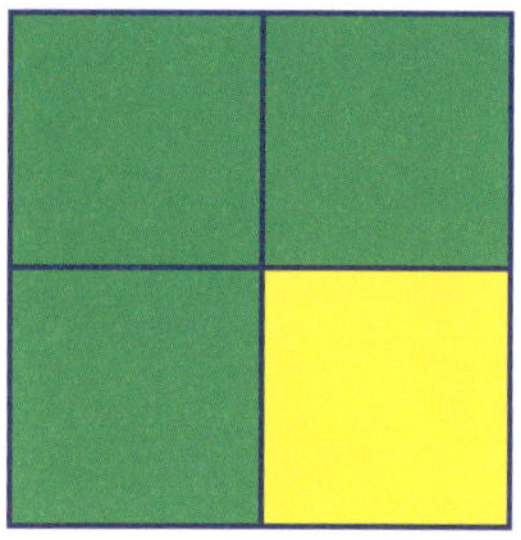

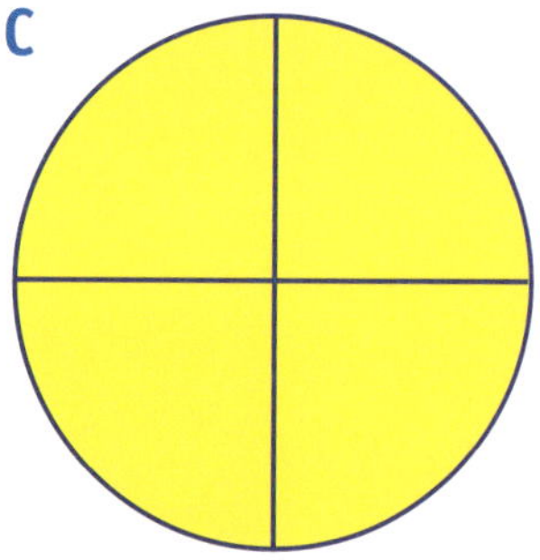

D  E  F

G 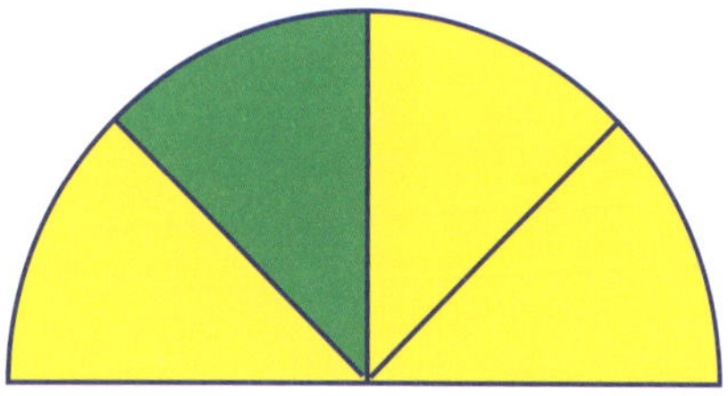 H 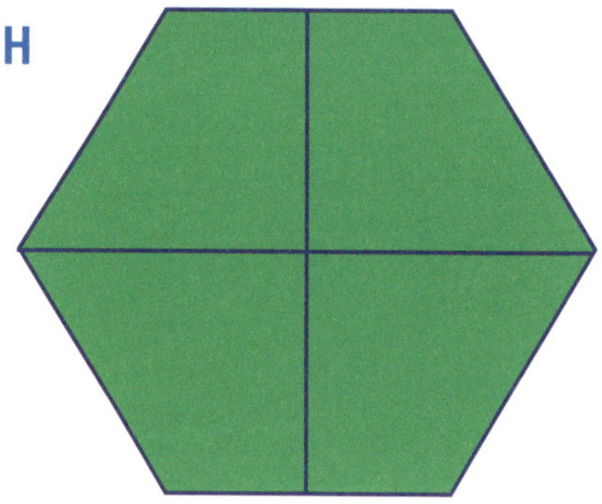 I

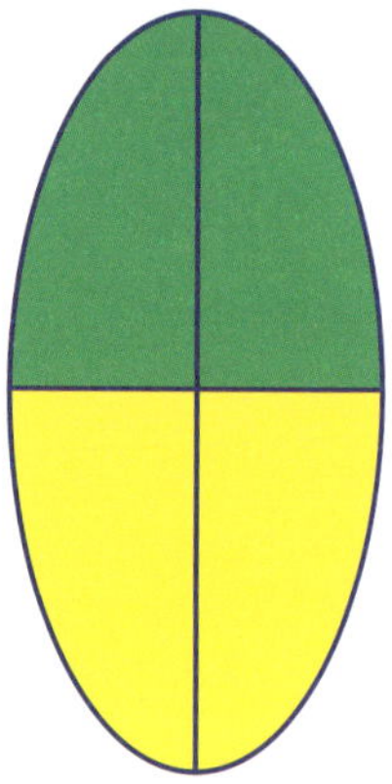

1 Which shapes are one quarter green? D and ____________

2 Which shapes are one half yellow? ____________

3 Which shapes show one whole? ____________

4 Which shapes are one half green? ____________

5 In F what fraction is yellow? ____________

6 In G what fraction is green? ____________

7 How many quarters are in one whole? ____________

8 How many halves are in one whole? ____________

9 How many quarters are in one half? ____________

10 How many halves are in 2 wholes? ____________

3 wholes? ____________

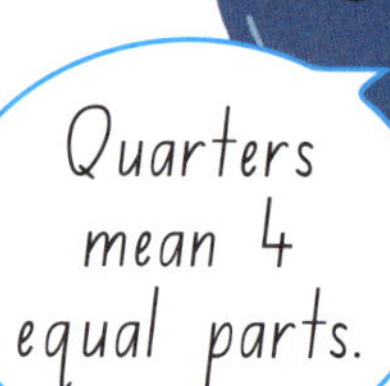

 Number AC9M3N02 recognise and represent unit fractions and their multiples in different ways; combine fractions with the same denominator to complete the whole

Unit 5 Halves and quarters

1 Colour the letters that are cut in half.

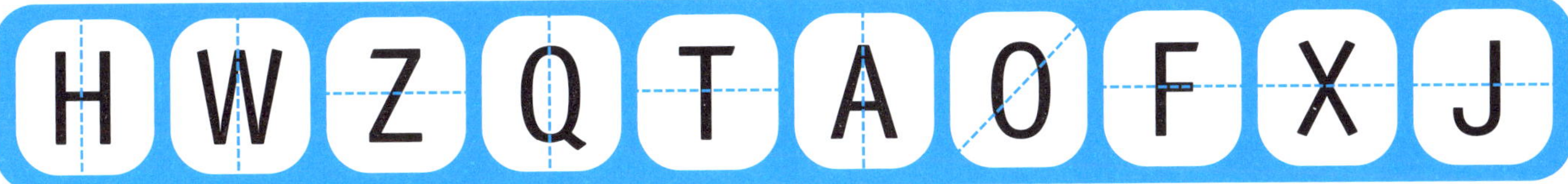

2 Draw a line to cut these letters in half.

3 Circle the halves. Tick the quarters.

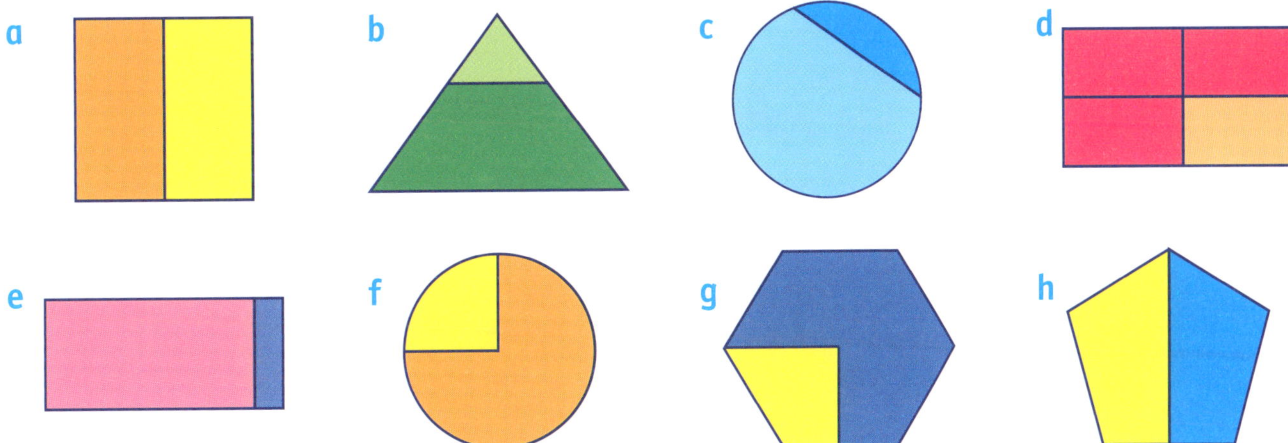

4 Use red to circle the objects that have been cut in half. Use blue to circle the objects that have been cut into quarters.

Unit 5 Fractions as part of a whole

1 Colour part of each shape to match the fraction.

a 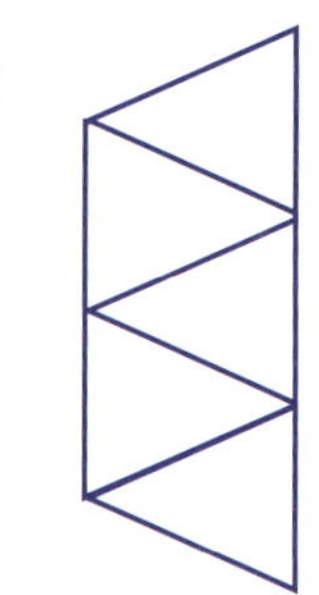

I out of 5
one fifth

b 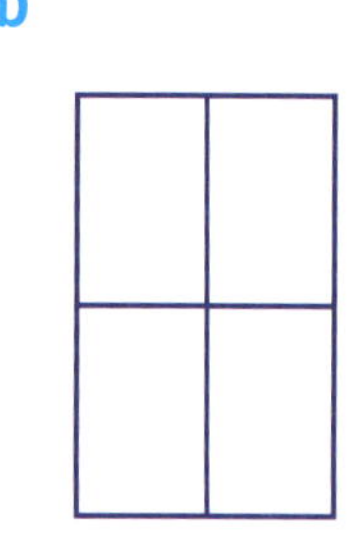

I out of 4
one quarter

c 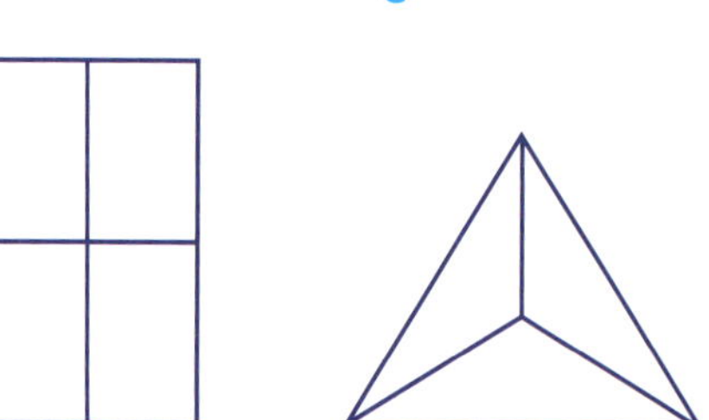

I out of 3
one third

d 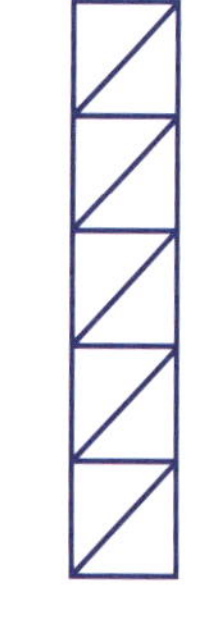

I out of 10
one tenth

e 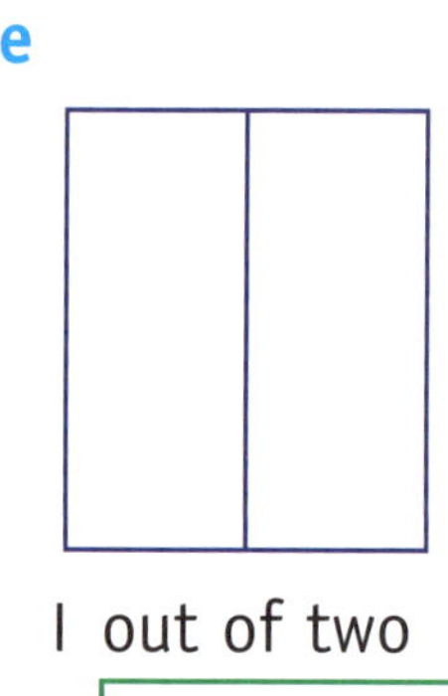

I out of two
one ______

2 Write the fraction for the part coloured.

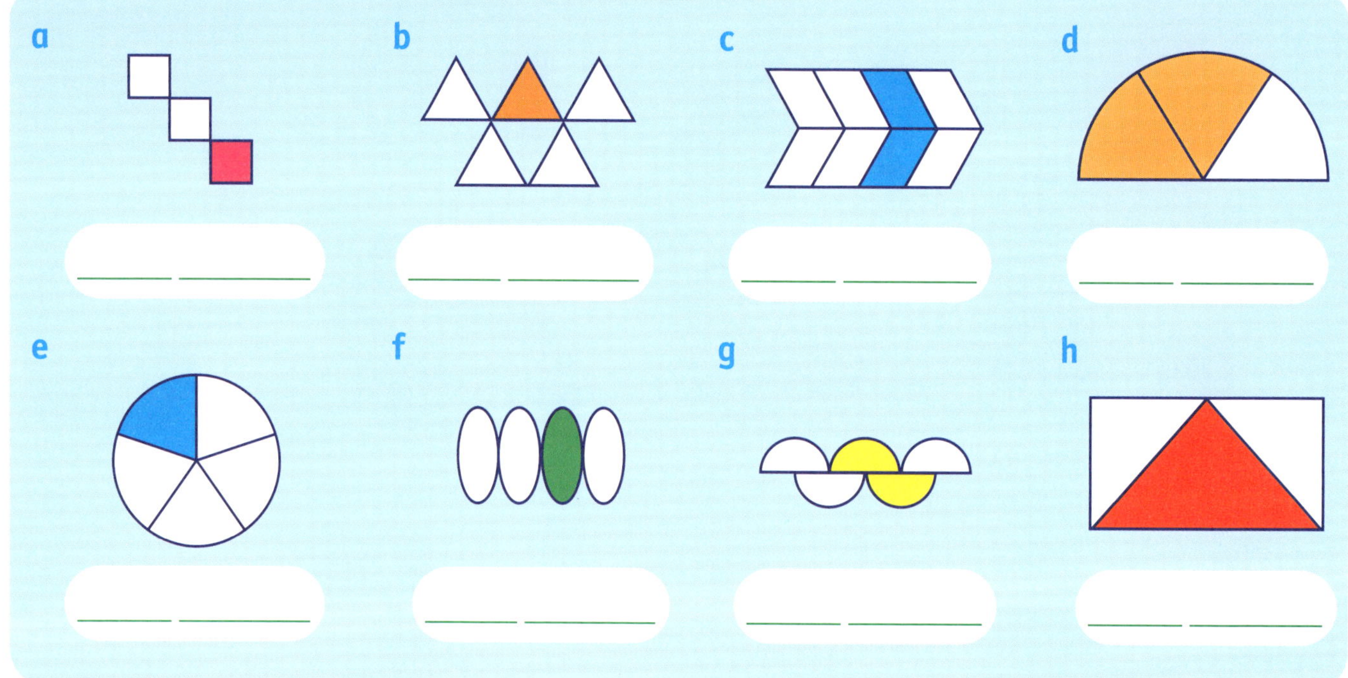

3 Draw lines to make equal parts. Colour and name a fraction you like.

a ______ ______

b ______ ______

Mastery Checklist I can:
- ☐ understand that fractions are equal parts
- ☐ recognise diagrams of halves and quarters
- ☐ divide letters into halves
- ☐ recognise halves and quarters in the real world
- ☐ recognise unit fractions as one part of a whole.

 Number AC9M3N02 recognise and represent unit fractions and their multiples in different ways; combine fractions with the same denominator to complete the whole

Problem solving

Fraction rewards

1 As a reward each person in the red team got one piece of a Jolly Chew Bar. Colour the pieces each child received.

a Nelly got one piece of a four piece bar.

b Feng got one piece of a three piece bar.

c Sara got one piece of an eight piece bar.

d Mei got one piece of a six piece bar.

2 Write the names in order from smallest piece to largest piece.

__________ __________ __________ __________

3 a Are these rewards fair? Why? ____________________

b What would you have done? ____________________

____

4 How many different ways can you divide this Jolly Chew Bar into quarters to share with three other people and yourself?

I can solve problems by:

☐ dividing in equal shares ☐ using drawings and diagrams.

Measure length with people measures Investigation 1

Your classroom is getting new carpet. The principal needs the measurements of your room.

Estimate first. The room is ________________ long and ________________ wide.

How could you measure the room without using a tape measure?

____

measure without a tape measure

Draw your room here and show the different measurement tools you used.

Write what you found out.

____

____

____

____

Measurement AC9M3M01 & AC9M3M02 identify which metric units are used to measure everyday items; use measurements of familiar items and known units to make estimates • measure and compare objects using familiar metric units of length, mass and capacity, and instruments with labelled markings

Measure length with people measures Investigation 1

Your teacher says you could rearrange the furniture in your classroom, so you have to measure it too. Do this with parts of your body: feet, hands, arms, forearms. Make a table to record the measurements. Explain how you measured the objects.

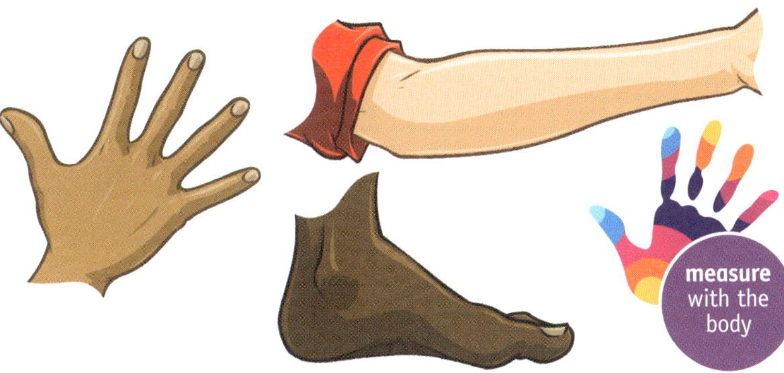

Why are people measures useful?

____

____

____

....

To carry out these tasks I need to:

- ☐ estimate lengths
- ☐ measure lengths with parts of my body
- ☐ explain how I measure lengths
- ☐ use a table to record lengths of different objects
- ☐ work well in a group.

I enjoyed this task!

☆ ☆ ☆ ☆ ☆

Revision

1 Which number completes the pattern?

Shade one bubble.

228 ○ 282 ○ 238 ○ 283 ○

2 Which group shows 54?

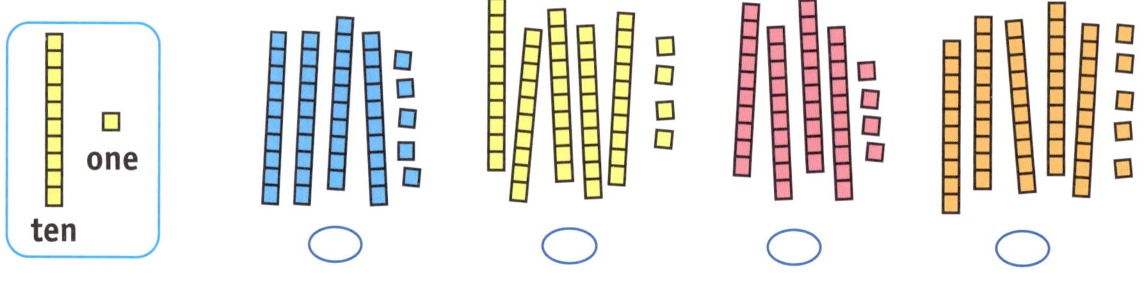

○ ○ ○ ○

3 Huey had $1 to spend and bought this toy.

How much change did he get?

5c ○ 25c ○ $1.15 ○ 15c ○

4 A cake costs $13. How much for two cakes?

$15 ○ $23 ○ $26 ○ $25 ○

5 How much altogether?

$523 ○ $532 ○ $343 ○ $432 ○

Revision

6 Which shape has one quarter coloured green?

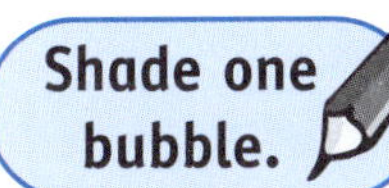

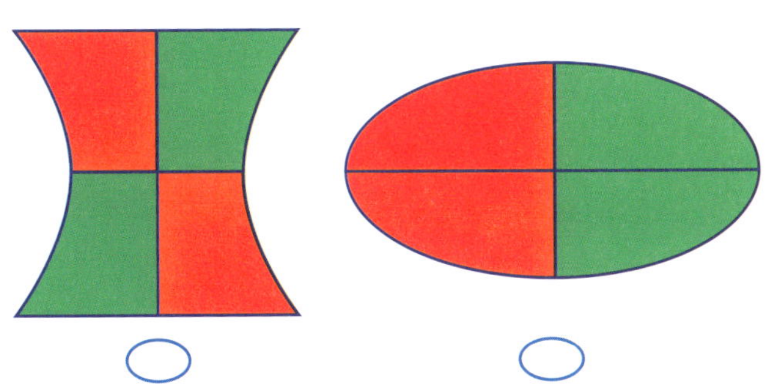

7 Which shape has been cut in half?

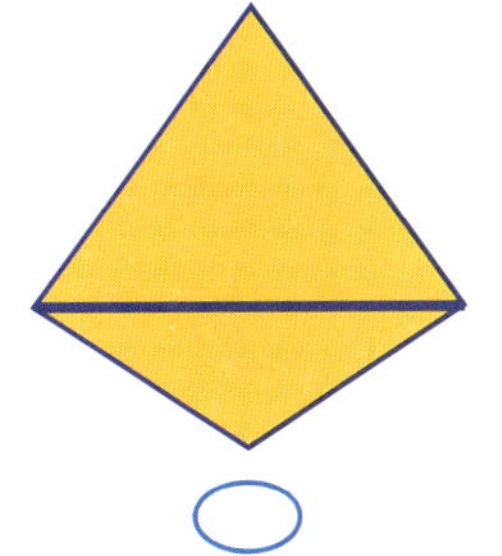

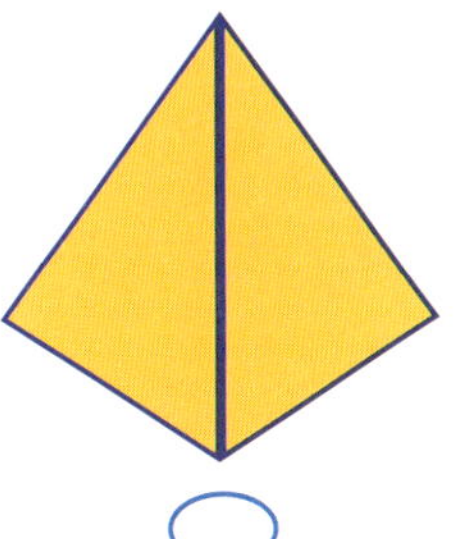
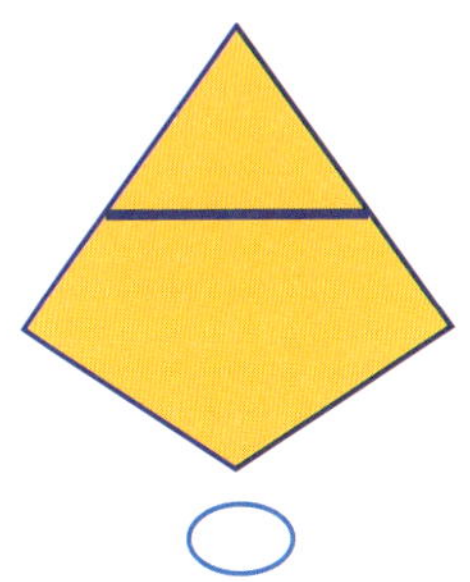

8 Which number is closest to 500?

475 520 560 490

9 Which snake is 5 m long?

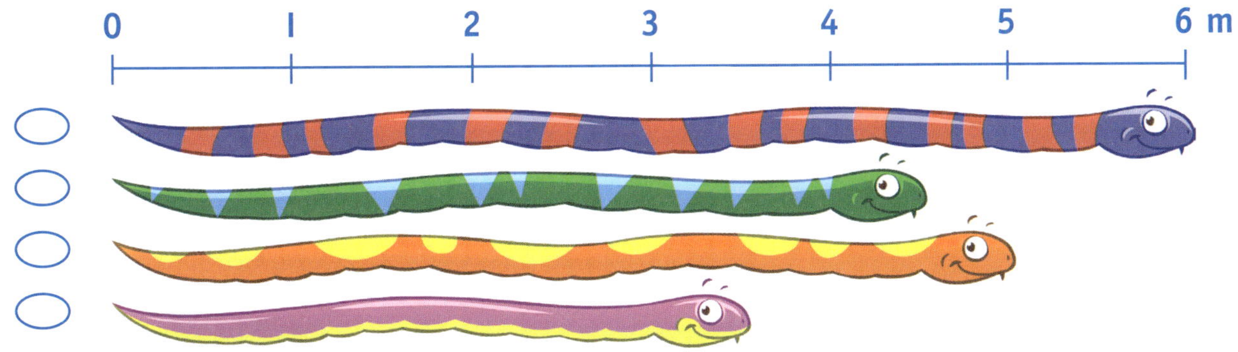

10 Write the number sentence to match.

Write your answer in the box.

Unit 6 Patterns

A

0 4 8 12 16 20

B

C

2 5 8 11 14 17

D

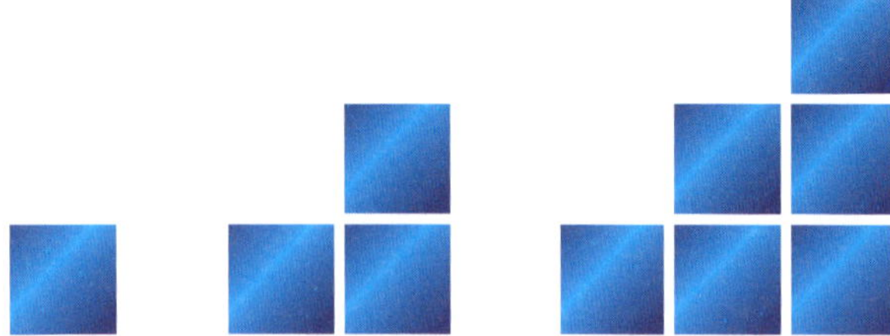

1 a How is pattern **A** made? ____________

b What are the next three numbers? ______ ______ ______

c What will the 12th number be? ______

2 Draw the next term for **B**.

3 a What is the next number in **C**? ______

b What is the pattern for **C**? ______

c Will 27 be in **C**? ______ Why? ____________

4 a How many squares will be in the next term for **D**? ______

b Draw it.

Unit 6 Patterns using shapes and numbers

1 a Start at 2. Make a pattern by adding four.

b Start at 1. Make a pattern by adding four.

c

3 7 11 15 19 23

How was this pattern made? ______________________

d Each pattern rule is add 4. Why are the patterns different? ______________________

____

Look at page 28.

2 a What is happening to change the terms in **B**? ______________________

b Write the pattern in numbers. ______ ______ ______ ______

c How many spots will there be in the 10th term? ______ 14th term? ______

d Draw another pattern like **B** using triangles.

3 a What shape is used for **D**? ______

b Will the next term use a circle? ______

Why? ______________________

Challenge!

How many squares will be in the 10th shape for **D**? ☐

Unit 6 Patterns with numbers

1 Finish each pattern and write the rule.

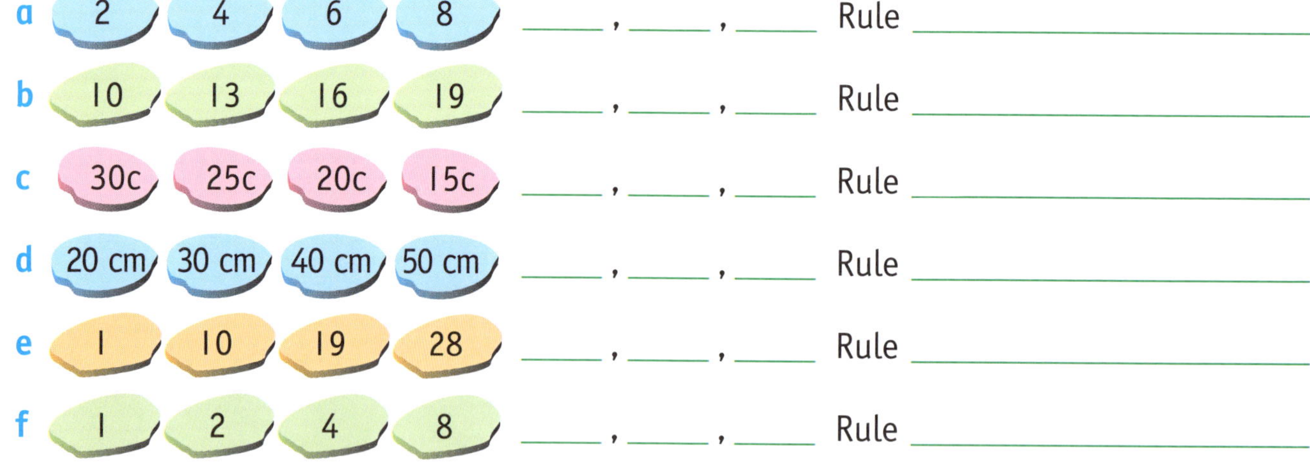

a 2, 4, 6, 8, ____, ____, ____ Rule ____________

b 10, 13, 16, 19, ____, ____, ____ Rule ____________

c 30c, 25c, 20c, 15c, ____, ____, ____ Rule ____________

d 20 cm, 30 cm, 40 cm, 50 cm, ____, ____, ____ Rule ____________

e 1, 10, 19, 28, ____, ____, ____ Rule ____________

f 1, 2, 4, 8, ____, ____, ____ Rule ____________

g 48, 42, 36, 30, ____, ____, ____ Rule ____________

h 2, 9, 16, 23, ____, ____, ____ Rule ____________

i $\frac{1}{5}$, $\frac{2}{5}$, $\frac{3}{5}$, $\frac{4}{5}$, ____, ____, ____ Rule ____________

j 39, 35, 31, 27, ____, ____, ____ Rule ____________

2 a Start with 20. Make a pattern by adding 4.

b Start with 86. Make a pattern by taking away 10.

86, ____, ____, ____, ____

c Write the instructions for this pattern. ____________

____

0, 11, 22, 33, 44

Looking for patterns

Finish this pattern. 1, 3, 7, 15, ____, ____

What did you do? ____________

Mastery Checklist I can:

- ☐ work out the rule for a number pattern
- ☐ continue patterns
- ☐ follow a rule to make a number pattern
- ☐ make my own patterns with numbers and shapes.

Number AC9M3N07 follow and create algorithms involving a sequence of steps and decisions to investigate numbers; describe any emerging patterns

Frog jumps

Froggy jumps by **twos** to visit Ducky. He jumps to lily pad **2**, then **4** and so on until he gets there.

Froggy's jumps: **2, 4, 6** ______________________ How many jumps? ______

Next, Froggy jumps by **fours** from Ducky to the flies for a snack, starting at **12.**

Froggy's jumps: **12** ______________________ How many jumps? ______

Now Froggy jumps by **fives** from the flies to visit his mum, starting at **5.**

Froggy's jumps: **5** ______________________ How many jumps? ______

Make up your own pattern for Froggy's next set of jumps.

____

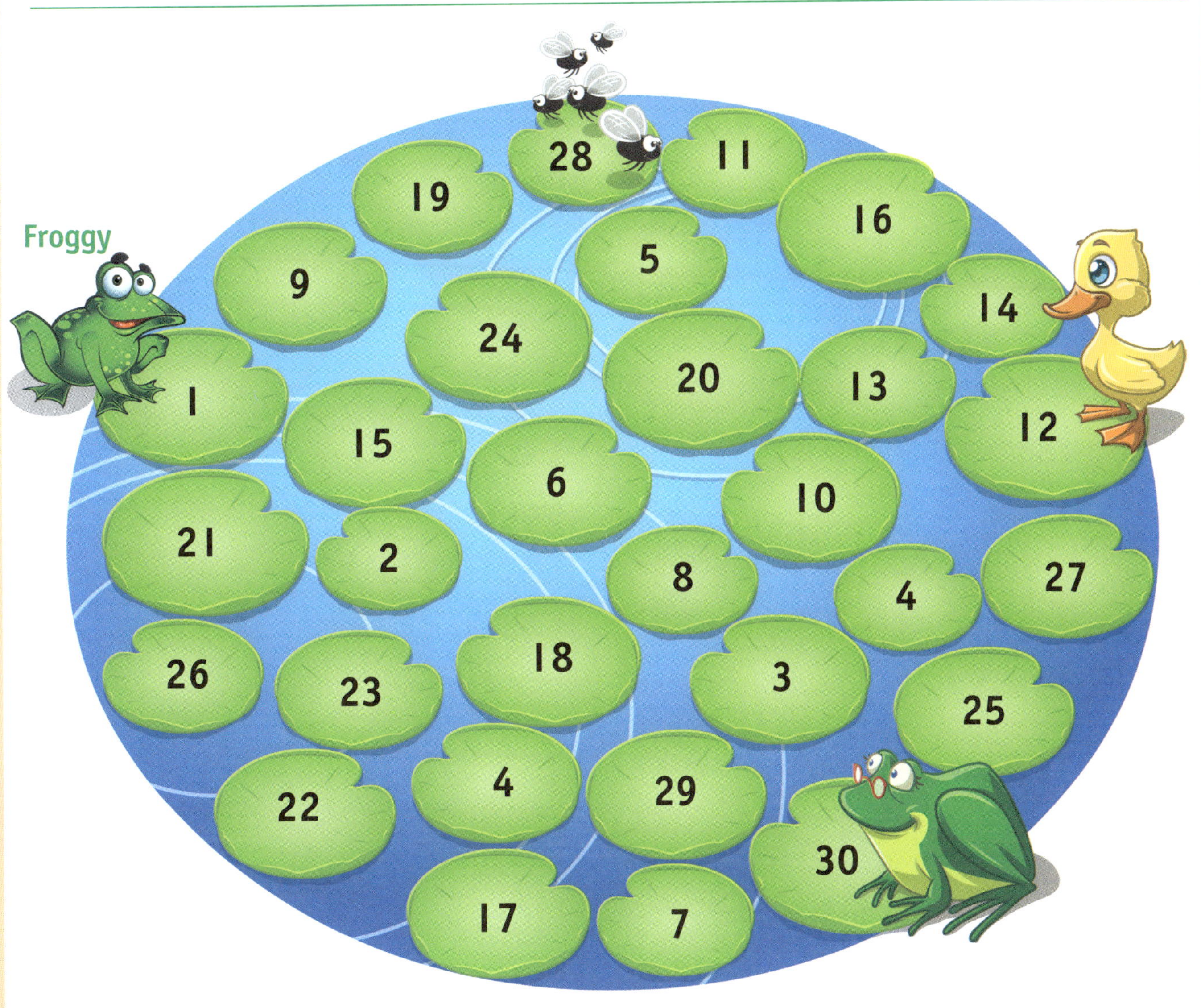

I can solve problems by:

☐ completing patterns by adding ☐ describing the patterns I see.

Unit 7 Half hours and quarter hours

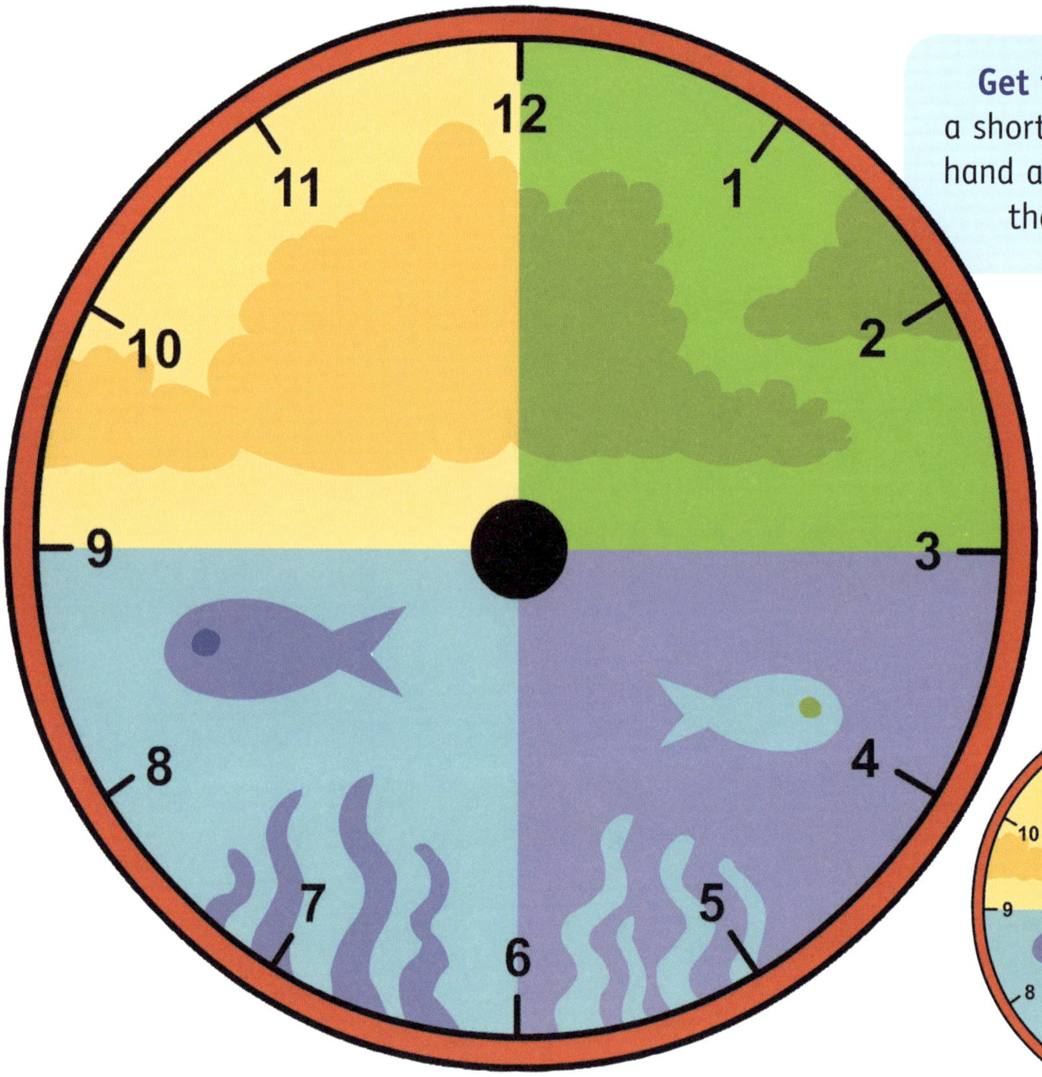

Get two craft sticks:
a shorter one for the hour hand and a longer one for the minute hand.

use sticks to show the time

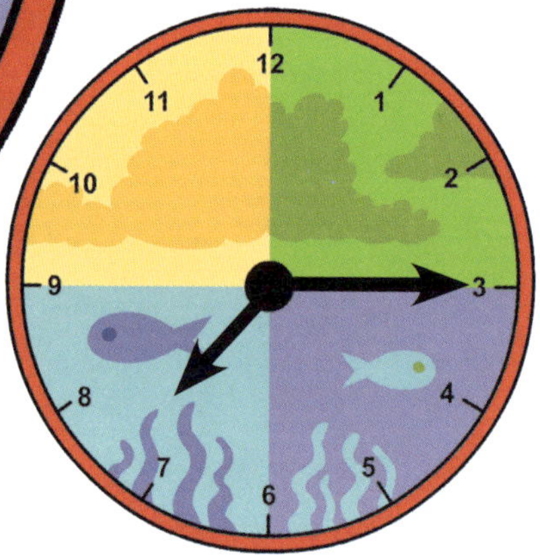

1 With your craft sticks show: **a** 4 o'clock **b** 7 o'clock **c** 10 o'clock

d Where is the minute hand each time? ______

e Where is the hour hand at 4 o'clock? ______

2 With your craft sticks show: **a** $\frac{1}{2}$ past 8 **b** $\frac{1}{2}$ past 11 **c** $\frac{1}{2}$ past 5

d Where is the minute hand each time? ______

e Where is the hour hand at $\frac{1}{2}$ past 8? ______

3 **a** What is the time on the small clock? ______

b Why is the minute hand on 3? ______

c Where is the hour hand? ______

4 With your craft sticks show: **a** $\frac{1}{4}$ past 9 **b** $\frac{1}{4}$ past 2 **c** $\frac{1}{4}$ past 10

d $\frac{1}{4}$ to 5 **e** $\frac{1}{4}$ to 3 **f** $\frac{1}{4}$ to 12

Unit 7 Five-minute intervals

1 How many minutes pass as the minute hand moves from:

a 12 to 1 ____________ b 12 to 3 ____________ c 12 to 6 ____________

d 12 to 9 ____________ e 12 to 7 ____________ f 12 to 2 ____________

g 12 to 12 ____________ h 12 to 11 ____________ i 12 to 4 ____________

j 12 to 10 ____________ k 12 to 5 ____________ l 12 to 8 ____________

2

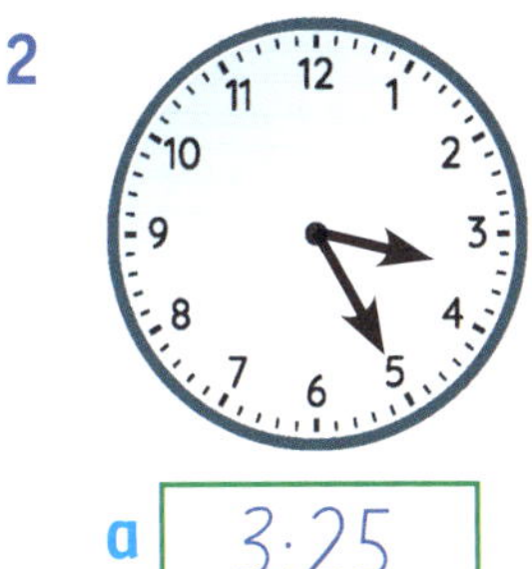

a 3:25

b 

c

d

e 

3 Use 'past' and 'to' to tell these times, eg $\frac{1}{4}$ to 5.

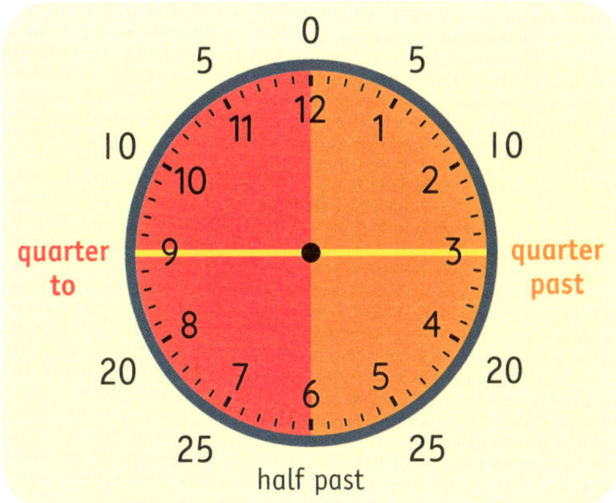

a

b

c

4 Draw these times.

a 

25 to 5

b 

5 past 10

c 

$\frac{1}{4}$ to 5

d

20 past 12

e

10 past 7

Unit 7 Analogue and digital times

1

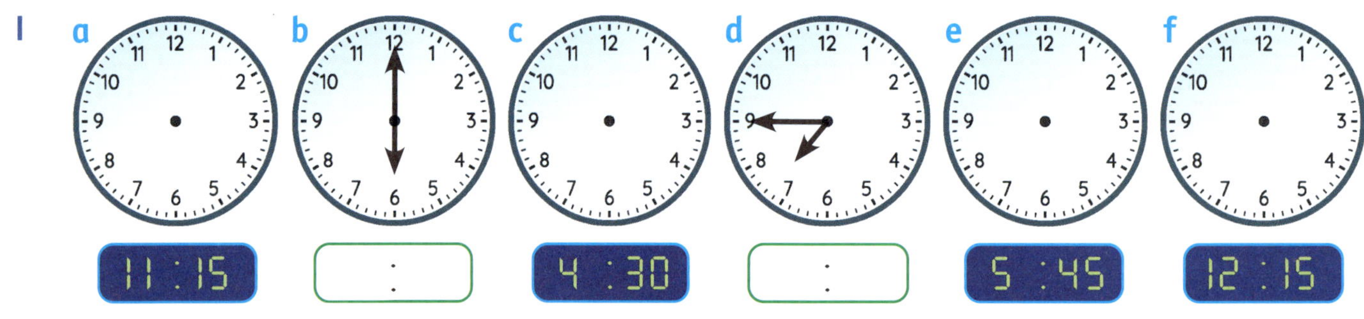

2 a 7 : 05 b 11 : 15 c 3 : 45 d 9 : 05 e 5 : 30

	Read	Means
a	*seven-oh-five*	*5 minutes past 7*
b		
c		
d		
e		

3 Match the time to the correct clock.

Measurement AC9M3M04 describe the relationship between the hours and minutes on analogue and digital clocks, and read the time to the nearest minute

Unit 7 Time to the minute

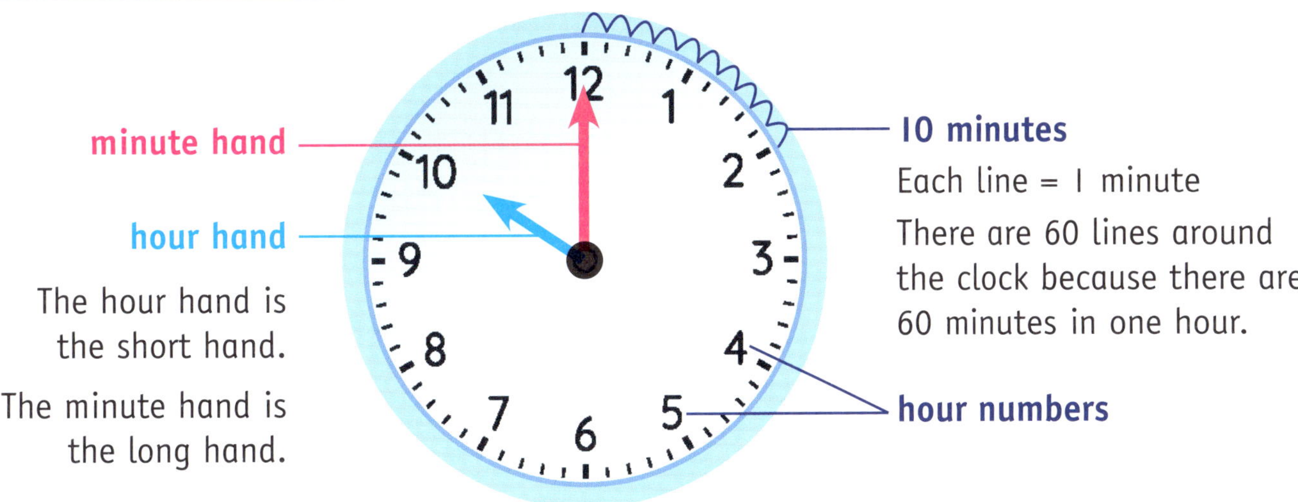

1 Write the minutes past the hour time. Then show the digital time.

a

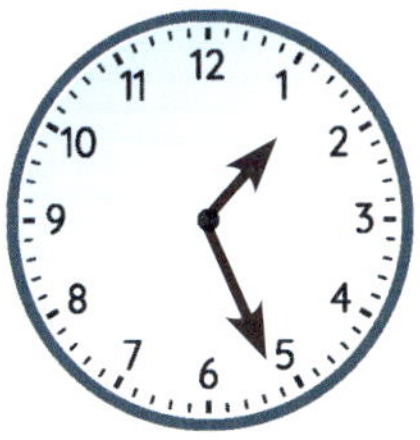

b

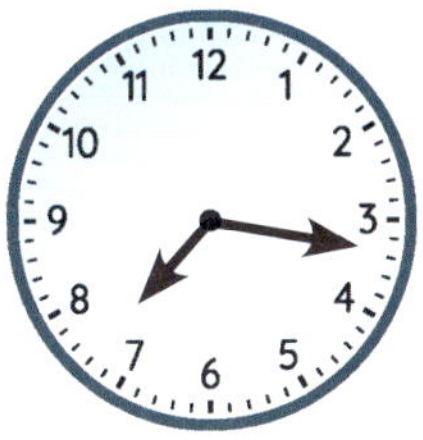

c

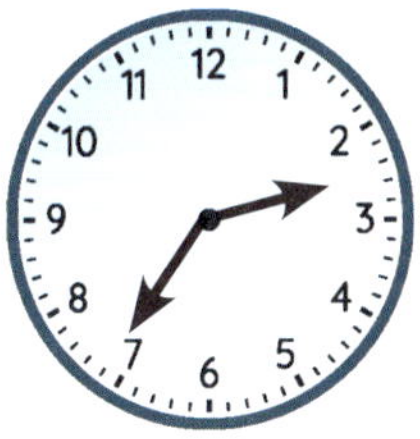

d

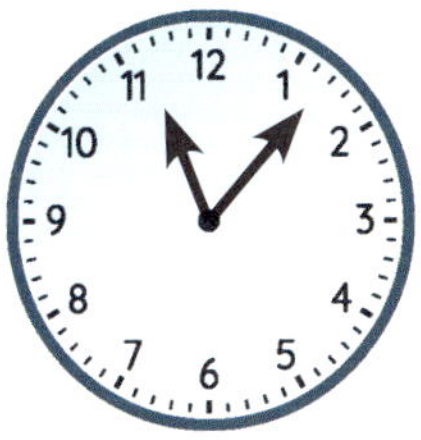

e

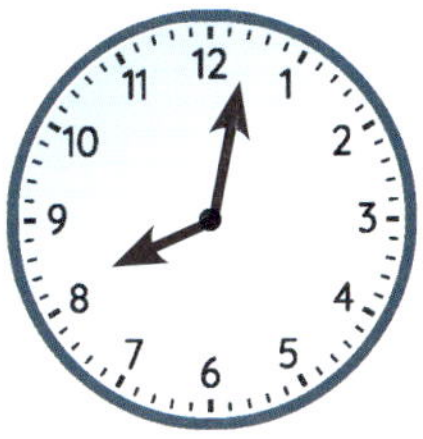

f

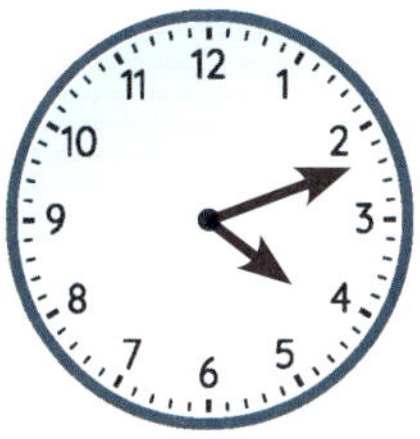

2 Draw these times.

a 26 to 5

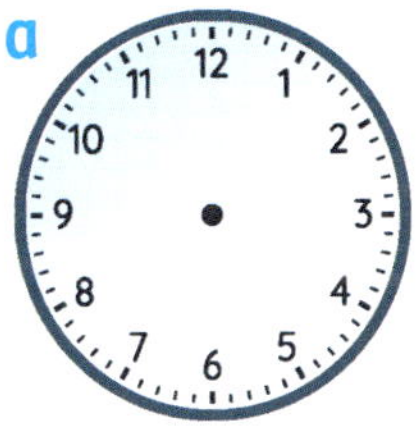

b 6 past 11

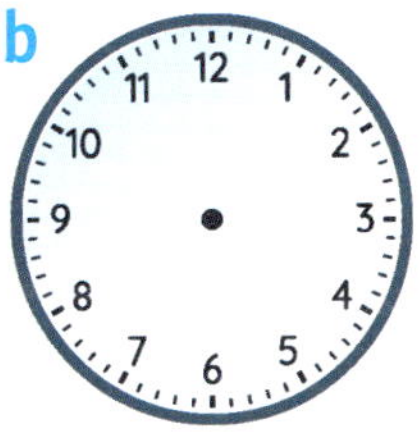

c 14 to 4

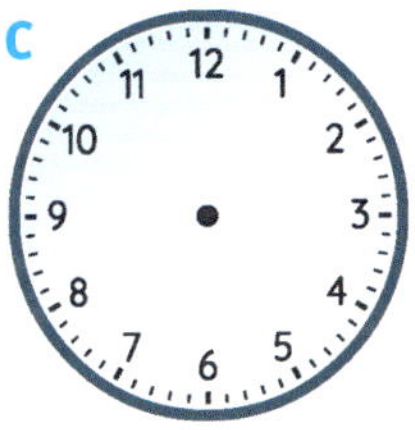

d 21 past 1

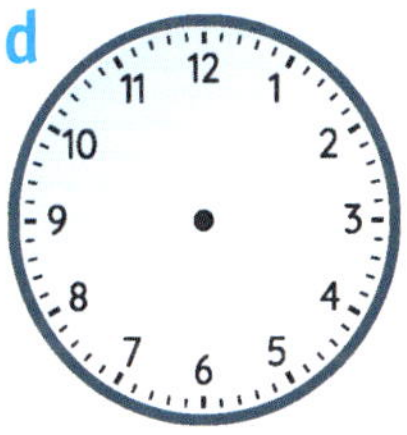

e 9 past 6

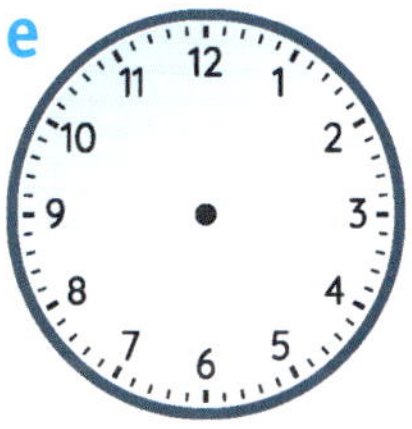

Mastery Checklist I can:
- ☐ show half hours and quarter hours on a clock
- ☐ recognise and show times to the nearest 5 minutes
- ☐ match analogue and digital times
- ☐ recognise and show times to the minute.

Unit 8 Prisms

Faces, corners, edges, views

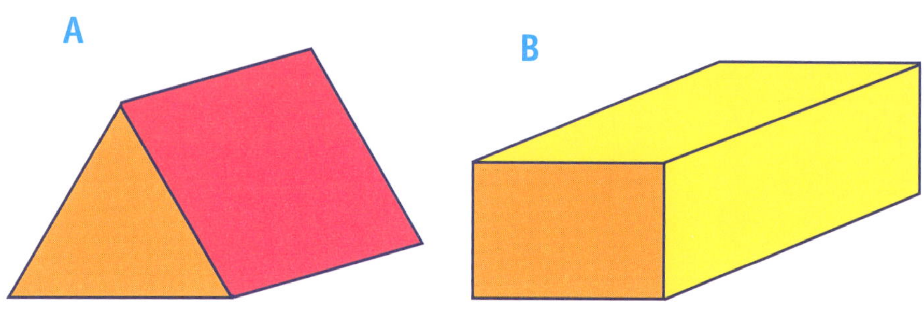

Prisms:
- **have two matching ends**
- **all other faces are rectangles**
- **are named by the shape of the matching ends.**

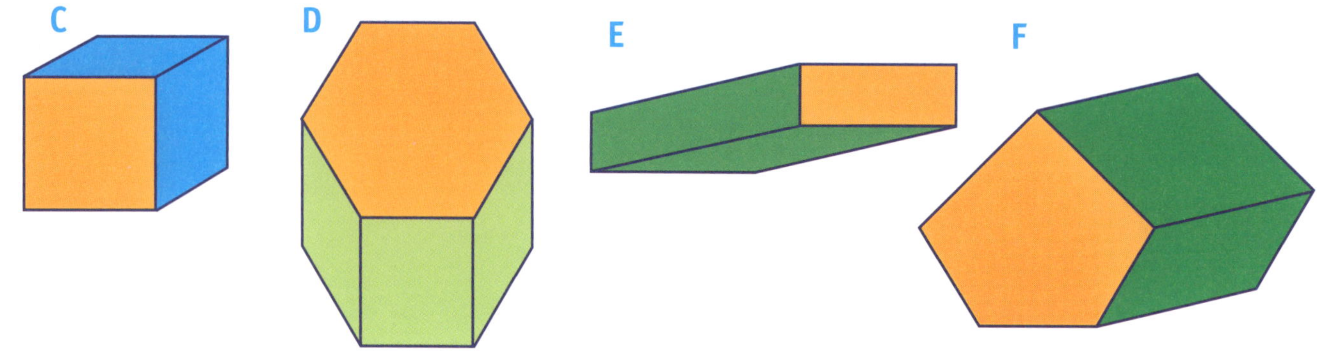

1 Name the shape of each orange face (end).

A ______ B ______
C ______ D ______
E ______ F ______

2 Use the orange face name (end) to name each prism.

A *Triangular prism* B ______
C ______ D ______
E ______ F ______

3 How many faces and ends altogether does each prism have? Remember that you can't see them all.

A ______ B ______ C ______
D ______ E ______ F ______

4 What shape are all the faces that aren't ends? ______

5 What is a prism? ______

______

______

Space AC9M3SP01 make, compare and classify objects, identifying key features and explaining why these features make them suited to their uses

Unit 8 Pyramids

Pyramids:
- have one base and all other faces are triangles
- are named by the shape of the base.

1 Name these pyramids.

a 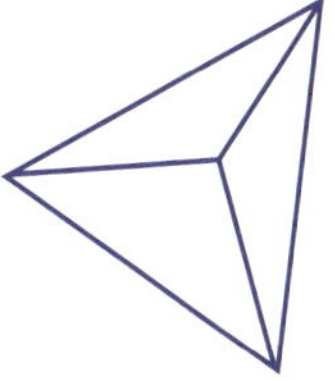

____

____

b 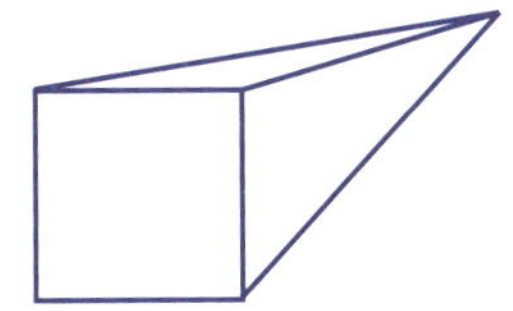

____

____

c 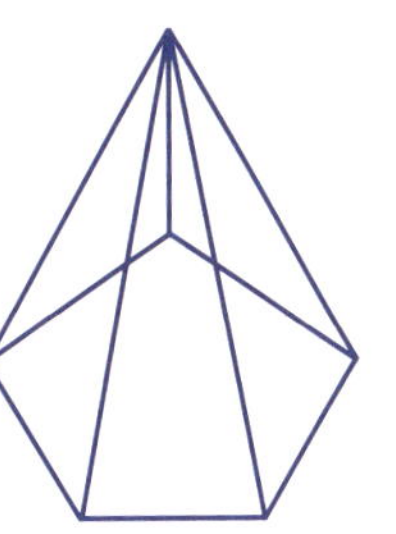

____

____

2 Circle the pyramids. Draw a square around the prisms.

A 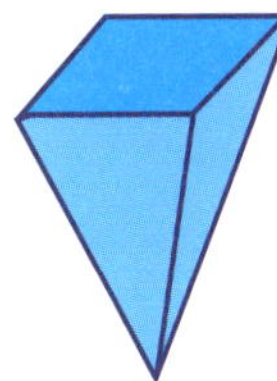

B 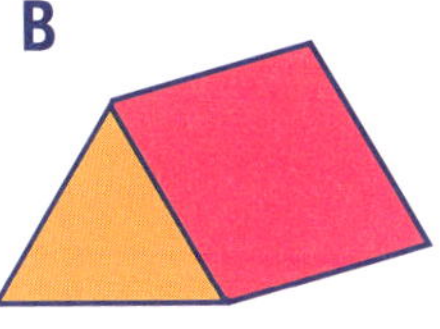

C 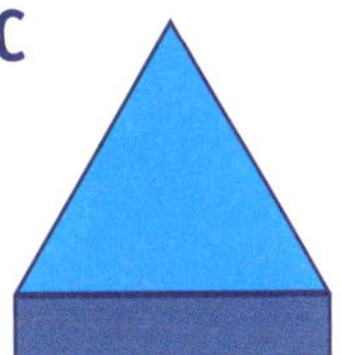

D 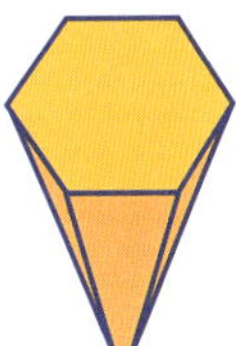

E 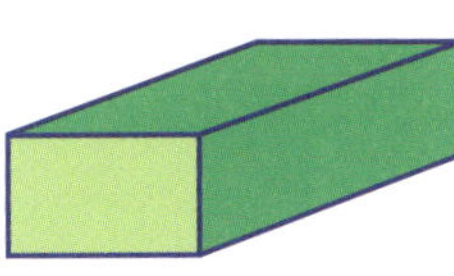

a How many faces has shape **D**? __________

b How many faces has shape **A**? __________

c Which picture shows a square pyramid? __________

d Which picture shows a rectangular prism? __________

3 Draw each face.

Challenge! How many everyday items can you name that are pyramid-shaped or triangular prisms?

____

____

____

Unit 8 Constructing 3D objects

Use clay and small pieces of sticks or straws to construct the 3D objects. Then write how many faces, edges and corners.

Prism	Faces	Edges	Corners
	6	12	8

Pyramid	Faces	Edges	Corners
	5	8	5

Space AC9M3SP01 make, compare and classify objects, identifying key features and explaining why these features make them suited to their uses

Unit 8 Cones, cylinders and spheres

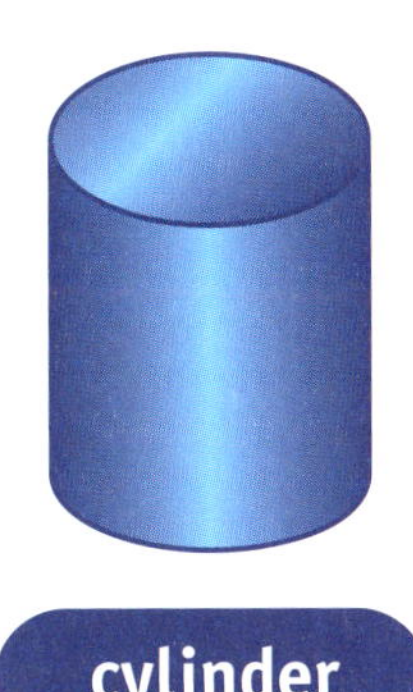

cylinder

cone

sphere

1 Name three things that are cylinders.

a ______ b ______ c ______

2 Name three things that are cones.

a ______ b ______ c ______

3 Name three things that are spheres.

a ______ b ______ c ______

4 Which object above can be most easily stacked? ______

Why? ______

5 A 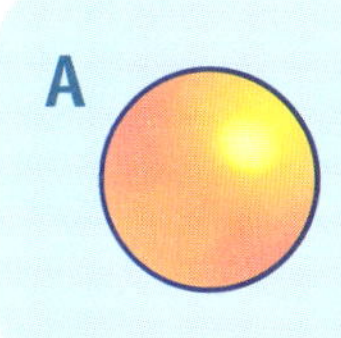 B 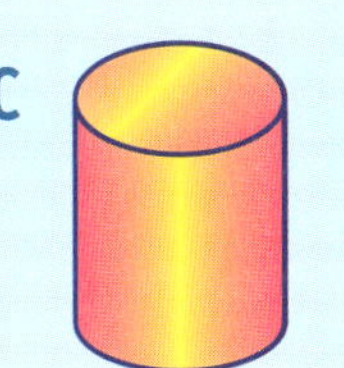 C

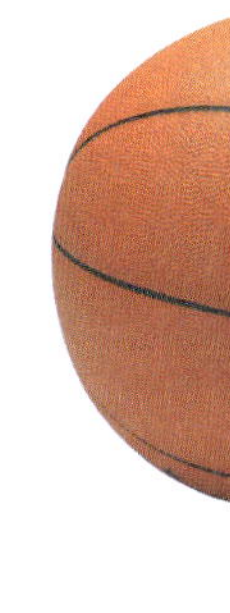

Am I **A**, **B** or **C**?

a I have 1 curved surface and 1 flat surface. ______

b I have only 1 surface. ______

c I have 2 flat surfaces and 1 curved surface. ______

6 How many surfaces has **A**? ______ **B**? ______ **C**? ______

Mastery Checklist I can:

- ☐ describe the features of prisms
- ☐ describe the features of pyramids
- ☐ make prisms and pyramids
- ☐ describe the features of cones, cylinders and spheres.

Problem solving

How can you make prisms?

1 Write the time when you start this page, using 'to' or 'past'. ____________

2 Make a prism. Choose from the following ways.
Use pattern blocks.
Use paper.
Use clay or another solid material.

build a prism

3 Describe what you did and how you did it. Draw it.

____
____
____
____
____
____
____

4 Draw your prism from a different view.

5 What did you find out about prisms?

____
____

6 Write the time when you finished working on this page. ____________

How long were you working on this page? ____________

I can solve problems by:

☐ understanding properties of prisms ☐ drawing prisms from different views.

Space AC9M3SP01 make, compare and classify objects, identifying key features and explaining why these features make them suited to their uses

Unit 9 Graphs

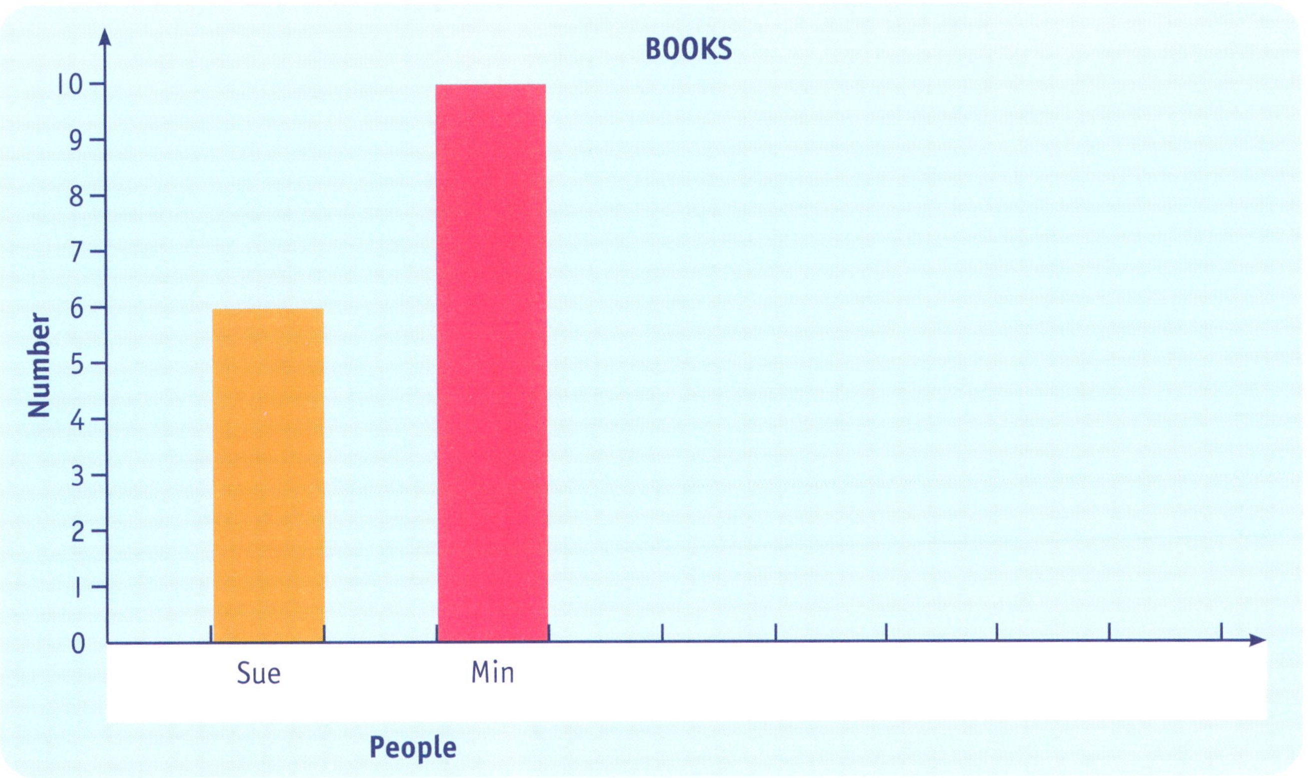

1 Complete the column graph. Write the children's names under the columns.

2 What is this graph telling us? ______

3 Who has: a the most books? ______ b the least books? ______

4 Who has two less books than Amy? ______

5 Which two children together have 9 books? ______

6 How many books do the children have altogether? ______

7 If John gives half his books to Min, how many will he now have? ______

8 Does the graph tell us who likes reading most? Why or why not?

______

______

______

Unit 9 Column graph

At the beginning of the year Mr Wright gave the students in his class new pencils.

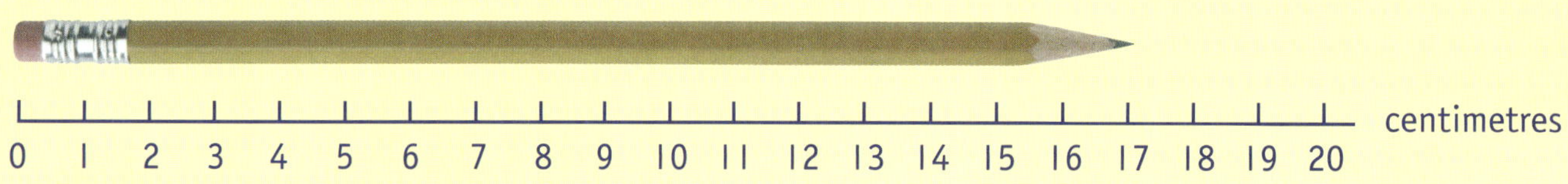

1 How long were the pencils? ______________

One month later Mr Wright asked some students how long their pencils were now. He graphed the results.

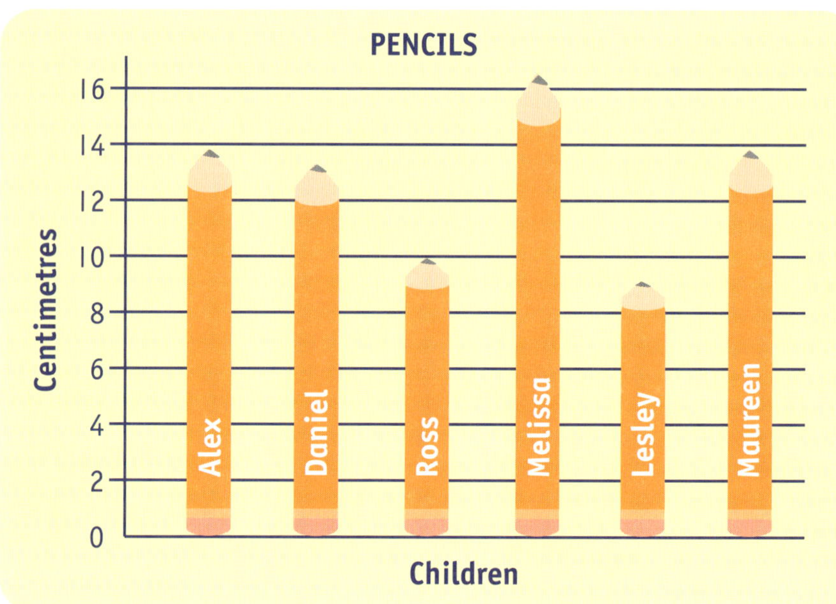

2 How long is Alex's pencil? ______________

3 How long is Daniel's pencil? ______________

4 Who has the longest pencil? ______________

5 Whose pencil is the shortest? ______________

6 a How long is Lesley's pencil? ______________

b How much shorter is it now than when she got it? ______________

7 How much shorter is Ross's pencil now than when Mr Wright gave it to him? ______________

8 Give one reason why Lesley's pencil is so short.

____

____

9 Why do you think Melissa's pencil is so long?

____

____

10 Why did Mr Wright measure pencils? ______________

____

Statistics AC9M3ST01 & AC9M3ST02 acquire data for categorical and discrete numerical variables; record the data using appropriate methods • create and compare different graphical representations of data sets including using software where appropriate; interpret the data in terms of the context

Problem solving

Class favourites survey

Find out about your class. Survey the class about a topic: Sports, Food or Games. What question will you ask?

Carry out a survey.

Tally

Show your results as a picture graph or column graph.

What did you find out?

I can solve problems by:

☐ understanding data and data displays ☐ collecting and organising data.

Unit 9 Certain, likely, unlikely, impossible

1 Write *certain*, *likely*, *unlikely* or *impossible*.

a The sky will be green tomorrow. ____________

b The sun will rise in the morning. ____________

c I may not be able to go to the party. ____________

d I will grow taller than a giraffe. ____________

e It might rain tonight. ____________

f We will have a holiday this year. ____________

2 There are 6 red, 4 green and 2 yellow balls in the bag.

Without looking, what is your chance of choosing a:

a	red ball?	50-50	likely	unlikely	impossible
b	yellow ball?	50-50	likely	unlikely	impossible
c	green ball?	50-50	likely	unlikely	impossible
d	purple ball?	50-50	likely	unlikely	impossible
e	ball?	50-50	likely	unlikely	impossible

3 Colour the flowers so that it would be likely you choose purple, unlikely you choose orange, impossible to choose white.

4 Colour the marbles so you have an equal chance of choosing red or blue.

Probability AC9M3P01 identify practical activities and everyday events involving chance; describe possible outcomes and events as 'likely' or 'unlikely' and identify some events as 'certain' or 'impossible' explaining reasoning

Unit 9 Chance outcomes

The different ways a thing can happen are called **outcomes**.

1 A coin is tossed.

a What two ways can it fall? ____________ ____________

b How many outcomes can there be? ____________

2 a What colours show on traffic lights? ________________________

b How many are there? ____________

c How many possible outcomes are there? ____________

3 a How many faces are on this die? ____________

b If you toss the die, what are the possible outcomes?

____________ ____________ ____________ ____________ ____________ ____________

c How many possible outcomes are there? ____________

4 This basket contains two apples and two oranges. Without looking, you pick out one piece of fruit.

a What could it be? ________________________

b How many possible outcomes are there? ____________

5 Write something where:

a the outcome is certain. ________________________

b the outcome is impossible. ________________________

c the outcome is likely. ________________________

d the outcome is unlikely. ________________________

Challenge!

Work with a partner. Throw a die 10 times. Record the outcomes. There are 6 possible outcomes. Does each outcome occur the same number of times? Why or why not?

chance experiment

Mastery Checklist I can:
- ☐ complete a column graph
- ☐ answer questions about a column graph
- ☐ carry out a survey and present the results
- ☐ identify events as certain, likely, unlikely or impossible
- ☐ show an equal chance
- ☐ work out possible outcomes.

Probability AC9M3P01 & AC9M3P02 describe possible outcomes and events as 'likely' or 'unlikely' and identify some events as 'certain' or 'impossible' explaining reasoning • conduct repeated chance experiments; identify and describe possible outcomes, record the results, recognise and discuss the variation

Revision Term 1

1 Write the number: p 2

a 10 more than 115 ______

b 100 less than 810 ______

c 10 less than 370 ______

d 100 more than 370 ______

2 Write in numerals: p 6

a three hundred and seventy-one

______

b five hundred and six ______

c two hundred and forty ______

3 Write in words: p 6

a 98 ______

b 613 ______

______

c 480 ______

______

4 Write in the missing numbers. p 8

a 95 90 ______ 80 75 ______

b 59 ______ 39 ______ 19

c 19 17 ______ ______ 11 9

5 Double: a 7 ______ b 19 ______ p 9

6 Use the number lines. p 12

a 32 − 17 = ______

b 53 − 25 = ______

p 13

7 a 17 − 9 = ______ b 15 − 8 = ______

c 20 − 13 = ______ d 16 − 7 = ______

8 p 13

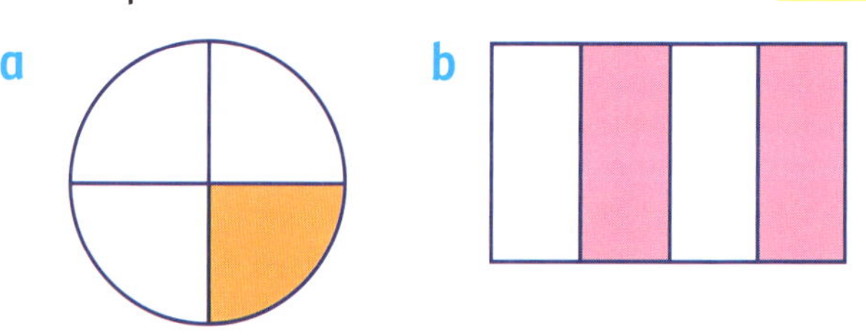

Write a story and a number sentence.

______

______

______

9 Circle the correct answer. p 18

a A door is about 2 cm 2 m high.

b A book cover is about 20 cm 1 m wide.

c A bedroom is about 50 m 4 m long.

p 19

10 Measure the lines to the nearest cm.

a ______ b ______

11 What part has been shaded? p 22

a ______ b ______

c

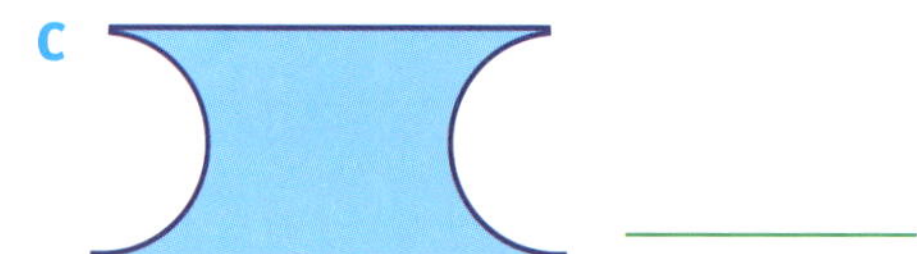

______

12 Draw lines to cut this into quarters. Shade $\frac{1}{2}$. p 22

Revision Term 1

13 Write a fraction for the part coloured. p 22

a 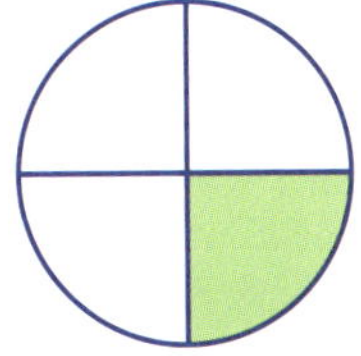 ______

b 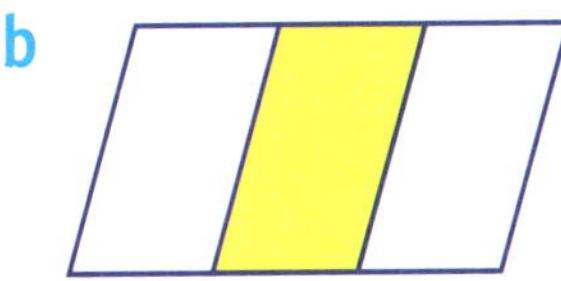 ______

c 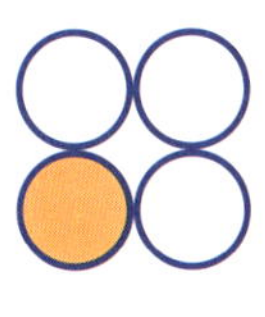 ______

d 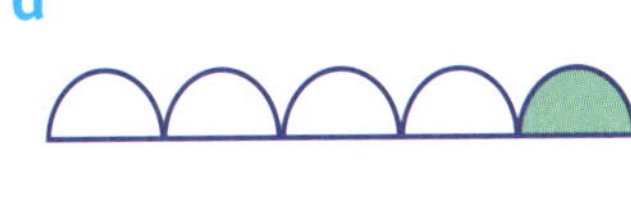 ______

14 Write the next two terms and the rule. p 30

a 5 8 11 14 17 ______ ______

Rule ____________

b 20 25 30 35 ______ ______

Rule ____________

c 63 58 53 48 ______ ______

Rule ____________

15 Make your own pattern on the grid. Write the rule. p 30

1	2	3	4	5
6	7	8	9	10
11	12	13	14	15
16	17	18	19	20
21	22	23	24	25

____

16 What is the time? p 33

a  ____________

b  ____________

17 Name these 3D objects. p 37

a 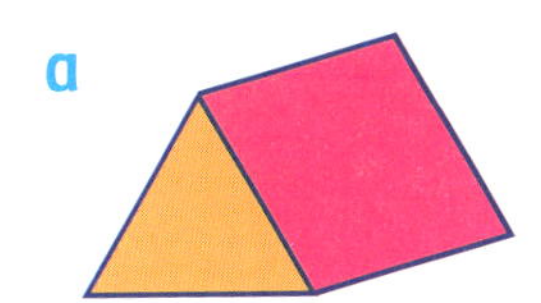 ____________

b 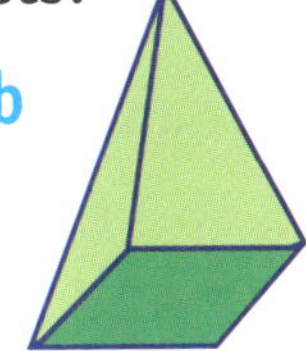 ____________

18 How many faces has: p 38

a a cube? ______

b a triangular pyramid? ______

19 Draw the top view of: p 39

a cone	a cylinder

20 What am I? p 39

a I have 1 curved surface only. ______

b I have 4 triangular faces. ______

21 Write one thing for tomorrow: p 44

a that is certain to happen.

____

b that is unlikely to happen.

____

c that is impossible.

____

p 45

22 a How many possible outcomes are there if you throw a die? ______

b What are they? ____________

NAPLAN* practice

This is a test to see how well you understand what you have learnt.

Instructions

Read each question carefully. There are three different ways to show your answer:

- Shade the bubble next to the correct answer.
- Write a word in a box.
- Write a number in a box.

Use a pencil. DO NOT use a pen. If you make a mistake, rub it out and try again.

Shade one bubble.

1 Jess arranged her star stickers.

How many star stickers does Jess have?

37 ◯ 43 ◯ 47 ◯ 50 ◯

2 4 children drew some shapes.

Glen | Zac | Kell | Bella

Who drew a triangle and a square?

Kell ◯ Zac ◯ Bella ◯ Glen ◯

3 What colour is the longest crayon?

0 1 2 3 4 5 6 7 8 9 10

CRAYON CRAYON CRAYON CRAYON

yellow ◯ blue ◯ red ◯ green ◯

* This is not an officially endorsed publication of the NAPLAN program and is produced independently of Australian governments.

Test practice

4 Here are four numbers.

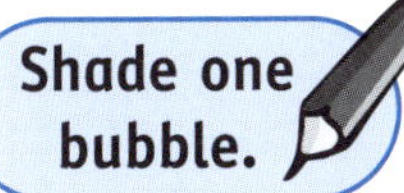

What is the second largest number?

85 805 588 815

5 28 + 9 = ☐

Write your answer in the box.

6 Double 9 and add 4. ☐

Shade one bubble.

7 Which letter can be cut into halves?

8 If we count by threes, what will we say after 24?

25 26 27 28

9 How many wheels on 4 cars?

5 + 4 + 4 + 4 = 5 × 4 = 4 + 4 + 4 + 4 = 5 + 4 =

10 Jimmy's shape has a right angle. Which is Jimmy's shape?

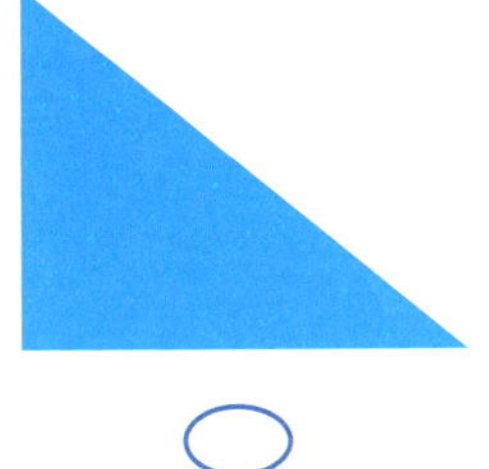

Test practice

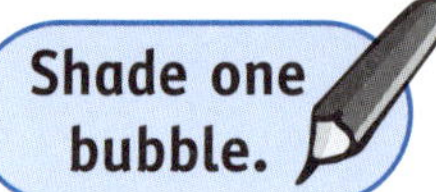

11 Gary has 8 more fish than mice. Which statement is true?

There are less mice than fish. ◯

There are the same numbers of fish and mice. ◯

There are less fish than mice. ◯

Mice plus fish is more than fish plus mice. ◯

Write your answer in the box.

12 Nan has 20 metres of ribbon and cuts off 5 metres for Nadeem, then another 5 metres for Stacey.

How much does she have left? ☐

13 47 – 34 = ☐

14 There was 2 L of juice in this bottle. How much did I pour out?

◯ one litre

◯ half a litre

◯ 750 mL

◯ 2 litres

Write your answer in the box.

15 If this Friday is 9th April, what is the date next Friday? 

Test practice

16 This is a counting pattern.

38, 35, 32, △, 26, 23, ○

What numbers go in the shapes?

26 and 23	30 and 29	31 and 30	29 and 20
	○	○	○

17 Which pattern has one quarter coloured?

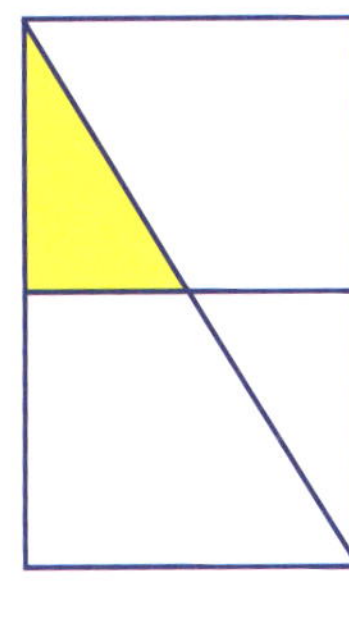 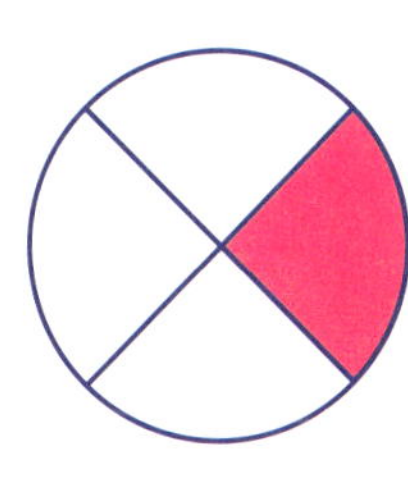 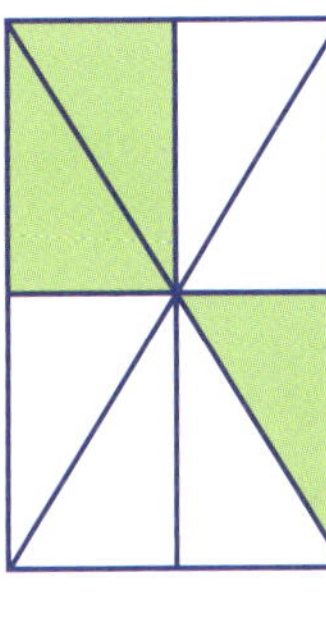 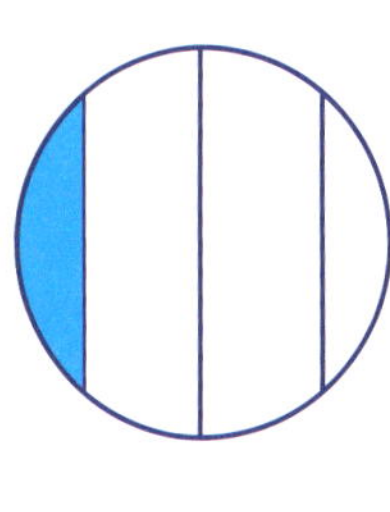

 ○ ○ ○

18 Which object is a cylinder?

   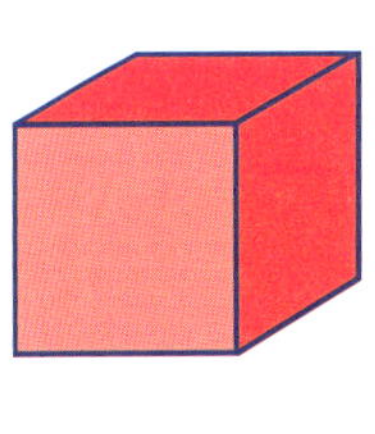

○ ○ ○ ○

19 Which object is a triangular pyramid?

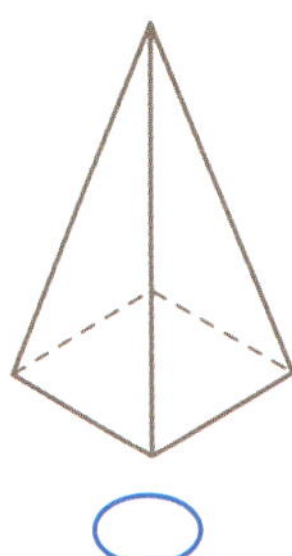 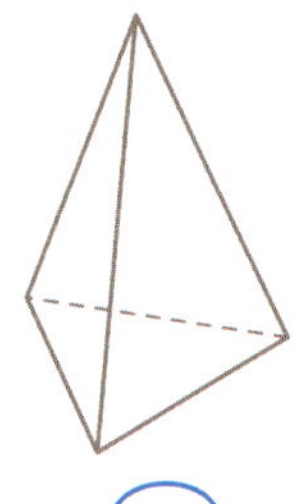 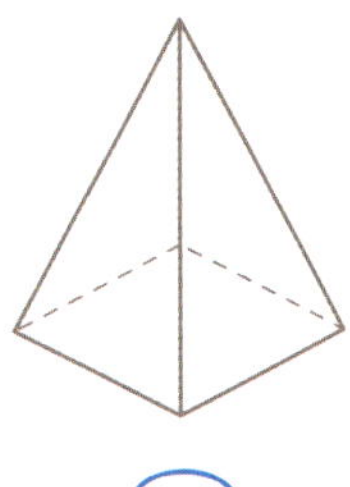 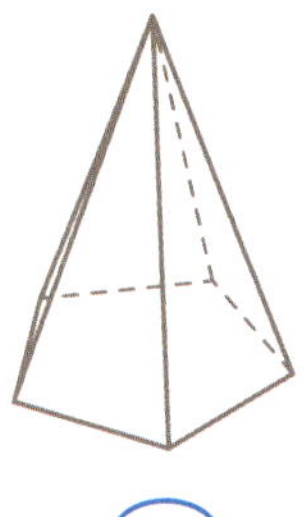

○ ○ ○ ○

Test practice

20 How many faces, edges and corners does a triangular prism have?

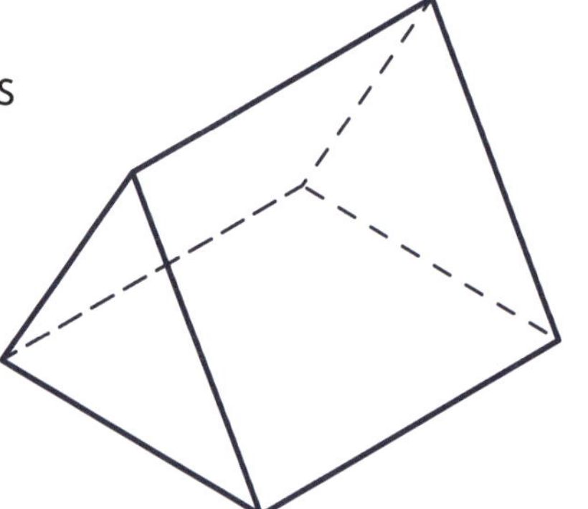

- 6 faces, 5 edges, 9 corners
- 9 faces, 5 edges, 6 corners
- 5 faces, 6 edges, 9 corners
- 5 faces, 9 edges, 6 corners

21 This graph shows runs scored by 5 children.

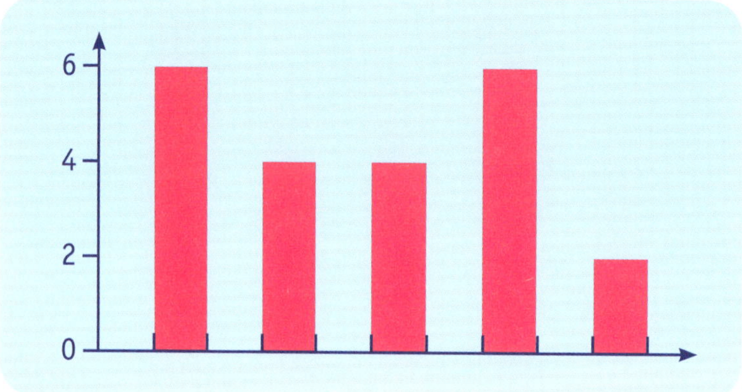

How many children scored 6 runs?

1 6 2 5

22 This arrow shows how many metres a snail has travelled.

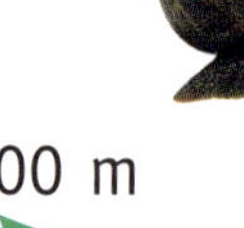

200 300 m

How many metres has the snail travelled?

250 280 207 290

Test practice

23 Which clock is showing a quarter to 4?

Write your answer in the box.

24 Talya has 24 stickers to share equally. If she has 8 friends, how many stickers can she give each friend?

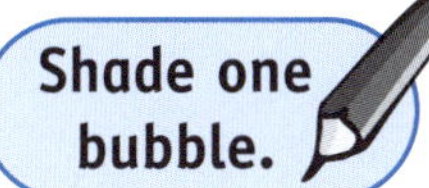

25 To be certain of pulling out a red ball from a bag of six balls, what should be in the bag?

6 red

26 Cow needs 25 squares. Horse needs 30 squares. Pig needs 18 squares. Sheep needs 17 squares. Which paddock does the sheep live in?

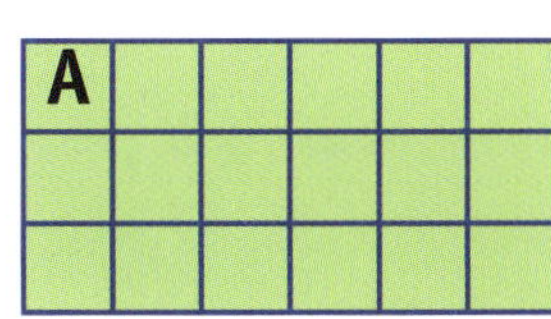

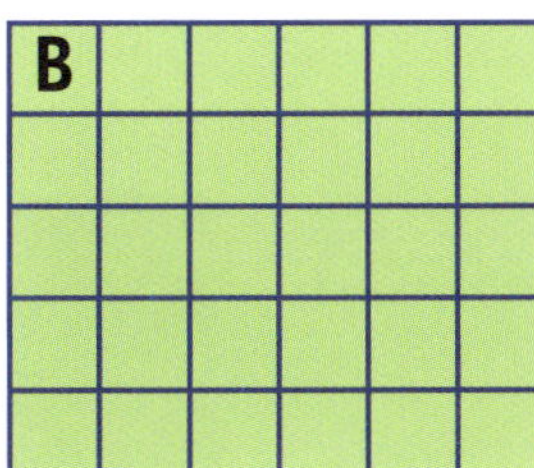

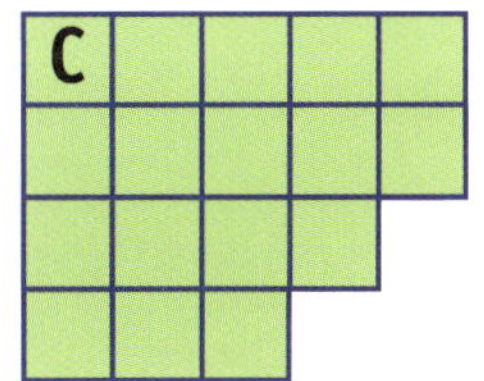

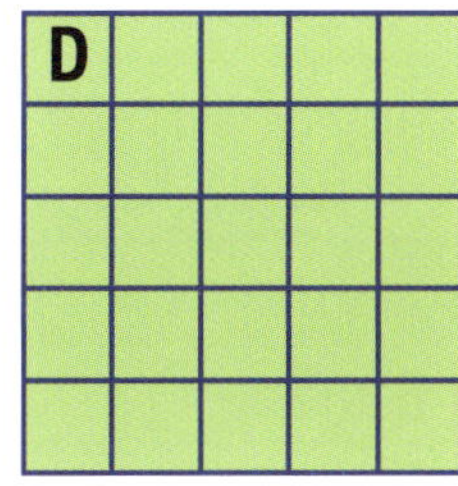

A B C D

27 We spent $4.80 on biscuits and $3.95 on drinks. How much more did we spend on biscuits than drinks?

$0.85 $1.05 $0.90 $1.15

Test practice

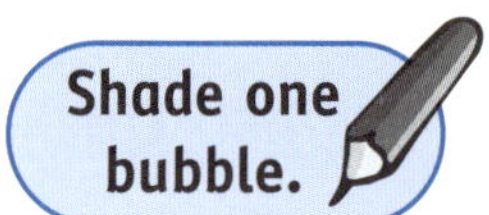

28 The cow is heavier than the pig, the pig is heavier than the cat, but the cat is lighter than the dog. Which animal is lightest?

the dog ◯ the cow ◯ the cat ◯ the pig ◯

29

How much money do I have?

$530 ◯ $511 ◯ $503 ◯ $500 ◯

30 Kerry built a cube from straws. She used one straw for each edge. How many straws did she use?

12 ◯ 8 ◯ 21 ◯ 24 ◯

31 This is a train timetable.

Train to:	Time leaving:
Banker	10:00
Havely	10:10
Spickle	10:15
Kenso	10:40

Which train is leaving at a quarter past ten?

Banker ◯ Havely ◯ Spickle ◯ Kenso ◯

Test practice

32 Some friends had 10 strawberries to share equally. There was 1 left over. How many friends were there?

3	4	5	2
◯	◯	◯	◯

33 This is a map of Jackie's town.

On her way to the Library after school, what does Jackie walk past?

- ◯ the Café and home
- ◯ the field and the Police Station
- ◯ the Café and the Church
- ◯ the field and the Mall

34 To make this number pattern, what is the rule?

7, 11, 15, 19, 23

- ◯ add all numbers to 20
- ◯ double and add 1
- ◯ add 5
- ◯ add 4

Unit 10 Bridging 1000

Numbers to 1000

B $75

A $946

C $608

E $1035

D $1261

G $2413

F $1197

1 Which wallet holds the most money? ______

2 Which wallet holds the least money? ______

3 Order the wallets from holds least to holds most.

4 Add $10 to:

a B ______ b C ______ c D ______ d G ______ e A ______

5 Take $100 from:

a A ______ b C ______ c F ______ d G ______ e E ______

6 Which wallet holds: a closest to $100? ______ b closest to $1000? ______

7 A TV costs $980. Which wallets could you use? ____________________

Why? ____

 Number AC9M3N03 & AC9M3N05 add and subtract two- and three-digit numbers using place value to partition, rearrange and regroup numbers to assist in calculations without a calculator • estimate the quantity of objects in collections and make estimates when solving problems to determine the reasonableness of calculations

Unit 10 Thousands

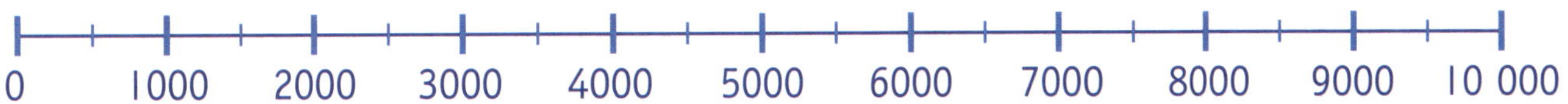

1 Write the number 1000 more than:

a 2000. ________ b 5000. ________ c 7000. ________ d 3000. ________

2 Write the number 1000 less than:

a 10 000. ________ b 5000. ________ c 9000. ________ d 2000. ________

3 What number is halfway between:

a 0 and 1000? ________

b 6000 and 7000? ________

c 3000 and 4000? ________

d 9000 and 10 000? ________

e 1000 and 2000? ________

f 8000 and 9000? ________

4 Add.

	Add 1		Add 10		Add 100
a 99	100	→	110	→	210
b 109		→		→	
c 199		→		→	
d 1009		→		→	
e 1099		→		→	
f 1999		→		→	

5 Write the number for:

a two hundred and forty-eight. ________

b eight hundred and eleven. ________

c four hundred and fifty. ________

d seven hundred and nine. ________

e one thousand three hundred and sixty-five. ________

f two thousand one hundred and ninety-seven. ________

g four thousand five hundred and eighteen. ________

h seven thousand six hundred and twenty. ________

Challenge! What is my number?

a My ones digit is 4, my hundreds digit is 7, my tens digit is 5 and my thousands digit is 9. ________

b My tens digit is 8 and my thousands digit is 2. ________

Number AC9M3N01 & AC9M3N03 recognise, represent and order natural numbers using naming and writing conventions for numerals beyond 10 000 • add and subtract two- and three-digit numbers using place value to partition, rearrange and regroup numbers to assist in calculations without a calculator

Unit 10 Numbers to 10 000

1 Write the number shown.

a

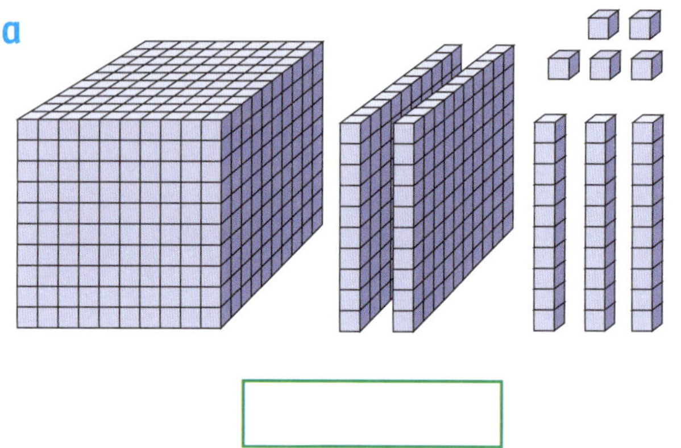

b

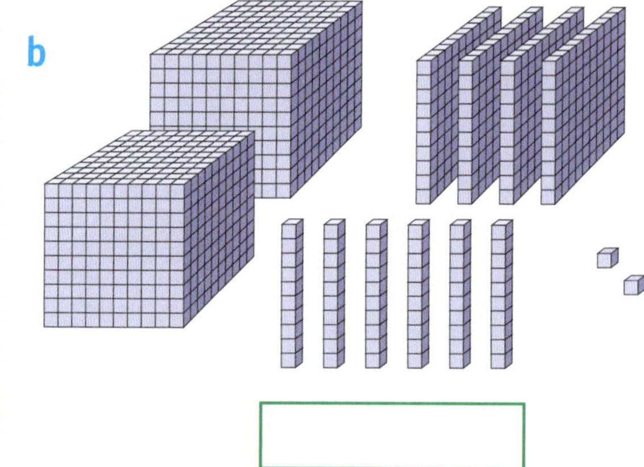

c

d

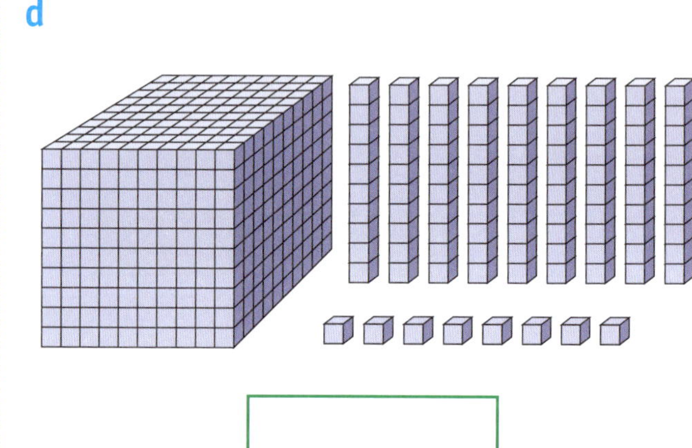

2 Write the numbers from question 1 in words.

a ______________________

b ______________________

c ______________________

d ______________________

3 Circle the larger number.

a 690 609

b 937 793

c 2985 2002

d 4157 5147

e 8061 6810

f 2594 2954

4 Join the numeral to its name.

one thousand and one

one thousand one hundred and ten

one thousand and ten

one thousand one hundred

Unit 10 Place value

3648
3000 + 600 + 40 + 8
The value
of the 3 is 3000
of the 6 is 600
of the 4 is 40
of the 8 is 8

1 Complete.

a 9526 = 9000 + 500 + ______ + ______

b 3749 = ______ + ______ + ______ + ______

c 5618 = ______ + ______ + ______ + ______

d 7293 = ______ + ______ + ______ + ______

e 6054 = ______ + ______ + ______ + ______

2 Write the number.

a 2000 + 800 + 10 + 7 = ______

b 8000 + 400 + 60 + 1 = ______

c 4000 + 900 + 70 + 2 = ______

d 1000 + 300 + 80 + 5 = ______

e 3000 + 40 + 8 = ______

f 7000 + 200 + 6 = ______

3 What is the value of the underlined numeral?

a	2618 ______	b	1584 ______	c	6372 ______	d	9493 ______
e	3265 ______	f	7726 ______	g	159 ______	h	5087 ______
i	4903 ______	j	2600 ______	k	7008 ______	l	304 ______

4 Write these in ascending order.

a	8420	2048	3915	______	______	______
b	7506	983	9375	______	______	______
c	5130	5301	5013	______	______	______
d	4142	1244	4214	______	______	______
e	8080	8800	8008	______	______	______

Challenge!

Use these numerals to write as many different four-digit numbers as you can.

2 9 0 3

How many could you find? ______

Mastery Checklist I can:
- ☐ add 10 and 100 to 4-digit numbers
- ☐ order 4-digit numbers
- ☐ add 1000 to 4-digit numbers
- ☐ find the number halfway between
- ☐ recognise numbers in base 10 blocks
- ☐ expand 4-digit numbers to show place value.

Unit 11 Number facts 3×

1

0	a	0 × 3 = 3 × 0 = 0
3	b	1 × 3 = 3 × 1 = 3
6	c	2 × 3 = 3 × 2 = ☐
9	d	3 × 3 = 3 × 3 = ☐
12	e	4 × 3 = 3 × ☐ = ☐
15	f	☐ × 3 = 3 × 5 = ☐
18	g	6 × 3 = 3 × ☐ = ☐
21	h	7 × 3 = 3 × ☐ = ☐
24	i	☐ × 3 = 3 × ☐ = 24
27	j	☐ × 3 = 3 × ☐ = ☐
30	k	10 × 3 = 3 × 10 = ☐

NOTICE!
Memorise the 3× table.

2 30 – ☐ – 24 – ☐ – ☐ – 15 – 12 – ☐ – 6 – ☐ – ☐

3 Pick (3) and another number from the bag. Multiply them.
Colour the two numbers in the bag and the answer in the rhombus the same colour.

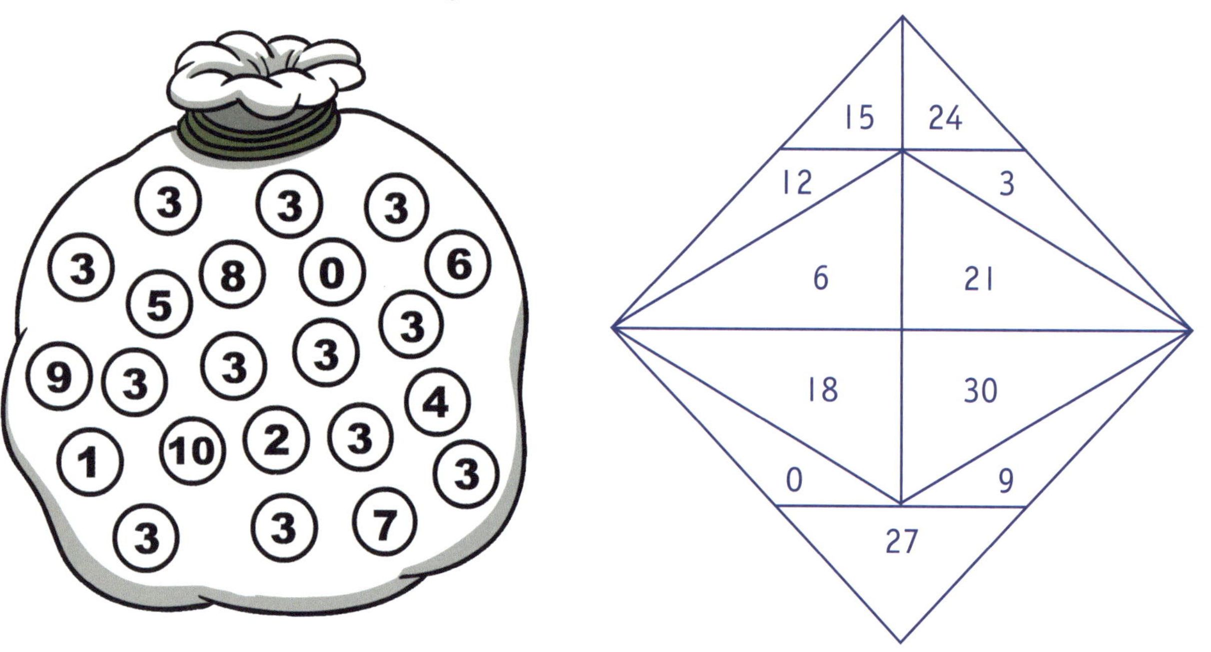

 Number AC9M3N04 multiply and divide one- and two-digit numbers, representing problems using number sentences, diagrams and arrays, and using a variety of calculation strategies
Algebra AC9M3A03 recall and demonstrate proficiency with multiplication facts for 3, 4, 5 and 10

Unit 11 Number facts 0×, 5×

0, 5 tables

1 How many petals on:

a 1 flower? ____ b 7 flowers? ____

c 3 flowers? ____ d 10 flowers? ____

e 2 flowers? ____ f 4 flowers? ____

g 9 flowers? ____ h 6 flowers? ____

i 5 flowers? ____ j 8 flowers? ____

k How many petals on no flowers? ____

l 11 × 5 = ____ m 12 × 5 = ____

Any number times zero is always equal to zero.

2 a 0 × 6 = ☐ b 3 × 0 = ☐ c 2 × 0 = ☐ d 0 × 8 = ☐

e 9 × 0 = ☐ f 0 × 4 = ☐ g 66 × 0 = ☐ h 999 × 0 = ☐

3 Count by 5s.

4

1	2	3	4	5	6	7	8	9	10
11	12	13	14	15	16	17	18	19	20
21	22	23	24	25	26	27	28	29	30
31	32	33	34	35	36	37	38	39	40
41	42	43	44	45	46	47	48	49	50
51	52	53	54	55	56	57	58	59	60

a Colour the ×3 numbers yellow.

b Colour the ×5 numbers blue.

c Which numbers turn green?

____

____

____

____

____

Unit 11 Number facts 3×, 4×, 5×, 10×

0×

0 × 3 = 0

0 × 5 = 0

0 × 10 = 0

1 Count backwards in:

a 3s from 21, ____, ____, ____, ____, ____, ____

b 4s from 38, ____, ____, ____, ____, ____, ____

c 10s from 100, ____, ____, ____, ____, ____, ____

2 Write the number sentence. How many:

a	wheels on 8 trikes?	3 x 8	on 3 trikes?	3 x 3
b	eyes on 9 owls?	____	on 5 owls?	____
c	10c coins in $7?	____	in $4?	____
d	toes on 6 feet?	____	on 8 feet?	____
e	hands on 5 clocks?	____	on 10 clocks?	____
f	arms on 4 starfish?	____	on 9 starfish?	____
g	corners on 7 squares?	____	on 4 squares?	____
h	ears on 10 horses?	____	tails on 10 horses?	____
i	feet on 1 dog?	____	feet on 3 dogs?	____

3 a One ticket to a show costs $10. What is the cost of 6 tickets? ☐

b Ten children get 5 lollies each. How many lollies altogether? ☐

4 Complete this from memory.

×	0	1	2	3	4	5	6	7	8	9	10
5											

Mastery Checklist I can:
- ☐ remember the 3× table
- ☐ remember the 5× table
- ☐ remember the 0× table
- ☐ count back in 3s, 5s and 10s
- ☐ write number sentences
- ☐ complete number facts from memory.

Number AC9M3N04 & AC9M3N07 multiply and divide one- and two-digit numbers • follow and create algorithms involving a sequence of steps and decisions to investigate numbers; describe any emerging patterns **Algebra AC9M3A03** recall and demonstrate proficiency with multiplication facts for 3, 4, 5 and 10

Unit 12 Subtraction facts to 20

1 Ronnie made a pile of cans for target practice.

a How many cans are there? ______

How many would be left if she knocked down:

b 6? ______ c 11? ______ d 15? ______ e 2? ______ f 13? ______

g the top row? ______ h the top two rows? ______

i the top three rows? ______ j the top four rows? ______

k all the cans? ______

2 How many would she need to rebuild if these were left?

a 7 ______ b 12 ______ c 19 ______ d 4 ______ e 9 ______

3 She rebuilds only the bottom three rows. How many are left if she knocks down:

a 6? ______ b 9? ______ c 13? ______ d 7? ______ e 3? ______

4 She doesn't put up the top row. How many are left if she knocks down:

a 18? ______ b 11? ______ c 6? ______ d 13? ______ e 4? ______

Algebra AC9M3A01 recognise and explain the connection between addition and subtraction as inverse operations, apply to partition numbers and find unknown values in number sentences
AC9M3A02 extend and apply knowledge of addition and subtraction facts to 20 to develop efficient mental strategies for computation

Unit 12 Subtraction linked with addition

1 Write three more related facts.

a 20 – 6 = 14   20 – 14 = 6   6 + 14 = 20   14 + 6 = 20

b 20 – 13 = ______ ______ ______ ______

c 20 – 9 = ______ ______ ______ ______

d 20 – 16 = ______ ______ ______ ______

e 20 – 5 = ______ ______ ______ ______

f 20 – 12 = ______ ______ ______ ______

2 Complete these puzzles.

–	–	
18	6	
14	3	
		☐

–	–	
20	9	
15	7	
		☐

–	–	
19	7	
11	4	
		☐

–	–	
16	8	
9	5	
		☐

3 Jay has $20. How much change would she get if she bought the:

a top? ______   b teddy bear? ______   c robot? ______   d goggles? ______

e top and chocolates? ______   f table tennis bat and goggles? ______

4 Vinny has $16. What item can't he buy? ______

5 True or false?

a Jay could buy three items. ______

b Why? ______

c Vinny bought the goggles and has $8 left. ______

d Why? ______

Algebra AC9M3A01 recognise and explain the connection between addition and subtraction as inverse operations, apply to partition numbers and find unknown values in number sentences
AC9M3A02 extend and apply knowledge of addition and subtraction facts to 20 to develop efficient mental strategies for computation

Unit 12 Counting on

1 a 16 take away 9 ______ b 11 minus 7 ______
c 19 subtract 12 ______ d take 8 from 12 ______
e 80 subtract 10 ______ f 7 less than 47 ______
g 15 minus 10 ______ h take 0 from 18 ______

–
subtract
minus
less than
take from
take away
difference

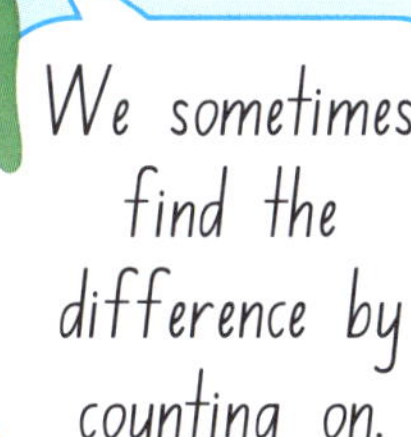

20, 21, 22, 23, 24, 25.
That's 6 more!

2 Count on to complete.

a

	39	43	40	42	46	45
–37						

b

	62	68	60	66	64	61
–59						

c

	26	21	25	20	23	28
–18						

d

	80	87	89	83	90	84
–76						

3 Count on to find the answers. Then write the subtraction.

a Carl had 19 marbles.
Ingrid had 24 marbles.
How many more did Ingrid have? ______

☐ – ☐ = ☐

b Bella had 37 Smarties.
Bill had 29 Smarties.
How many more did Bella have? ______

☐ – ☐ = ☐

c Shona ate 53 cherries.
Seb ate 61 cherries.
How many more did Seb eat? ______

☐ – ☐ = ☐

d Nicole read 48 pages.
Ned read 39 pages.
How many more did Nicole read? ______

☐ – ☐ = ☐

Looking for patterns

What is the pattern? Make up another subtraction pattern.

	11	61	81	31	51	91	21	71
–7								

Unit 12 Two-digit subtraction

Jump strategy 

1 Quick practice.

a	b	c	d	e	f	g
16 − 7 = ___	20 − 12 = ___	18 − 13 = ___	14 − 9 = ___	13 − 6 = ___	15 − 8 = ___	12 − 5 = ___

2 Use the number line.

a 37 minus 23

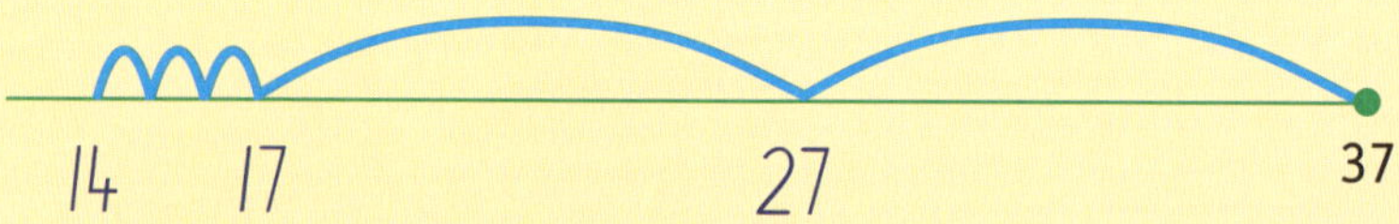

14 17 27 37

37 − 23 = ___

b 52 take away 34

52

52 − ___ = ___

c subtract 15 from 61

61

61 − ___ = ___

d 94 less 47

94

− ___ = ___

e difference between 72 and 23

− ___ = ___

Draw a diagram

Jay's ant farm had 96 ants. 47 escaped and 25 died.

How many are left? ☐

Hint: Draw a number line.

Mastery Checklist

I can:
- ☐ use subtraction facts to 20
- ☐ connect addition and subtraction
- ☐ work out change from $20
- ☐ count on to subtract
- ☐ use algorithms to subtract
- ☐ use number lines to subtract.

Number AC9M3N03 add and subtract two- and three-digit numbers using place value to partition, rearrange and regroup numbers to assist in calculations without a calculator
Algebra AC9M3A02 extend and apply knowledge of addition and subtraction facts to 20 to develop efficient mental strategies for computation

Unit 13 Subtraction strategies

Subtract to 100

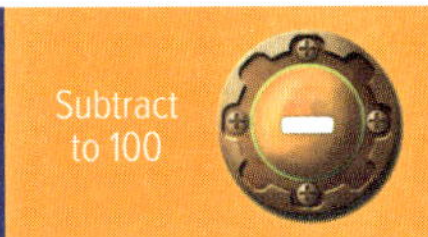

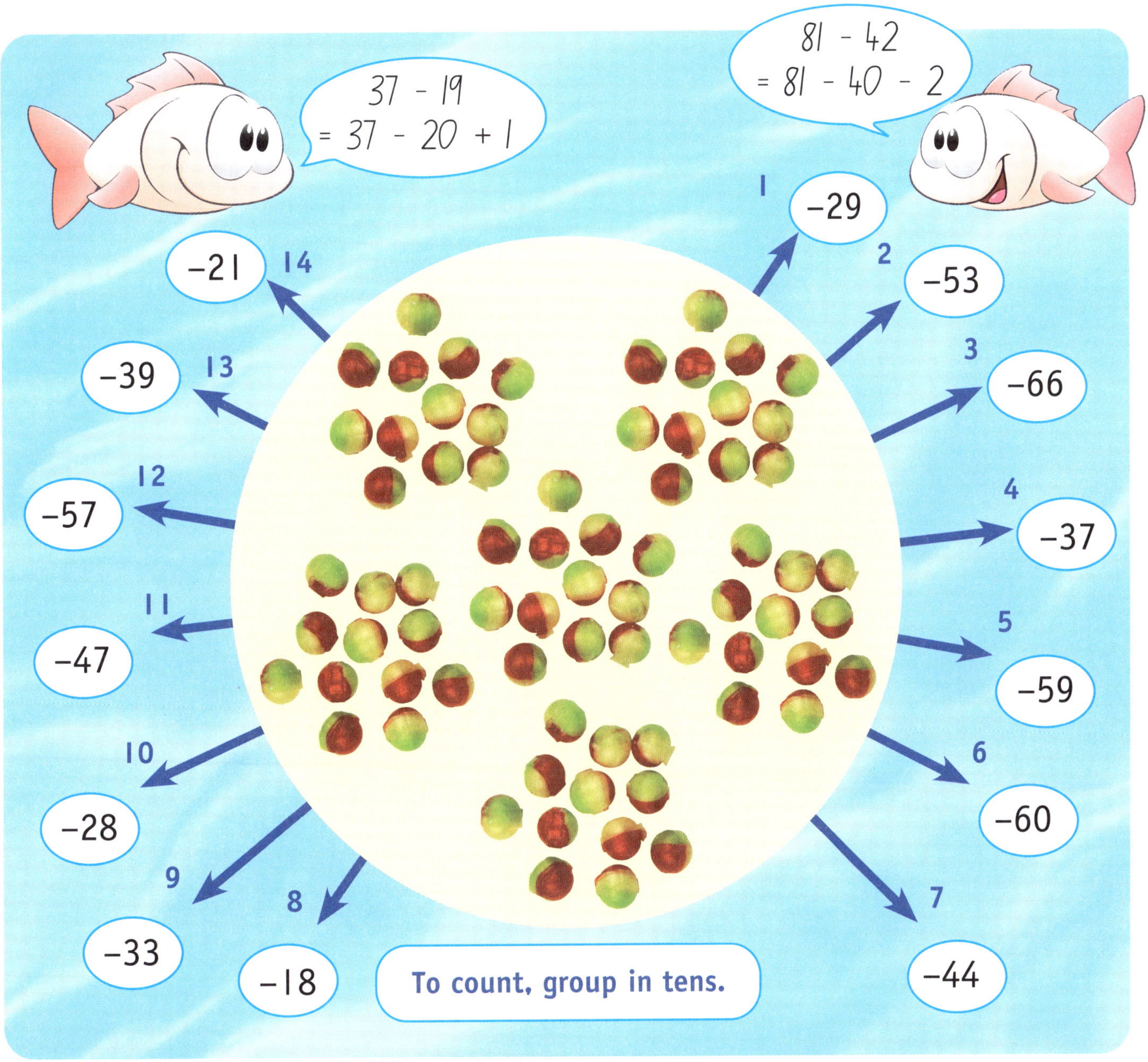

37 - 19
= 37 - 20 + 1
81 - 42
= 81 - 40 - 2
1 −29
2 −53
3 −66
4 −37
5 −59
6 −60
7 −44
8 −18
9 −33
10 −28
11 −47
12 −57
13 −39
14 −21
To count, group in tens.

1 72 − 30 + 1 = ____ ☐ − ☐ = ☐

2 72 − 50 − 3 = ____ ☐ − ☐ = ☐

3 ________ = ____ ☐ − ☐ = ☐

4 ________ = ____ ☐ − ☐ = ☐

5 ________ = ____ ☐ − ☐ = ☐

6 ________ = ____ ☐ − ☐ = ☐

7 ________ = ____ ☐ − ☐ = ☐

8 ________ = ____ ☐ − ☐ = ☐

9 ________ = ____ ☐ − ☐ = ☐

10 ________ = ____ ☐ − ☐ = ☐

11 ________ = ____ ☐ − ☐ = ☐

12 ________ = ____ ☐ − ☐ = ☐

13 ________ = ____ ☐ − ☐ = ☐

14 ________ = ____ ☐ − ☐ = ☐

Number AC9M3N03 add and subtract two- and three-digit numbers using place value to partition, rearrange and regroup numbers to assist in calculations without a calculator
Algebra AC9M3A02 extend and apply knowledge of addition and subtraction facts to 20 to develop efficient mental strategies for computation

Unit 13 Two-digit subtraction

Subtract to 100

1 Write stories.

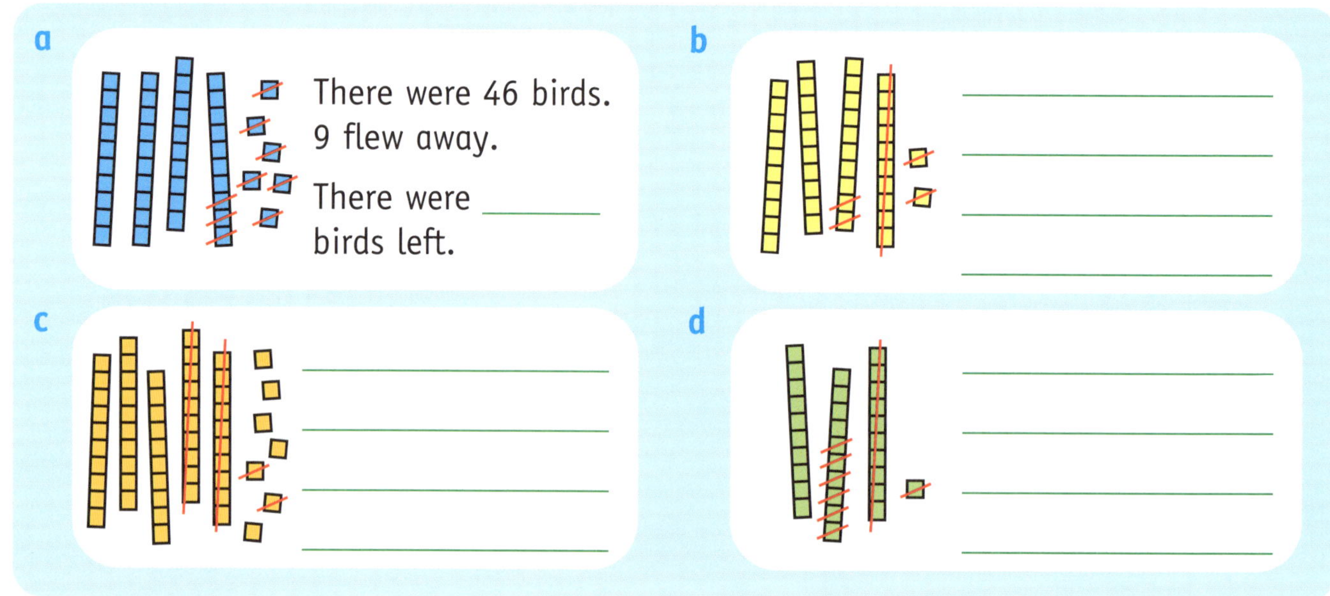

2 Use the blocks to find the answers.

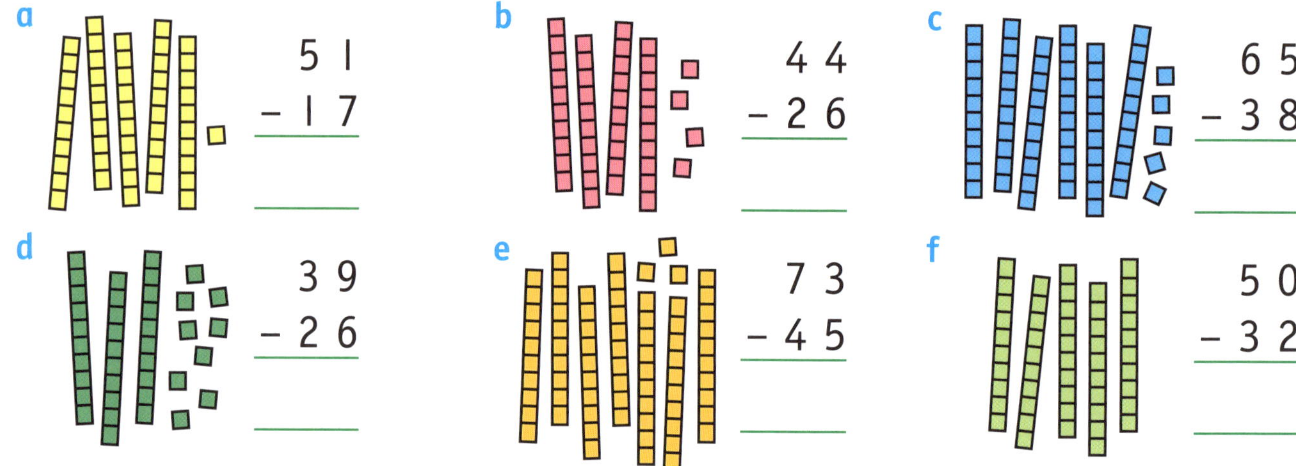

a 51 − 17 = ____

b 44 − 26 = ____

c 65 − 38 = ____

d 39 − 26 = ____

e 73 − 45 = ____

f 50 − 32 = ____

3 Use Base 10 blocks if you need help.

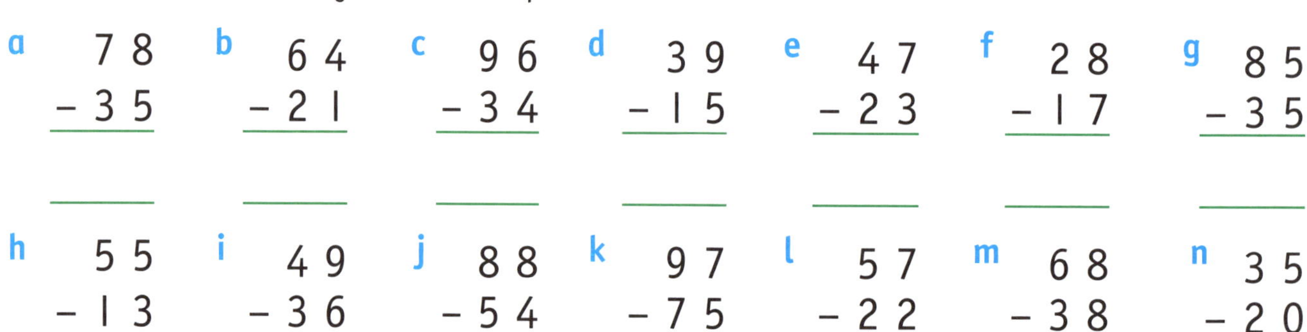

a 78 − 35 = ____

b 64 − 21 = ____

c 96 − 34 = ____

d 39 − 15 = ____

e 47 − 23 = ____

f 28 − 17 = ____

g 85 − 35 = ____

h 55 − 13 = ____

i 49 − 36 = ____

j 88 − 54 = ____

k 97 − 75 = ____

l 57 − 22 = ____

m 68 − 38 = ____

n 35 − 20 = ____

Challenge! Find 4 pairs of numbers with a difference of 27.

Number AC9M3N03 & AC9M3N06 add and subtract two- and three-digit numbers using place value to partition, rearrange and regroup numbers to assist in calculations without a calculator • use mathematical modelling to solve practical problems

Unit 13 Subtraction stories

Related facts

1	2	3	4	5	6	7	8	9	10
11	12	13	14	15	16	17	18	19	20
21	22	23	24	25	26	27	28	29	30
31	32	33	34	35	36	37	38	39	40
41	42	43	44	45	46	47	48	49	50
51	52	53	54	55	56	57	58	59	60
61	62	63	64	65	66	67	68	69	70
71	72	73	74	75	76	77	78	79	80
81	82	83	84	85	86	87	88	89	90
91	92	93	94	95	96	97	98	99	100

1 a Find pairs of numbers the same colour.

b Work out the difference for each pair.

c Write one subtraction sentence and one addition sentence for each pair.

☐ + ☐ = ☐

☐ − ☐ = ☐
☐ + ☐ = ☐

☐ − ☐ = ☐
☐ + ☐ = ☐

☐ − ☐ = ☐
☐ + ☐ = ☐

☐ − ☐ = ☐
☐ + ☐ = ☐

☐ − ☐ = ☐
☐ + ☐ = ☐

☐ − ☐ = ☐
☐ + ☐ = ☐

☐ − ☐ = ☐
☐ + ☐ = ☐

2 a

Tom threw the basketball 25 m and kicked the soccerball 67 m. Write the difference in metres. ☐

b

The red balloon drifted 39 m and the blue balloon drifted 24 m. Write the difference in metres. ☐

c

Sal

Sue

Sal jumped 44 cm and Sue jumped 66 cm. Write the difference in centimetres. ☐

Mastery Checklist

I can:
- ☐ regroup numbers to subtract
- ☐ write subtraction stories
- ☐ use blocks to subtract
- ☐ use algorithms to subtract
- ☐ connect addition and subtraction
- ☐ solve subtraction stories.

Number AC9M3N03 add and subtract two- and three-digit numbers using place value to partition, rearrange and regroup numbers
Algebra AC9M3A01 recognise and explain the connection between addition and subtraction as inverse operations, apply to partition numbers and find unknown values in number sentences

Problem solving

Work backwards

1 Three children ran a race. Jack ran the race 3 seconds faster than Dave. Dave ran 2 seconds slower than Jerry. Jerry took 14 seconds. What was Jack's time?

Working:

Jerry 14 secs   Dave 14 + 2 = 16   Jack 16 – 3 = 13

Dave 16 secs   Jack's time was ________

2 Four children joined the 'Read-a-thon' to improve their reading rate. Toby read 4 books more than Koli. Koli read 5 books less than Troy, who read 16. How many books did Toby read?

Working:

Troy ____________ Koli ____________ Toby ____________

Troy read ________ Koli read ________ Toby read ________

Write your own *work backwards* problems and show the solution.

3 The answer is 50 stickers. What might the problem be?

____

____

____

____

Working: ______________________________________

____

4 Write your own.

____

____

____

____

Working: ______________________________________

____

I can solve problems by:

☐ using addition facts and related subtractions ☐ working backwards.

Number AC9M3N06 use mathematical modelling to solve practical problems; formulate problems using number sentences and choose calculation strategies, using digital tools where appropriate; interpret and communicate solutions in terms of the situation **Algebra AC9M3A01** recognise and explain the connection between addition and subtraction as inverse operations

Unit 14 Fractions in a line

1 Write each set of fractions in order, smallest to largest.

a $\frac{1}{4}, \frac{3}{4}, \frac{2}{4}, \frac{4}{4}$ ______________________

b $\frac{3}{3}, \frac{1}{3}, \frac{2}{3}$ ______________________

c $\frac{1}{5}, \frac{2}{5}, \frac{3}{5}, \frac{5}{5}, \frac{4}{5}$ ______________________

d $\frac{1}{10}, \frac{9}{10}, \frac{3}{10}, \frac{2}{10}, \frac{4}{10}, \frac{5}{10}, \frac{6}{10}, \frac{7}{10}, \frac{8}{10}, \frac{10}{10}$ ______________________

e $\frac{3}{5}, \frac{2}{5}, \frac{1}{5}, \frac{4}{5}$ ______________________

f $\frac{2}{2}, \frac{1}{2}$ ______________________

2 Colour the fraction. Then write and colour a smaller fraction.

a $\frac{4}{5}$

______

b 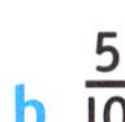

______

c $\frac{3}{4}$

d 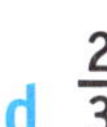

______

Unit 14 Count with fractions

1 Count by halves up to 1.

0 ________ ________

2 Count by thirds up to 1.

0 ________ ________ ________

3 Count by quarters up to 1.

0 ________ ________ ________ ________

4 Count by fifths up to 1.

0 ________ ________ ________ ________ ________

5 Count by tenths up to 1.

0 $\frac{1}{10}$ ________ ________ ________ ________ ________ ________ ________ ________ ________

6 a Five boys get 1 slice each.

How much pizza did each boy get?

____

b Two girls get 2 slices each.

How much pizza did each girl get?

____

Challenge! I cut a pizza into ten slices to share between five people.

How many pieces does each person get? ________

What fraction of the pizza is that? ________

Number AC9M3N02 recognise and represent unit fractions and their multiples in different ways; combine fractions with the same denominator to complete the whole

Unit 14 Fractions of a group

$\frac{1}{4}$ means one of four equal parts. We can make a fractional part of a group.
Find $\frac{1}{4}$ of a group by dividing it into 4.
eg $\frac{1}{4}$ of 8 is the same as 8 divided by 4.

$\frac{1}{4}$ of 8 is 2

1 One half of 8 is 8 divided into 2 equal parts.

$\frac{1}{2}$ of 8 is ________

2 Look at the number 12 and circle fractions of 12.

eg $\frac{1}{2}$ of 12      is 6

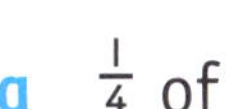

a $\frac{1}{4}$ of 12

is ________

b $\frac{1}{3}$ of 12

is ________

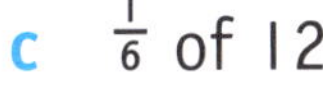

c $\frac{1}{6}$ of 12

is ________

d $\frac{1}{12}$ of 12

is ________

Mastery Checklist I can:
- ☐ compare and order fractions
- ☐ colour to show fractions
- ☐ count by fractions
- ☐ work out fractions of a group.

Cakes and Biscuits

Investigation 2

Parents are coming to visit your class and you have to make morning tea. You will need 50 muffins. This recipe makes 20 muffins.

Ingredients:

- 3 cups self-raising flour
- 1 cup of butter
- 1 cup of sugar
- 2 large eggs
- 1 cup of milk
- vanilla essence to taste
- some choc-bits, diced apple or banana

Method:

Place dry ingredients in a bowl.
Mix in wet ingredients. Add choc-bits, apple or banana.

Pour into regular muffin tins and cook for 10–15 minutes at 160 °C.

How will you make 50 muffins using this recipe? Write your answer here.

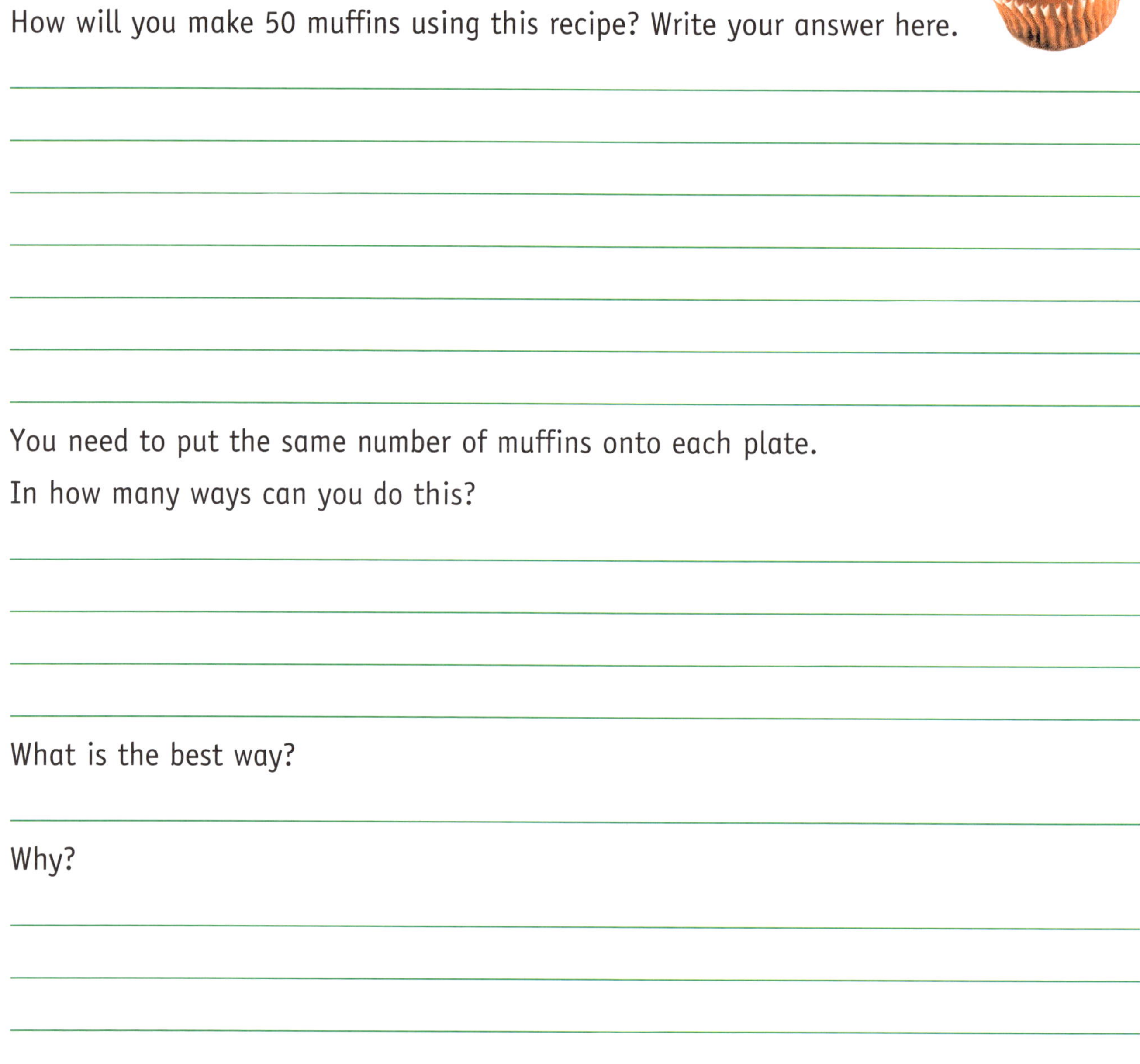

You need to put the same number of muffins onto each plate.

In how many ways can you do this?

What is the best way?

Why?

Number AC9M3N05 estimate the quantity of objects in collections and make estimates when solving problems to determine the reasonableness of calculations
Measurement AC9M3M02 measure and compare objects using familiar metric units of length, mass and capacity, and instruments with labelled markings

Cakes and Biscuits

Investigation 2

The Fete is coming and your class has the biscuit stall. Use one of these ingredient lists to work out how much money you can make selling 120 biscuits.

Ingredients – 20 biscuits in a batch

- 1 cup sugar
- 125 g butter, melted
- 1 teaspoon vanilla
- 1 cup plain flour
- 1 cup self-raising flour
- 1 egg, lightly beaten
- sprinkles and decorations

Cost of ingredients $5

Ingredients – 24 biscuits in a batch

- 125 g butter
- $\frac{1}{2}$ cup sugar
- $\frac{1}{2}$ cup brown sugar
- 1 egg
- $\frac{1}{2}$ tsp vanilla essence
- $\frac{1}{4}$ tsp salt
- $1\frac{3}{4}$ cups self-raising flour
- 150 g milk choc chips

Cost of ingredients $5.50

How will you make 120 biscuits?

How much will you charge for each biscuit? ____________

Money spent ____________ Money raised ____________

To carry out these tasks I need to:

- ☐ use doubling to multiply ingredients
- ☐ calculate how many batches to make
- ☐ calculate how to put biscuits onto trays evenly
- ☐ calculate how much money is spent and raised
- ☐ explain how I solve the problem.

I enjoyed this task! ☆☆☆☆☆

Number AC9M3N05 estimate the quantity of objects in collections and make estimates when solving problems to determine the reasonableness of calculations
Measurement AC9M3M02 measure and compare objects using familiar metric units of length, mass and capacity, and instruments with labelled markings

Revision

Shade one bubble.

1 How many minutes have passed when the minute hand moves from 5 to 8?

5	8	15	20
◯	◯	◯	◯

2 Which object is a pyramid?

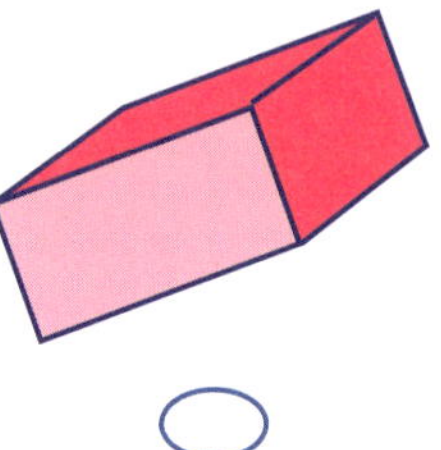

◯ ◯ ◯ ◯

3 Using only three cards, what is the largest number you can make?

714	471	741	704
◯	◯	◯	◯

4 Which operation does this number line show?

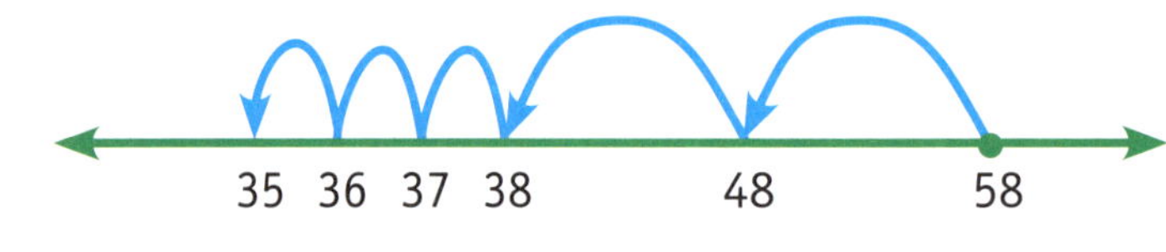

58 + 23	35 − 23	58 − 23	38 − 3
◯	◯	◯	◯

5 Write the next number in this pattern.

Write your answer in the box.

63 50 37 24 ?

Revision

Shade one bubble.

6 Which label is missing?

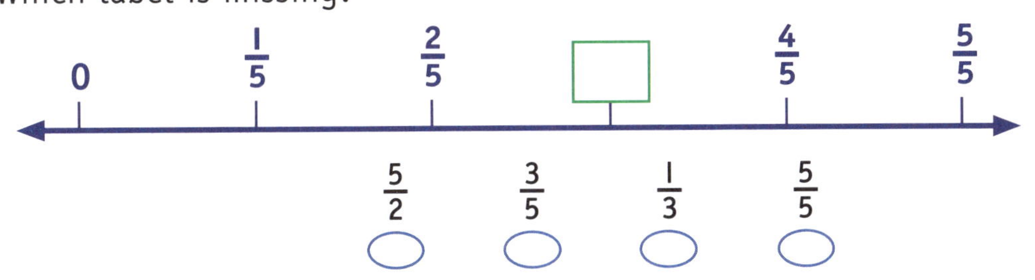

$\frac{5}{2}$ ◯ $\frac{3}{5}$ ◯ $\frac{1}{3}$ ◯ $\frac{5}{5}$ ◯

7 What fraction has been shaded?

Write your answer in the box.

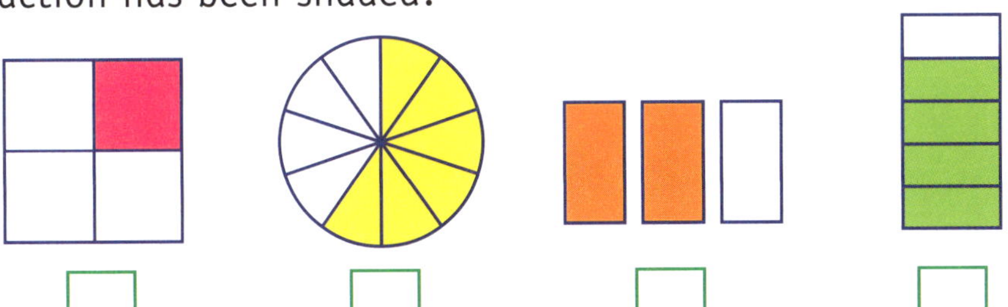

8 18 bunnies are in a row. If 11 hop away how many are left?

11 ◯ 9 ◯ 7 ◯ 8 ◯

Write your answer in the box.

9 Sam started his homework at 4 : 35 pm and finished at 5 : 05 pm.

How long did it take him? ☐ minutes

10 How many working dogs do they have altogether?

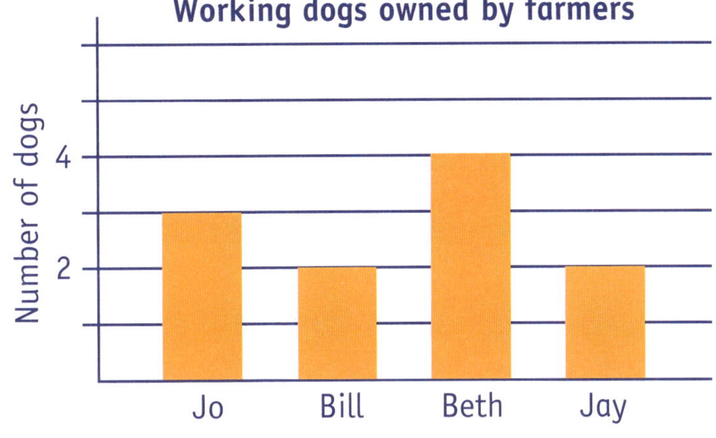

Unit 15 Eating in Japan

1 Which items cost less than ¥500?

____

2 Which items cost betwen ¥500 and ¥1000?

____

3 What three items could I buy for a total less than ¥1000?

____

____

4 If I bought the yakitori, the stir fry and a green tea, what change would I get from ¥5000?

____

5 If you had ¥2000, what would you buy? What is the total price of your choice?

____

____

6 Answer true or false.

a You pay more yen than Australian dollars for food in Japan. ______________

b This menu shows that food in Japan is more expensive than in Australia.

____

Number AC9M3N06 use mathematical modelling to solve practical problems involving additive and multiplicative situations including financial contexts; formulate problems using number sentences and choose calculation strategies, using digital tools where appropriate; interpret and communicate solutions in terms of the situation

Unit 15 Notes

1 Match.

2 Circle the coins to make the amount.

a $1.10	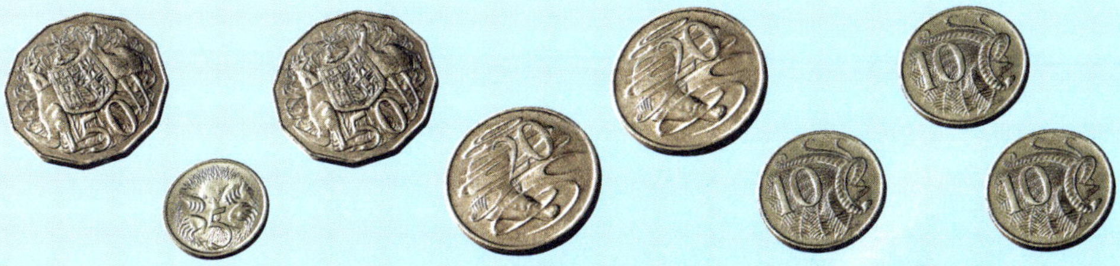
b $3.45	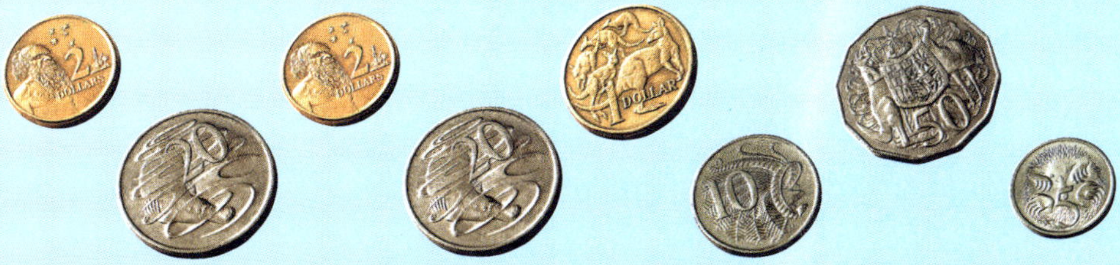
c $5.80	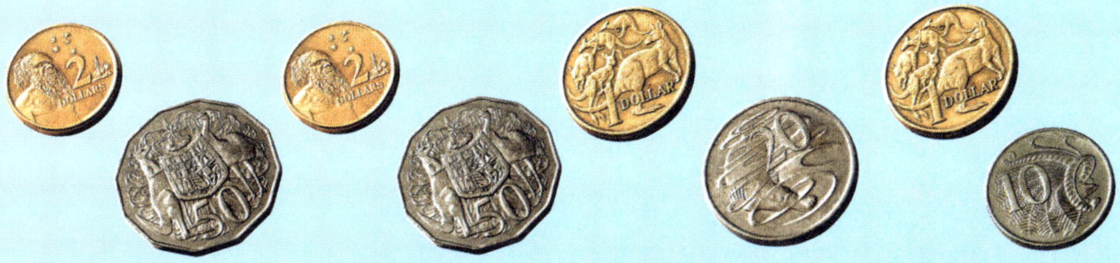
d $0.95	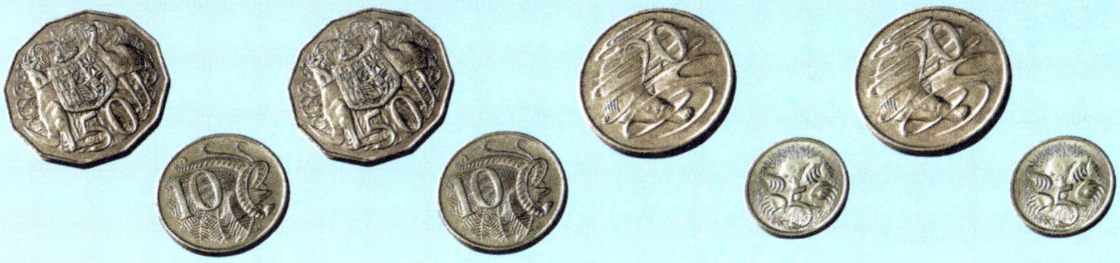

Unit 15 Money

Study this menu.

1 What coins would you use to pay for:

a the veggie burger? ______

b the milk shake? ______

c the snacks? ______

d the juice? ______

2 a My brother wants one of everything on the menu. Will a $20 note cover the cost? ______

b What is the total cost? ______

3 What is the cost of:

a a veggie burger and a juice?

______

b snacks and juice?

______

4 What change will I receive from $10 if I buy:

a a veggie burger?

______

b both drinks?

______

Working

Number AC9M3N06 use mathematical modelling to solve practical problems **Measurement AC9M3M06** recognise the relationships between dollars and cents and represent money values in different ways

Unit 15 Addition and subtraction of money

Change $

1 a 10c + 10c + 10c + 20c = _____ b 50c + 10c + 5c + 5c = _____

c 50c + 50c + 50c = _____ d 5c + 10c + 20c + 50c = _____

e 20c + 20c + 20c + 50c = _____ f 10c + 50c + 20c + 5c + 5c = _____

2 a $10 – $7 = _____ b $20 – $12 = _____ c $10 – $4 = _____

d $20 – $13 = _____ e $50 – $30 = _____ f $100 – $50 = _____

g $5 – $4.50 = _____ h $5 – $1.50 = _____ i $10 – $5.50 = _____

3 Complete.

a

+	$5	$36	$19	$1.50	$2.80
$7					

b

+	50c	25c	$2	$18	$1.45
35c					

4 Write two different ways to make each amount with coins.

Amount	Coin combination 1	Coin combination 2
a $1.85		
b $2.40		
c $5.95		
d $10.55		

5 Jay had $5 pocket money. He spent $2 on sweets and $1 on a drink. How much did he have left? ☐

6 For her birthday Kay was given $5. She already had $7.60. How much does she now have? ☐

7 Bozo's owner paid $35 at the vet and $17 for a new lead. How much did he spend? ☐

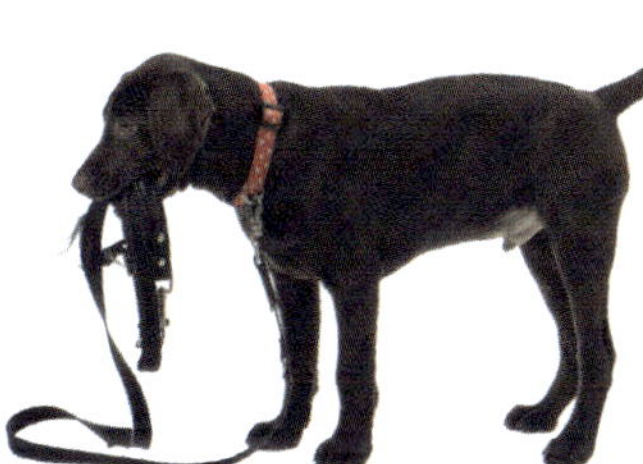

8 I bought an ice-cream for $2 and a sandwich for $4.40. How much change did I get from $10? ☐

Mastery Checklist I can:
- ☐ add costs and work out change
- ☐ recognise Australian notes and coins
- ☐ choose coins to equal an amount
- ☐ find different combinations of coins to equal an amount
- ☐ solve money word problems.

Unit 16 Number patterns

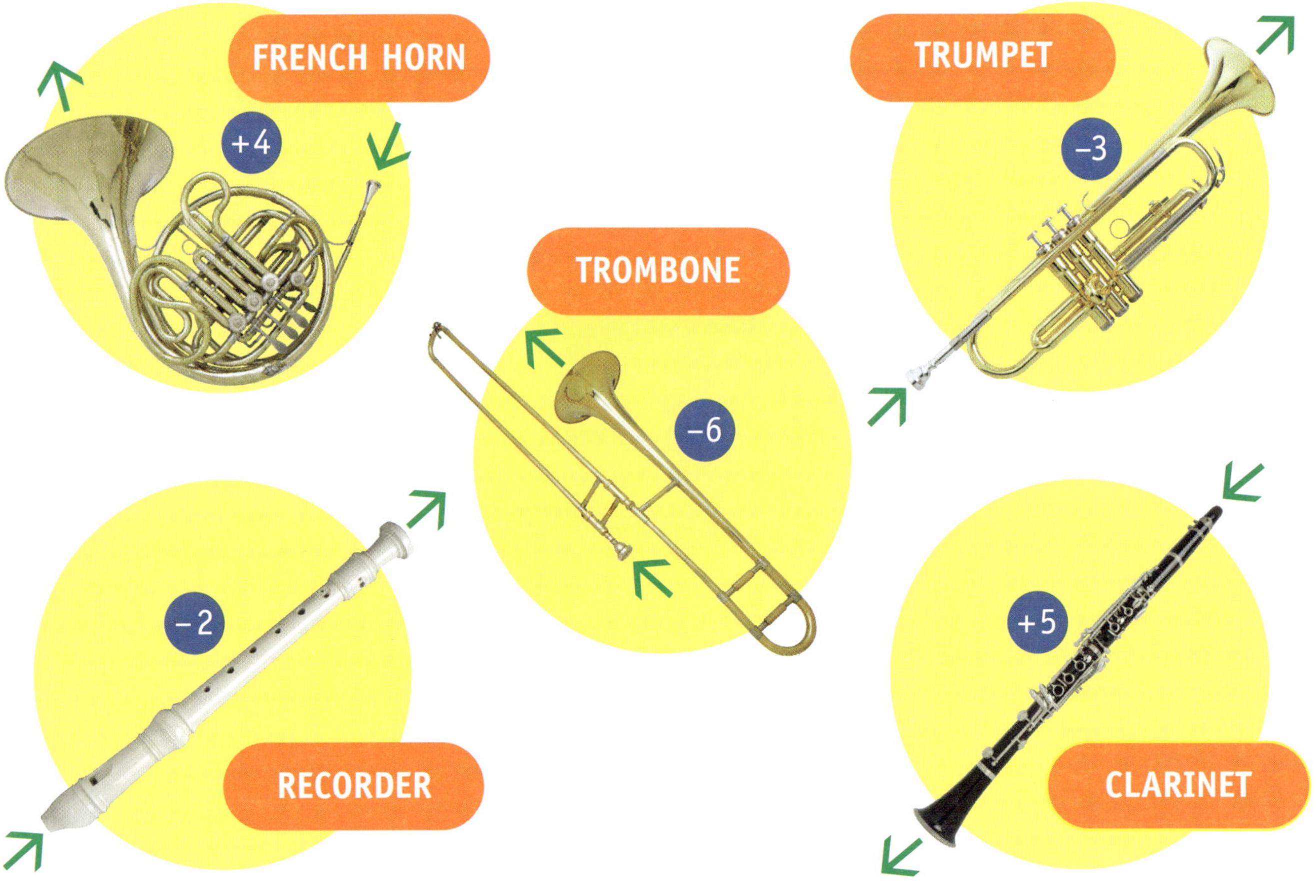

FRENCH HORN
+4

TRUMPET
−3

TROMBONE
−6

RECORDER
−2

CLARINET
+5

These are magical instruments.

When a number is blown in one end, it changes four times and all four numbers come out the other end. Each instrument has its own rule for making number patterns.

1 What numbers come out of the French horn if 7 is put in?

______ ______ ______ ______

2 What numbers come out of the trombone if 34 is put in?

______ ______ ______ ______

3 What happens to a 14 in a:

a trumpet? ______ ______ ______ ______

b clarinet? ______ ______ ______ ______

c recorder? ______ ______ ______ ______

4 What must be put in the clarinet for 40 to come out at the end of 4 changes?

____

Number AC9M3N07 follow and create algorithms involving a sequence of steps and decisions to investigate numbers; describe any emerging patterns

Unit 16 Pattern rules

1 Look at page 82. Complete these:

a for the trumpet. Start with 18. ____ ____ ____ ____

Rule = ____ Start with 25. ____ ____ ____ ____

b for the clarinet. Start with 18. ____ ____ ____ ____

Rule = ____ Start with 23. ____ ____ ____ ____

c for the recorder. Start with 18. ____ ____ ____ ____

Rule = ____ Start with 15. ____ ____ ____ ____

d for the French horn. Start with 16. ____ ____ ____ ____

Rule = ____ Start with 11. ____ ____ ____ ____

e for the trombone. Start with 24. ____ ____ ____ ____

Rule = ____ Start with 29. ____ ____ ____ ____

2 This is your kazoo. Decide how it changes numbers and how many changes it makes before it runs out of puff.

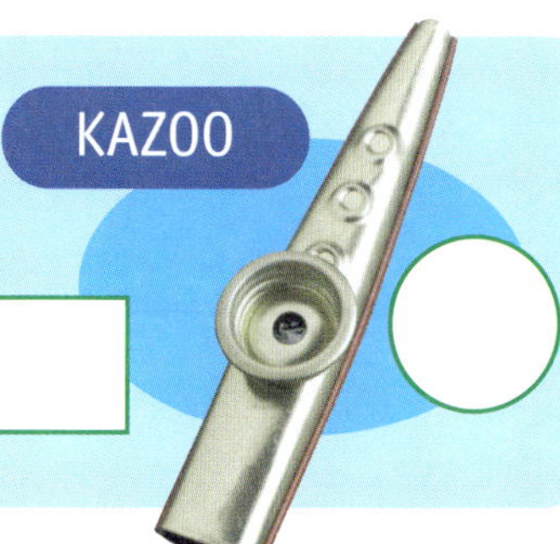

3 Use your kazoo.

a Start with 84. ____ ____ ____ ____

b Start with 110. ____ ____ ____ ____

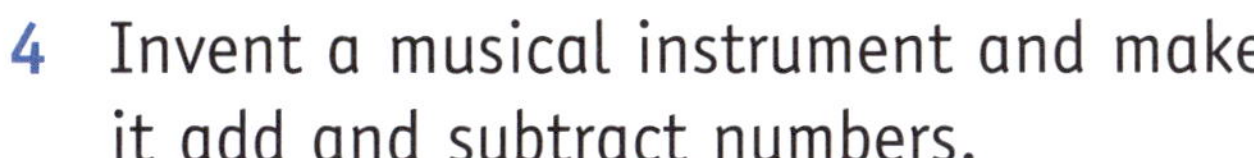

4 Invent a musical instrument and make it add and subtract numbers.

a Instrument name

____

b Changes it makes

____

c Use your instrument.

Start at 92.

____

Draw it here.

Unit 16 Number patterns

1 Write the next three rows.

a

4 + 9 = 13
14 + 9 = 23
24 + 9 = 33

______
______
______

b

8 + 7 = 15
18 + 7 = 25
28 + 7 = 35

______
______
______

c

9 + 7 = 16
19 + 7 = 26
29 + 7 = 36

______
______
______

d

46 – 12 = 34
56 – 12 = 44
66 – 12 = 54

______
______
______

e

89 – 5 = 84
89 – 15 = 74
89 – 25 = 64

______
______
______

f

6 + 6 + 6 = 18
7 + 7 + 7 = 21
8 + 8 + 8 = 24

______
______
______

A **multiple** is the answer you get when you multiply. 5 × 1 = **5**, 5 × 2 = **10**, 5 × 3 = **15**.
So 5, 10 and 15 are multiples of 5.

2 Start at 3. Use a straight line to join it to the next multiple of 3. Continue until you have reached 15.

What shape have you made?

______ Colour this shape.

3, 11, 4, 12, 5, 13, 6, 14, 7, 15, 8, 1, 9, 2, 10

3 Follow the patterns.

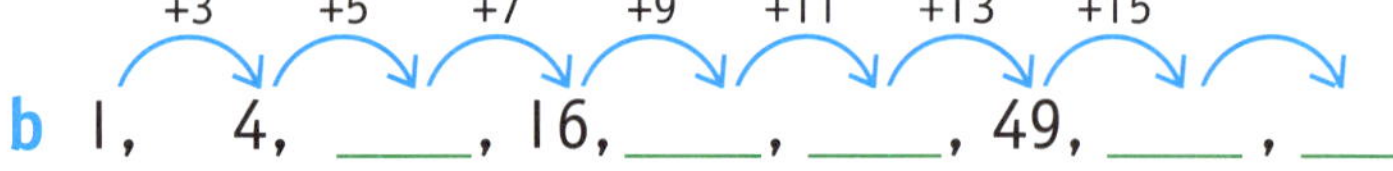

a 1, 2, 4, 7, ____, 16, ____, ____, ____
(+1, +2, +3, +4, +5, +6, +7)

b 1, 4, ____, 16, ____, ____, 49, ____, ____
(+3, +5, +7, +9, +11, +13, +15)

Mastery Checklist I can:
- ☐ follow a rule to make a number pattern
- ☐ start with different numbers to make a number pattern
- ☐ make my own number pattern
- ☐ continue number patterns with addition and subtraction.

Number AC9M3N07 follow and create algorithms involving a sequence of steps and decisions to investigate numbers; describe any emerging patterns
Algebra AC9M3A02 extend and apply knowledge of addition and subtraction facts to 20 to develop efficient mental strategies for computation with larger numbers

Problem solving

Patterns using multiples

Look for the patterns in tables.

1 Complete this multiplication square neatly in pencil.

×	1	2	3	4	5	6	7	8	9	10	11	12
1												
2		4										
3									27			
4												
5					25							
6												
7								56				
8												
9				36								
10										100		
11							77					
12												

12 3 18 42 9

2 Colour the multiples of 3.

3 Describe the pattern you coloured.

____

____

4 Use different colours, make some different patterns. Try colouring different patterns, using the multiples of 4 and 5.

5 What patterns did you find?

____

I can solve problems by:

☐ identifying multiples ☐ looking for and identifying patterns.

Number AC9M3N07 follow and create algorithms involving a sequence of steps and decisions to investigate numbers; describe any emerging patterns
Algebra AC9M3A03 recall and demonstrate proficiency with multiplication facts for 3, 4, 5 and 10; extend and apply facts to develop the related division facts

Unit 17 Capacity

1 Which container holds the most? _____

2 Which container holds the least? _____

3 Name two containers that hold about the same amount? ______________

4 Name two containers which hold more than any of these. ______________

____

5 Name two containers which hold less than any of these. ______________

____

6 About how many cups (E) would be needed to fill:

a B? __________ b D? __________ c A? __________ d F? __________

7 Write the containers in order from holds least to holds most.

____

measure capacity

8 Get an empty plastic soft drink bottle and a plastic cup.

a How many cups does the bottle hold? __________

b Does everyone in the class get the same answer? __________

c Why or why not? ______________________________

____

____

Number AC9M3N05 estimate the quantity of objects in collections and make estimates when solving problems to determine the reasonableness of calculations
Measurement AC9M3M02 measure and compare objects using familiar metric units of length, mass and capacity, and instruments with labelled markings

Unit 17 The litre

1 Ali used a plastic cup to fill coloured containers with water.

Container	Number of cups needed
Blue	
Green	
Yellow	
Red	
Orange	
Pink	

L stands for litre.
5 L is 5 litres.

a How many cups does the green container hold? ________

b Which container holds the most? ________

c Which container holds the least? ________

d How many cups does the orange one hold? ________

e Which two hold about the same?

____

2 Lucy used a different cup. She needed 8 cups to fill the green container.

a Is her cup bigger or smaller than Ali's cup? ________

b About how many of her cups will fill the yellow container? ________

c Is a plastic cup a good measure? ________

Give a reason. ________________

3 a How much milk was in the carton? ☐

b How much does the jug hold? ☐

4 Fill an empty 1 litre container with water. Pour it into some empty cups. How many cups does it fill? ☐

5 Use water and your 1 litre container to find things that hold:

less than 1 litre	about 1 litre	more than 1 litre

Unit 17 Millilitres

These containers measure millilitres.

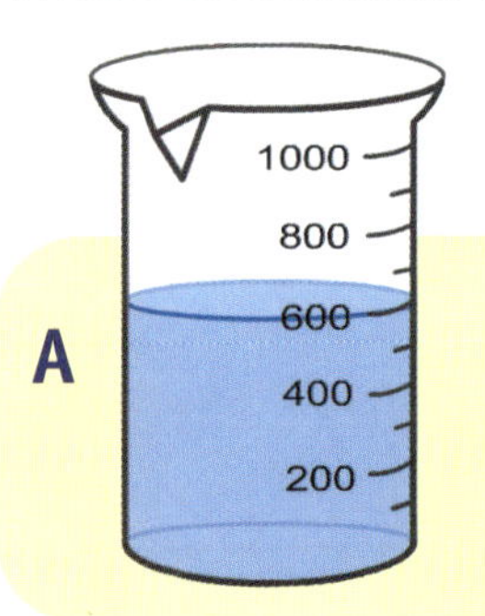

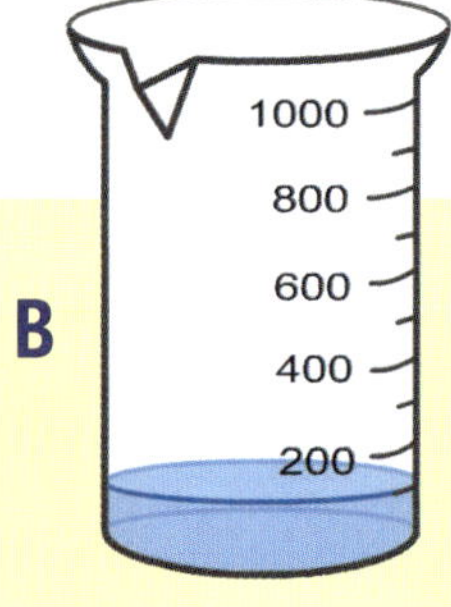

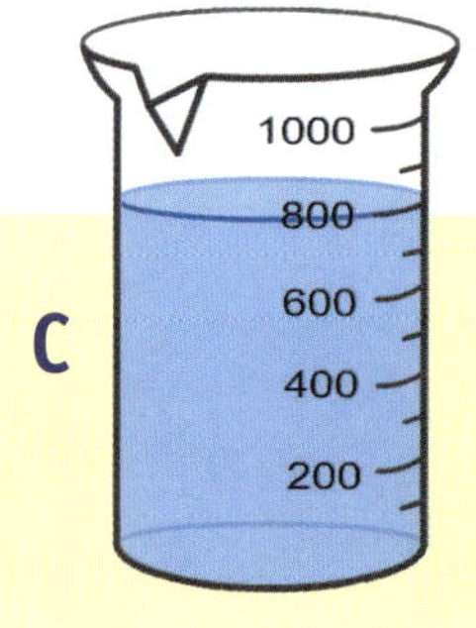

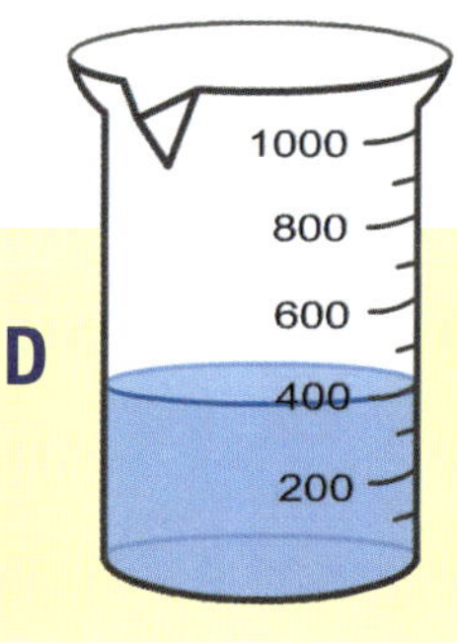

mL is millilitre.
1000 mL = 1 L
500 mL = $\frac{1}{2}$ L

1 How much water is in:

a **A**? ________ b **B**? ________ c **C**? ________ d **D**? ________

2 How much more is in: a **A** than **B**? ________ b **C** than **D**? ________

3 How much must be added to:

a **B** to make 1 L? ________ b **C** to make 1 L? ________

4 Which container is closest to: a 1 L?_____ b $\frac{1}{2}$ L?_____

5 Name 4 things which could be measured in millilitres.

6 a What is the capacity of **A**? ______

b What is the capacity of **B**? ______

c Which container holds more? ______

d How much more does it hold? ______

7 True (T) or false (F)?

a A dose of medicine is 5 L. ____

b A car can hold 40 L of petrol. ____

c A glass holds about 250 mL. ____

d The capacity of a cup is 200 L. ____

e My dog drank 1 mL of water today. ____

f The tall vase can hold 1 L of water. ____

Challenge!

On a large plastic bottle place an elastic band to show where you think $\frac{1}{2}$ L is. Check. Try with different containers.

estimate capacity, measure to check

Mastery Checklist

I can:

- ☐ compare the capacities of different containers
- ☐ use a cup to measure capacity
- ☐ compare capacities to 1 litre
- ☐ relate millilitres to litres
- ☐ choose between millilitres and litres.

Number AC9M3N05 estimate the quantity of objects in collections and make estimates when solving problems to determine the reasonableness of calculations
Measurement AC9M3M02 measure and compare objects using familiar metric units of length, mass and capacity, and instruments with labelled markings

Problem solving

Drinks for all

There will be 40 people at a party and you need to buy drinks for them all.

A 2 litre bottle holds 8 cups and a 3 litre bottle holds 12 cups.

How many bottles do you need to buy so that everyone can have two cups?

Find 3 different ways to buy enough bottles of drink.

A	B	C

If 2 litre bottles are $2 and 3 litre bottles are $3, what is the cheapest option?

How many mL in each drink? ________

I can solve problems by:

☐ understanding capacity ☐ writing algorithms.

Unit 18 am and pm

am is ante meridiem – before midday

pm is post meridiem – before midnight

1 Write am or pm.

a go to bed ________ b eat breakfast ________

c wake up ________ d finish school ________

e get dressed ________ f morning recess ________

g do homework ________ h eat afternoon tea ________

2 Write the above activities in the order you do them.

a ________ b ________

c ________ d ________

e ________ f ________

g ________ h ________

3 Name two things which take you:

a about one hour to do. ________

b about 10 minutes to do. ________

c about 2 minutes to do. ________

d only a few seconds to do. ________

4 Number these from shortest time (1) to longest time (6).

Watch one TV show.	
Clean my shoes.	
Feed the dog.	
Clean my teeth.	
Eat my lunch.	
Drink a glass of water.	

5 Circle the shortest time and cross the longest time.

a 1 week 1 month 1 hour 1 day

b 1 day 1 second 1 hour 1 week

c 1 month 1 year 1 fortnight 1 week

Unit 18 Time facts

1 a Draw a circle around the earliest time.

10 : 31 pm | 3 : 10 am | 1 : 30 pm | 10 : 30 am

b Draw a circle around the latest time.

2 : 45 am | 6 : 40 pm | 11 : 30 pm | 11 : 50 am

2 Number these times in order from earliest to latest.

5 : 10 pm ☐ 12 : 00 noon  7 : 45 am  1 : 10 am ☐

3 Complete.

$\frac{1}{4}$ past 7	get dressed	7 : 15
	go to school	:
	start school	:
	have lunch	:
	eat dinner	:

4 Yindi has three chores to do on Saturday:

- vaccuming – 1 hour
- wash the car – 45 minutes
- stack the dishwasher – 25 minutes.

Write the chores where they will fit into Yindi's schedule.

Saturday
8 am: breakfast
9 am: soccer
11 am:
12 noon: lunch
1 pm: shopping
2 pm:
2:40 pm: dance
4 pm:
4:45 pm: Nan visiting

Mastery Checklist I can:
- ☐ use am and pm
- ☐ estimate how long activities will take
- ☐ compare and order lengths of time
- ☐ read digital time
- ☐ complete a schedule.

Unit 19 Presenting data

1 Some friends drew a picture graph of the fish they caught.

a How many people went fishing? ____

b How many fish did Julio catch? ____

c Who caught the most fish? ____

d Who caught twice as many fish as Arthur? ____

e How many fish were caught altogether? ____

f Who said this? "I caught more fish than Julio, but fewer than Mary." ____

2 Mary decided to show the information as a column graph. She drew this.

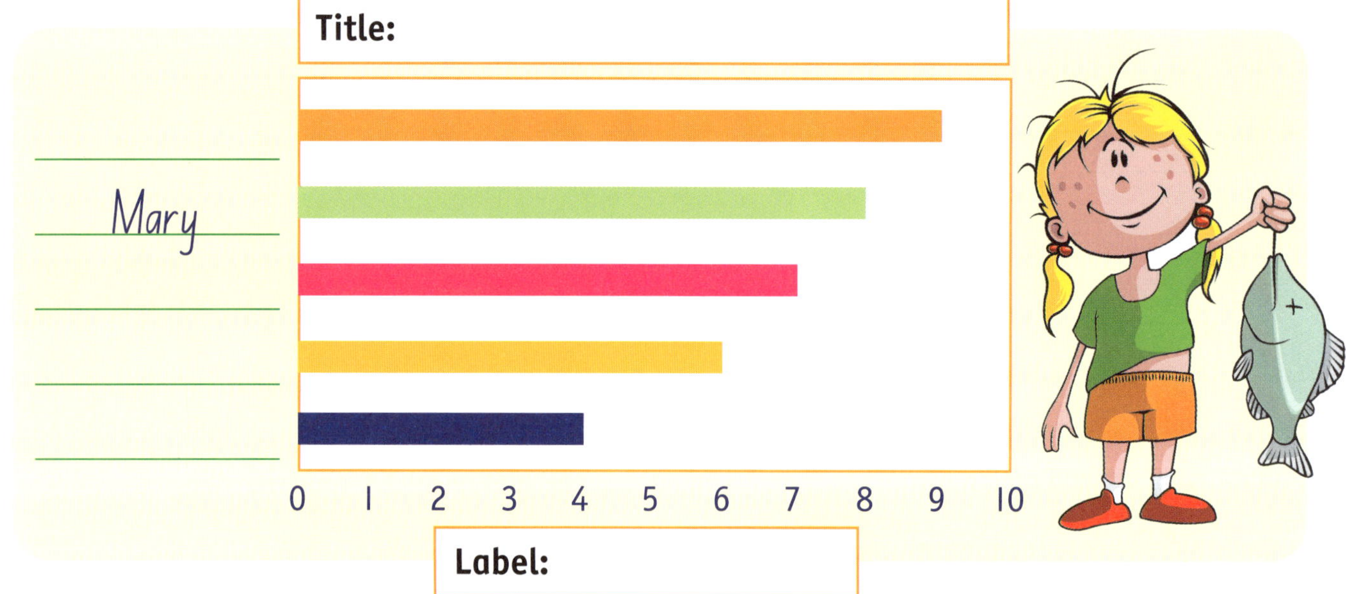

a Complete the column graph by writing the name of each person.

b Write a title on the graph.

c Write the missing label.

3 Conn said he would write a table for the information.

a Complete the table for Conn.

b In which order did he write the names of the people who went fishing? ____

Name	Number of fish caught
Arthur	
Julio	
Conn	7
Mary	
Tessie	

 Statistics AC9M3ST01 acquire data for categorical and discrete numerical variables to address a question of interest or purpose by observing, collecting and accessing data sets; record the data using appropriate methods including frequency tables and spreadsheets

Unit 19 Drawing a column graph

Data 

1 Eight children have heavy schoolbags.
Their teacher weighs each bag using books.

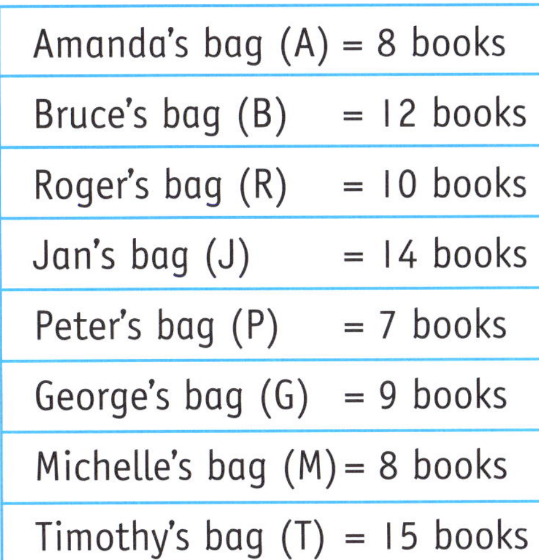

Amanda's bag (A) = 8 books
Bruce's bag (B) = 12 books
Roger's bag (R) = 10 books
Jan's bag (J) = 14 books
Peter's bag (P) = 7 books
George's bag (G) = 9 books
Michelle's bag (M) = 8 books
Timothy's bag (T) = 15 books

a How heavy is Roger's bag? __________ books

b Who has the heaviest bag? __________

c Who has the lightest bag? __________

d Which two bags have the same mass?

__________ and __________

e Write the three students with the heaviest bags from lightest to heaviest.

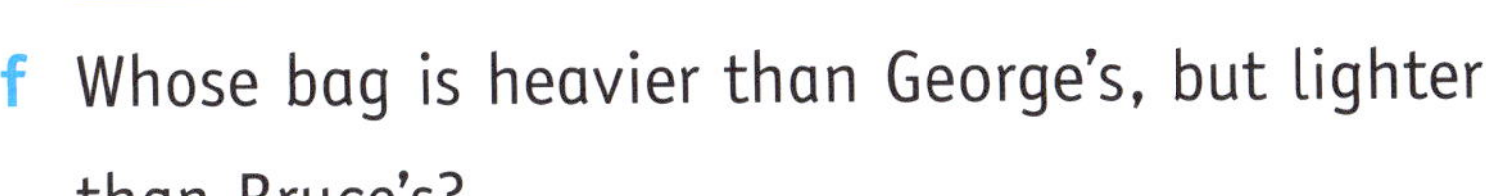

f Whose bag is heavier than George's, but lighter than Bruce's? __________

g What is the mass, in books, of Peter's bag and Roger's bag together? __________

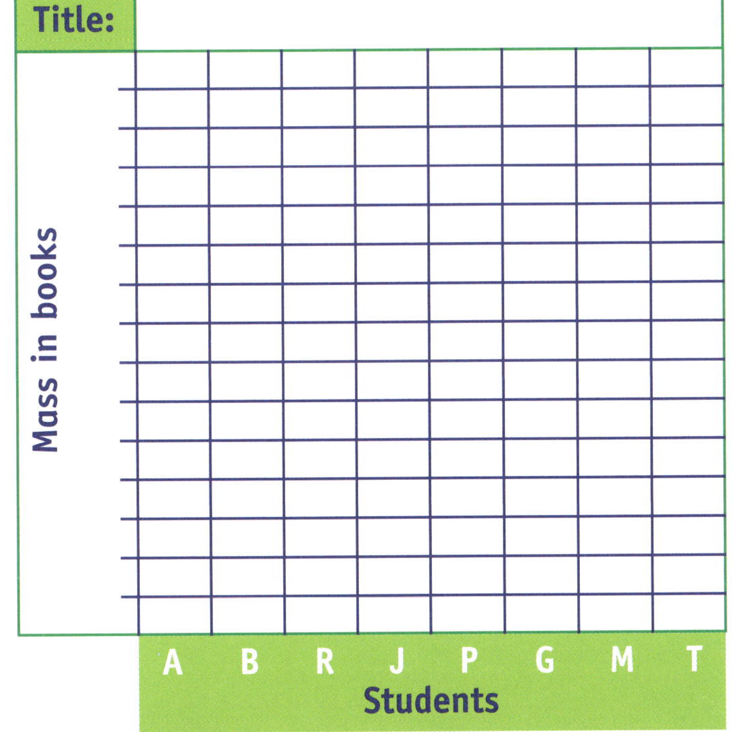

2 a Make a column graph by colouring the spaces.

b Write in the vertical scale.

c Write a title for your graph.

3 True or False?

a Jan's bag is twice as heavy as Peter's bag. __________

b Roger's bag is lighter than George's bag. __________

c Timothy's bag has the same mass as Michelle's bag and Peter's bag together. __________

d Three students have bags lighter than Roger's bag. __________

Mastery Checklist

I can:
- ☐ answer questions about a picture graph
- ☐ complete a column graph and a table
- ☐ answer questions about a column graph
- ☐ draw a column graph.

Draw a diagram

Find another way to present this information.

Statistics AC9M3ST01 acquire data for categorical and discrete numerical variables to address a question of interest or purpose by observing, collecting and accessing data sets
AC9M3ST02 create and compare different graphical representations of data sets; interpret the data in terms of the context

Revision Term 2

1 Order from smallest to largest. p 56

9390 9309 9399 9319 9380 9331

_____ _____ _____ _____ _____ _____

2 What is the value of the underlined number? p 59

a 57<u>8</u>2 _________

b <u>9</u>603 _________

3 Use the numerals 6, 7, 8, 9 to write a number with: p 59

a 6 in the hundreds place. _________

b 9 in the ones place. _________

c 7 in the thousands place. _________

4 p 61

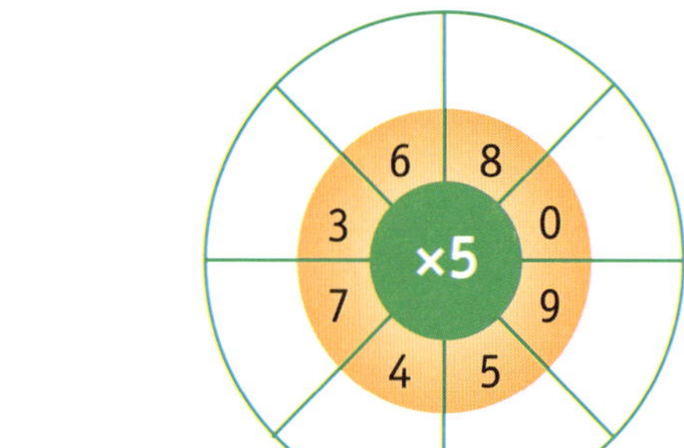

5 Write three more facts. p 63

20 − 13 = 7

_____ − _____ = _____

_____ + _____ = _____

_____ + _____ = _____

6 Count on to complete: p 65

	49	53	50	56	54
−47					

7 Use the number lines. p 66

a
$$\begin{array}{r} 42 \\ -\ 27 \\ \hline \end{array}$$

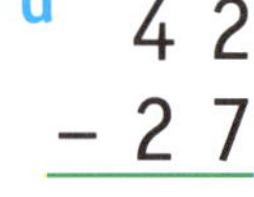

b p 66
$$\begin{array}{r} 81 \\ -\ 56 \\ \hline \end{array}$$

8 p 68

a
$$\begin{array}{r} 67 \\ -\ 14 \\ \hline \end{array}$$

b
$$\begin{array}{r} 88 \\ -\ 35 \\ \hline \end{array}$$

c
$$\begin{array}{r} 95 \\ -\ 20 \\ \hline \end{array}$$

9 My frog jumped 58 cm. p 69

Jill's frog jumped 37 cm.

What was the difference? _________

10 Write the next two fractions. p 71

a $\frac{1}{5}$, $\frac{2}{5}$, $\frac{3}{5}$, _________, _________

b $\frac{3}{10}$, $\frac{4}{10}$, $\frac{5}{10}$, _________, _________

11 Order these fractions from smallest to largest. p 71

a $\frac{2}{5}$, $\frac{5}{5}$, $\frac{1}{5}$, $\frac{4}{5}$, $\frac{3}{5}$

_____ _____ _____ _____ _____

b $\frac{7}{10}$, $\frac{2}{10}$, $\frac{1}{10}$, $\frac{5}{10}$, $\frac{9}{10}$

_____ _____ _____ _____ _____

c $\frac{2}{4}$, $\frac{3}{4}$, $\frac{4}{4}$, $\frac{1}{4}$

_____ _____ _____ _____

d $\frac{2}{3}$, $\frac{3}{3}$, $\frac{1}{3}$

_____ _____ _____

12 Circle the diagram for $\frac{1}{4}$. p 71

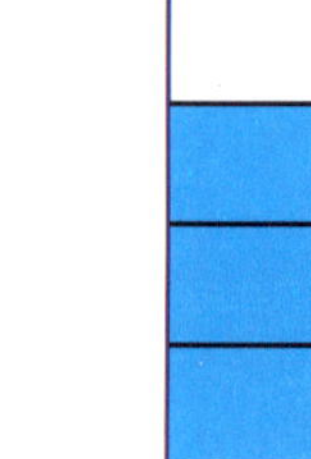

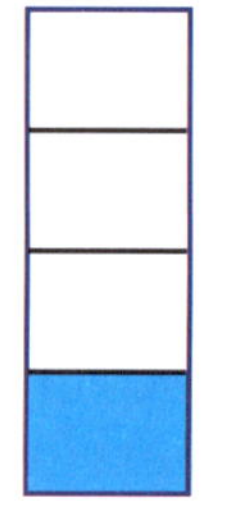

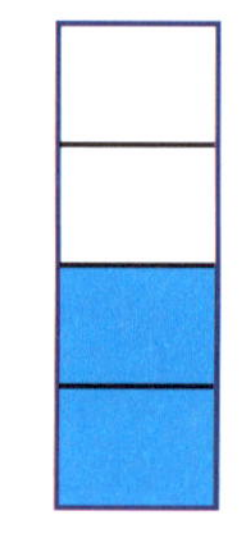

Revision Term 2

13 **a** Circle $\frac{1}{3}$ of this group. p 73

b Circle $\frac{1}{5}$ of this group.

p 79

14 Write the coins to make the amounts.

a 85c ______

b $2.40 ______

c $7.15 ______

15 Complete. p 81

a

+	$6	$1	$21	$2.20	$1.10	40c
$6						

b

−	$1	$3.70	$1.90	80c	$5	$7
70c						

16 Find the pattern. Write the next three rows. p 85

48 − 13 = 35

58 − 13 = 45

68 − 13 = 55

______

______

______

17 Write something that holds: p 87

a about 1 litre. ______

b more than 1 litre. ______

c less than 1 litre. ______

18 L or mL? p 88

a water in a cup ______

b petrol in a car ______

19 p 92

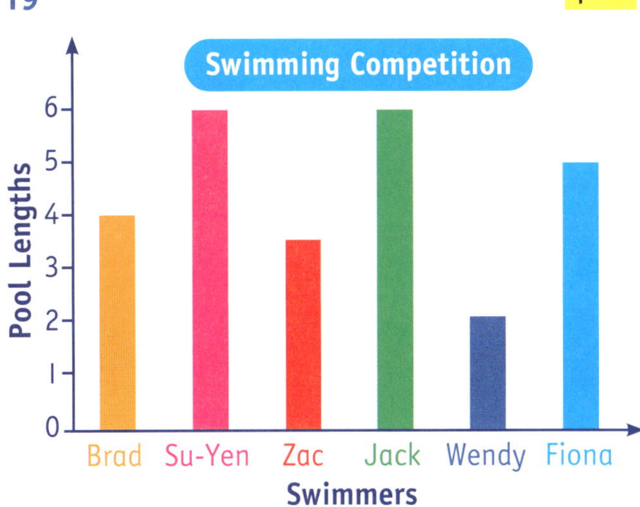

a Who swam the shortest distance?

______

b Which two swimmers swam the same distance?

______

c How many lengths did Zac swim? ______

d How many lengths were swum altogether? ______

e How many people swam in the competition? ______

f What is this graph for?

______

______

______

Unit 20 Addition of money

1 Which two toys can each child buy?

a Mary ______________________

b John ______________________

c Ali ______________________

d Ng ______________________

2 How much change will they get?

a Mary ____________ b John ____________

c Ali ____________ d Ng ____________

3 How many different toys could Mary buy? __________

Number AC9M3N02 recognise and represent unit fractions and their multiples in different ways; combine fractions with the same denominator to complete the whole
Measurement AC9M3M06 recognise the relationships between dollars and cents and represent money values in different ways

Unit 20 Addition of 3-digit numbers

1 How many in each group? Find the total.

a

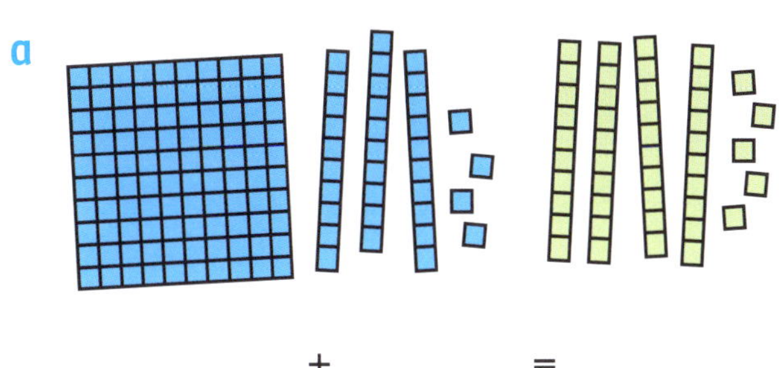

_____ + _____ = _____

b

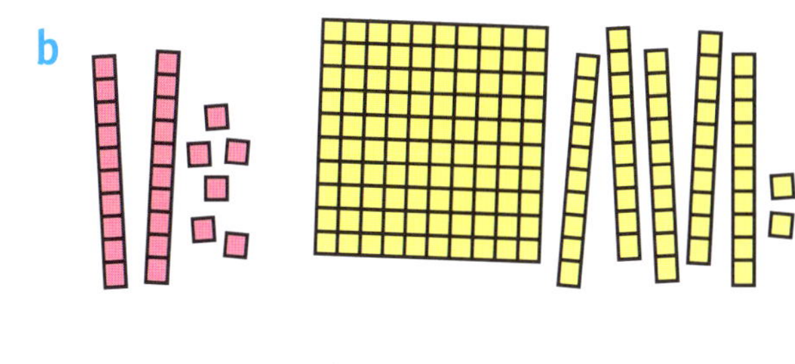

_____ + _____ = _____

c

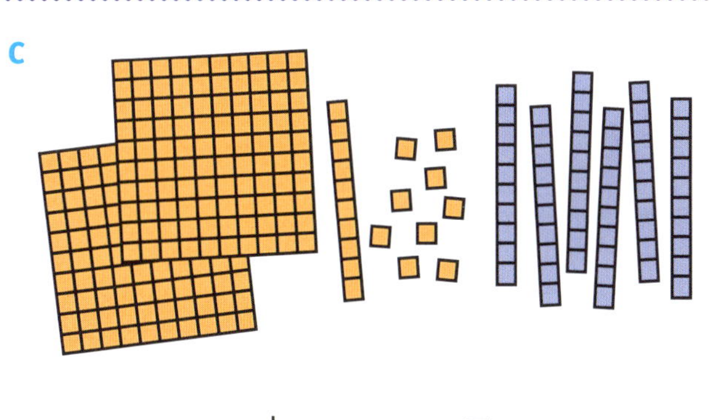

_____ + _____ = _____

d

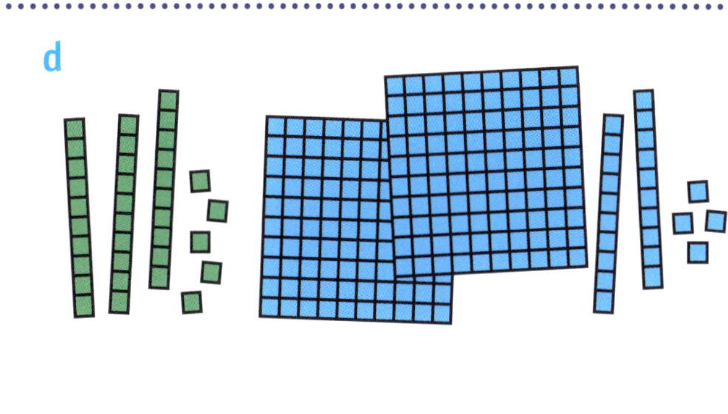

_____ + _____ = _____

2

a	b	c	d	e	f
173	231	127	284	353	126
+ 16	+ 45	+ 150	+ 115	+ 125	+ 472
___	___	___	___	___	___

3

a	b	c	d	e
3 0	2 □	□ □	1 2	□ 5
+ 2 □	+ 6 3	+ 2 4	+ □ 2	+ 2 □
□ 9	□ 7	9 9	8 □	6 8

4 Match each to its answer.

a 172 + 27

c 35 + 243

e 41 + 146

278 199 289

296 379 187

b 283 + 13

d 333 + 46

f 49 + 240

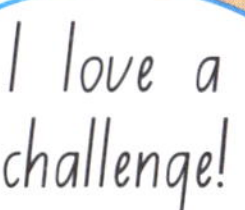

Challenge! Can you buy all the toys on page 99 with $20? Use a calculator.

Unit 20 Bar model for addition

Addition 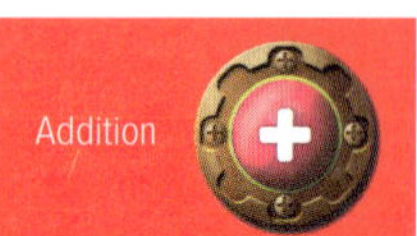

Problem	Bar model	Equation
1 Nullah counted crabs at the beach. He counted 75 crabs on Monday. After he counted some more on Tuesday, he had counted 139 crabs altogether. How many crabs did Nullah count on Tuesday?	75 | ? 139 ? = 64	75 + 64 = 139
2 Kylie saw 34 lizards on her hike, before lunch. Then after lunch she saw 27 more. How many lizards did she see altogether?	34 | 27 ? ? = ______	______ + ______ = ______
3 Nellie counted 22 kangaroo paintings, Kirra counted 36 echidna paintings and Maali counted 38 bird paintings. How many paintings did they see altogether?	22 | 36 | 38 ? ? = ______	______ + ______ + ______ = ______
4 Kai picked 39 berries on Saturday. He picked more berries on Sunday but forgot to count them. He had 129 berries altogether. How many berries did he pick on Sunday?	? = ______	______ + ______ = ______
5 Joey carved 14 coolamons in summer and 28 more in winter. How many coolamons did he carve altogether?	? = ______	______ + ______ = ______

Number AC9M3N06 use mathematical modelling to solve practical problems involving additive and multiplicative situations including financial contexts; formulate problems using number sentences and choose calculation strategies, using digital tools where appropriate; interpret and communicate solutions in terms of the situation

Unit 20 3-digit numbers and money

1 Write a number sentence and the answer.

+			
	230 + 24 = 254		

2

a Which two toys are the same price? ______________ ______________

b Which toy costs the most? ______________

c Which toy is the cheapest? ______________

d Which two toys together cost $8.50? ______________ ______________

e How much would it cost to buy the car and the yo-yo? ______________

f Can I buy the donkey and the softball with $7.50? ______________

g Which toys cost less than $5? ______________

h If you had $10, what would you buy? ______________

i If you had $20, what would you buy? ______________

Unit 20 Mental addition

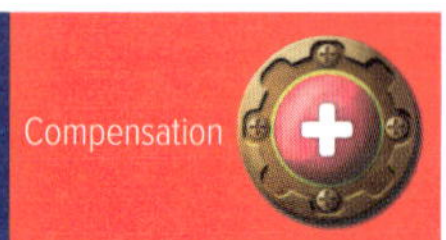

1 a 65 + 29 = 65 + 30 − 1 = ______ b 38 + 43 = 38 + 40 + 3 = ______

c 43 + 39 = ______ = ______ d 59 + 38 = ______ = ______

e 38 + 61 = ______ = ______ f 47 + 22 = ______ = ______

g 77 + 13 = ______ = ______ h 23 + 49 = ______ = ______

2 a

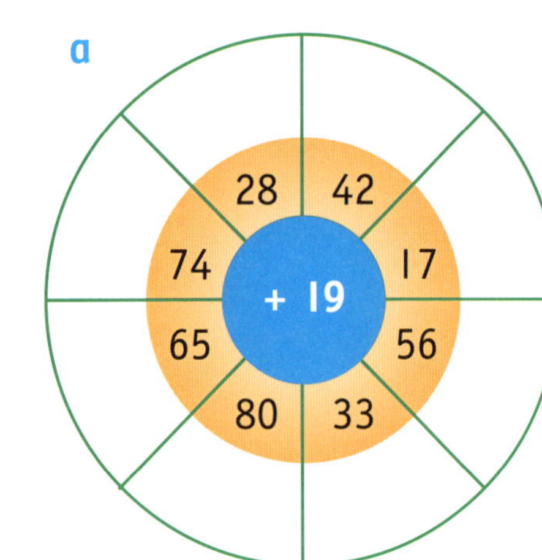

b

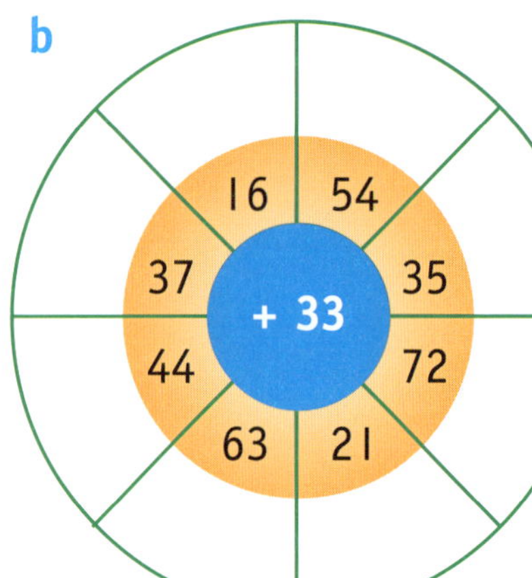

c

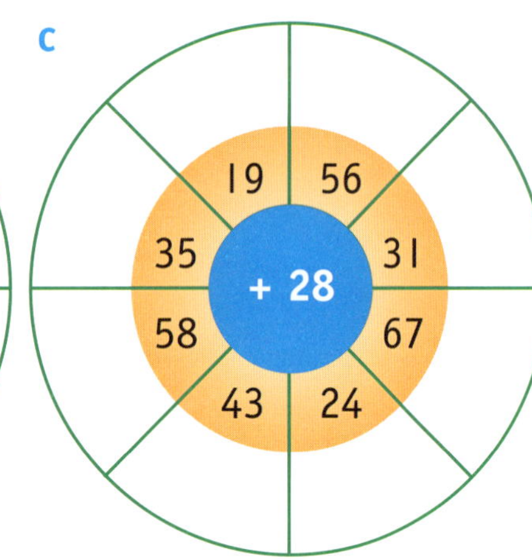

3 Estimate first.

	Estimate	Answer
a 17 + 15		
b 39 + 24		
c 35 + 63		

	Estimate	Answer
d 28 + 13		
e 51 + 37		
f 46 + 29		

4 Jon paid 25c for an apple, 30c for an orange and 45c for a banana.

a How much did he spend? ______

b How much change from $2? ______

Work backwards

Look at question 2 on page 99.
At the fair Mindy spent exactly $16 on 3 items. Which items did she buy?

Mastery Checklist

I can:

- ☐ add costs and work out change
- ☐ use base 10 blocks to add 3-digit numbers
- ☐ use algorithms to add 3-digit numbers
- ☐ use a bar model to add
- ☐ regroup numbers to add mentally
- ☐ estimate answer to addition.

Number AC9M3N03 & AC9M3N06 add and subtract two- and three-digit numbers using place value to partition, rearrange and regroup numbers to assist in calculations without a calculator • use mathematical modelling to solve practical problems involving additive and multiplicative situations including financial contexts

Unit 21 Multiplication

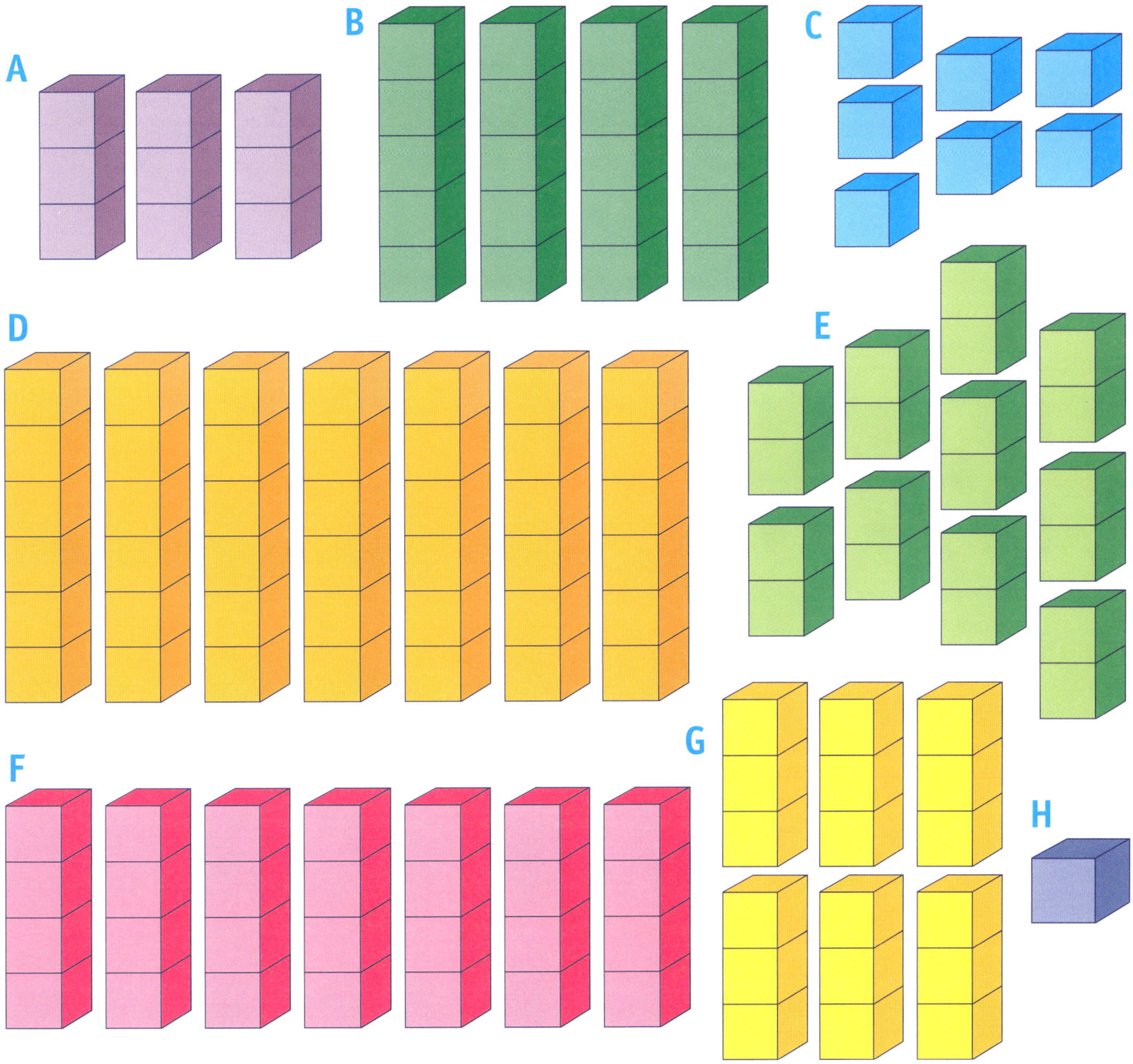

A

B

C

D

E

F

G

H

1

A	3 + 3 + 3 =	3 × 3 =
B	5 + 5 + 5 + 5 =	
C		
D		
E		
F		
G		
H		

2 Put A and G together and write an addition and a multiplication number sentence.

______

______

Unit 21 Multiplication

1 Use different colours to match.

a	2 + 2 + 2 + 2	6 bundles of 6	4 × 2	25
b	5 + 5 + 5 + 5 + 5	4 lots of 2	6 × 6	8
c	6 + 6 + 6 + 6 + 6 + 6	three nines	5 × 5	10
d	9 + 9 + 9	5 groups of 5	7 × 4	36
e	4 + 4 + 4 + 4 + 4 + 4 + 4	1 lot of 10	3 × 9	27
f	10	7 groups of 4	1 × 10	28

2

a	 8 + 8 + 8 = ☐ ice-creams	3 × 8 = ☐
b	 9 + 9 + 9 + 9 + 9 + 9 + 9 = ☐ hearts	☐ × 9 = ☐
c	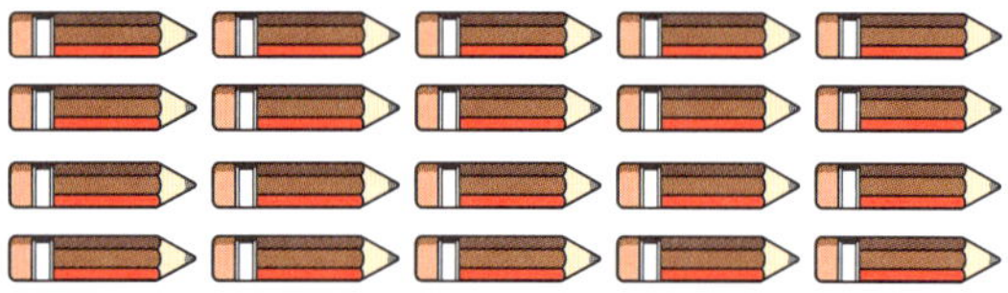 5 + 5 + 5 + 5 = ☐ pencils	4 × ☐ = ☐
d	 7 = ☐ cakes	☐ × ☐ = ☐
e	 ☐ + ☐ + ☐ = ☐ apples	☐ × ☐ = ☐
f	 ☐ + ☐ = ☐ balloons	☐ × ☐ = ☐

Algebra AC9M3A03 recall and demonstrate proficiency with multiplication facts for 3, 4, 5 and 10; extend and apply facts to develop the related division facts

Unit 21 Number facts 4×

3, 4 tables 

1	2	3	4	5	6	7	8	9	10	11	12	13
												14
27	26	25	24	23	22	21	20	19	18	17	16	15
28												
29	30	31	32	33	34	35	36	37	38	39	40	41
												42
							48	47	46	45	44	43

Kanga jumps along the path 4 spaces each time.

1 Colour the numbers she will land on.

2 How far did she go in:

a 0 jumps? ______ b 1 jump? ______ c 2 jumps? ______ d 3 jumps? ______

e 4 jumps? ______ f 5 jumps? ______ g 6 jumps? ______ h 7 jumps? ______

i 8 jumps? ______ j 9 jumps? ______ k 10 jumps? ______

3 A dog has 4 paws. Add groups of 4 to find how many paws on:

a 1 dog $4 \times 1 =$ ______ b 2 dogs $4 \times 2 =$ ______

c 3 dogs $4 \times 3 =$ ______ d 4 dogs $4 \times 4 =$ ______

e 5 dogs $4 \times 5 =$ ______ f 6 dogs $4 \times 6 =$ ______

g 7 dogs $4 \times 7 =$ ______ h 8 dogs $4 \times 8 =$ ______

i 9 dogs $4 \times 9 =$ ______ j 10 dogs $4 \times 10 =$ ______

k How many paws would no dogs have? $4 \times 0 =$ ______

4 a $4 \times 10 =$ ____ b $10 \times 4 =$ ____ c $4 \times 6 =$ ____ d $1 \times 4 =$ ____ e $4 \times 0 =$ ____

f $0 \times 4 =$ ____ g $9 \times 4 =$ ____ h $4 \times 4 =$ ____ i $7 \times 4 =$ ____ j $8 \times 4 =$ ____

5 A butterfly has 4 spots on its wings. How many spots on 5 butterflies? ☐

6 Each car has 4 wheels. How many wheels on 7 cars? ☐

Algebra AC9M3A03 recall and demonstrate proficiency with multiplication facts for 3, 4, 5 and 10; extend and apply facts to develop the related division facts
Number AC9M3N04 multiply and divide one- and two-digit numbers, representing problems using number sentences, diagrams and arrays, and using a variety of calculation strategies

Unit 21 Number facts 5×

1 How many hands? ________

2 How many fingers?

a 2 hands ________
b 12 hands ________
c 7 hands ________
d 0 hands ________
e 6 hands ________
f 3 hands ________
g 4 hands ________
h 10 hands ________
i 9 hands ________
j 8 hands ________
k 11 hands ________
l 5 hands ________

3 Count in 5s.

4 Complete from memory.

×	4	1	5	9	3	7	12	10	6	0	11	8	2
5													

Number AC9M3N06 use mathematical modelling to solve practical problems involving additive and multiplicative situations
Algebra AC9M3A03 recall and demonstrate proficiency with multiplication facts for 3, 4, 5 and 10

Unit 21 Number facts practice

3, 4, 5, 10 tables 

1 Write a multiplication fact for each badge. Do some have more than one?

a 

10 x 9 =

b 

c 

d 

e 

f 

g 

h 

i 

j 

k 

l 

2

×	2	8	5	10	0	7	3	1	6	9	4
4											
10											
5											
3											

3 a 

Mum drew a star with 3 points.

How many points on 9 stars?

b 

Aunt Jo drew a star with five points.

How many points on 9 stars?

c 

Uncle Bill drew a star with eight points.

How many points on 9 stars?

d 

How many more points are there on Uncle Bill's stars than on Aunt Jo's stars?

Unit 21 Vertical multiplication

1 Write a number sentence for this picture.

☐ × ☐ = ☐

2 Write a number sentence and the answer.

a 10 cars. 4 people in each car. How many people? ☐ × ☐ = ☐

b 5 tricycles. 3 wheels on each tricycle. How many wheels? ☐ × ☐ = ☐

c 3 cases each holding 8 pencils. How many pencils? ☐ × ☐ = ☐

d 5 rows with 10 boys in each row. How many boys? ☐ × ☐ = ☐

e 8 nests with 5 eggs in each nest. How many eggs? ☐ × ☐ = ☐

f 10 pies on each tray. There are 6 trays. How many pies? ☐ × ☐ = ☐

3 Write the answers and match.

6 × 3 ___	8 × 2 ___	7 × 5 ___	10 × 9 ___	4 × 1 ___	8 × 6 ___

7 × 5 = ☐ 6 × 3 = ☐ 8 × 2 = ☐ 8 × 6 = ☐ 10 × 9 = ☐ 4 × 1 = ☐

Draw a diagram

Draw pictures to show:

2 rows of 6	5 groups of 3 stars	4 lots of 7 apples
2 × 6 = ☐	5 × ☐ = ☐	☐ × ☐ = ☐

Mastery Checklist I can:

- ☐ use equal groups to multiply
- ☐ connect repeated addition with multiplication
- ☐ remember the 3× and 4× tables
- ☐ remember the 5× and 10× tables
- ☐ solve multiplication stories
- ☐ use multiplication algorithms.

Number AC9M3N04 & AC9M3N06 multiply and divide one- and two-digit numbers, representing problems using number sentences, diagrams and arrays • use mathematical modelling to solve practical problems involving additive and multiplicative situations

Problem solving

Vegetable garden

Victor is planning gardens of lettuces, tomatoes and radishes. He wants to plant them in rows of equal numbers of plants. He has 30 lettuce, 32 tomato and 36 radish plants. How can he plant them in these garden beds?

Key: ● = lettuce ▲ = tomato ◆ = radish

I can solve problems by:

☐ dividing numbers ☐ writing algorithms.

Unit 22 Sharing

1 These dogs all need good homes. How many dogs are there? _______

2 How many dogs would each person get if they were fairly shared by:

a 4 people? _______ b 3 people? _______

c 2 people? _______ d 24 people? _______

e 6 people? _______ f 8 people? _______

g 1 person? _______ h 12 people? _______

3 Tom took half the dogs. How many did he take? _______

4 Jacky took one quarter of the dogs. How many did she take? _______

5 If five people wanted the dogs, would they each get a fair share? _______

Why? ____

____

6 Are there other ways to share which are not fair? _______________

Number AC9M3N02 & AC9M3N04 & AC9M3N06 recognise and represent unit fractions and their multiples in different ways • multiply and divide one- and two-digit numbers, using a variety of calculation strategies • use mathematical modelling to solve practical problems

Unit 22 Fair shares

Fair shares means an equal number in each share.

1 a Are these shares fair? ______

b Why? ______

______

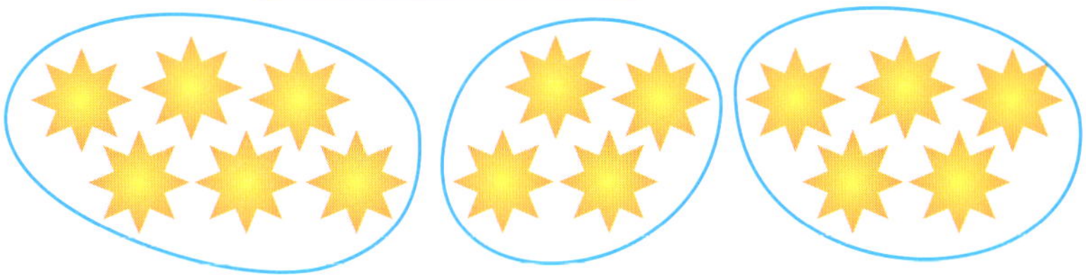

2 a Make 5 fair shares.

One share ______

b Make 4 fair shares.

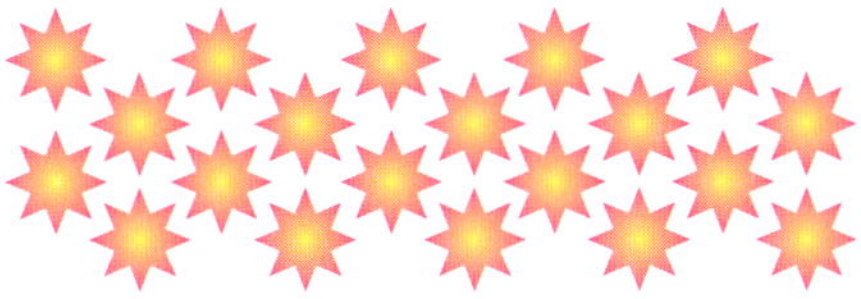

One share ______

c Make 10 fair shares.

One share ______

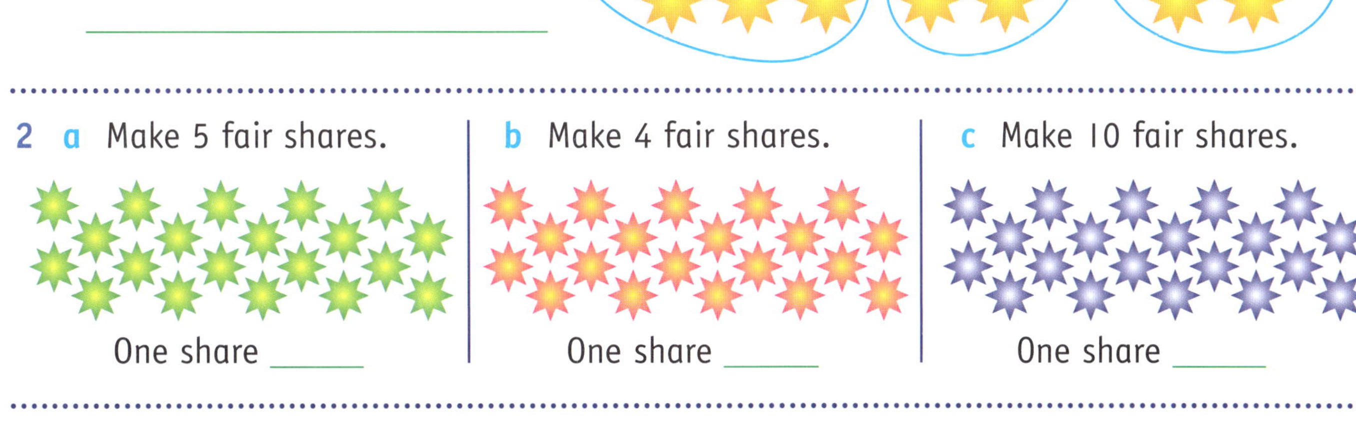

3 Circle to make fair shares. How many in each share?

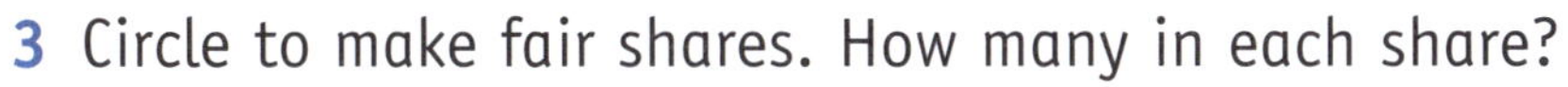

a 2 shares ______

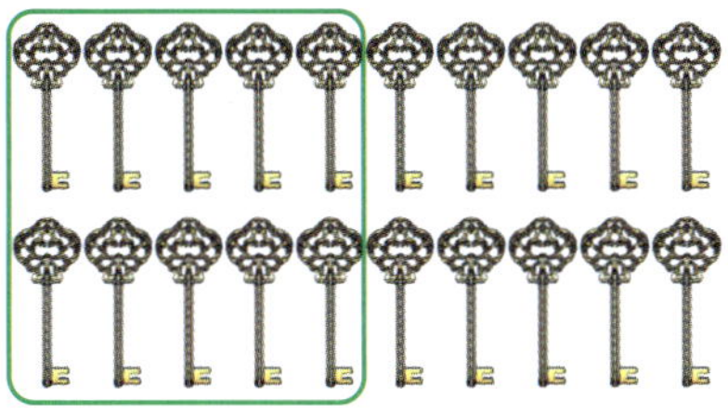

b 3 shares ______

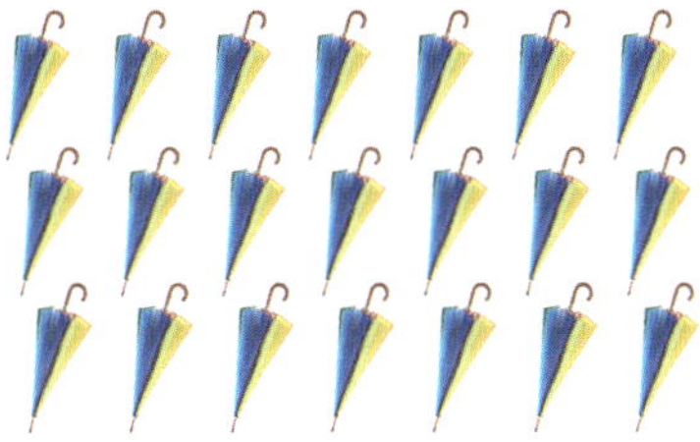

c 4 shares ______

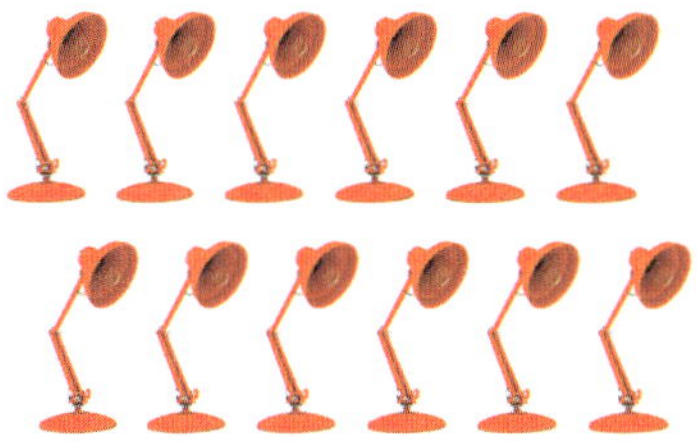

d 5 shares ______

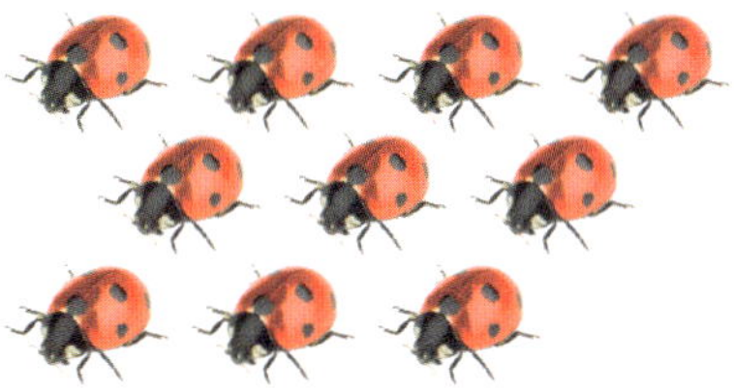

e 10 shares ______

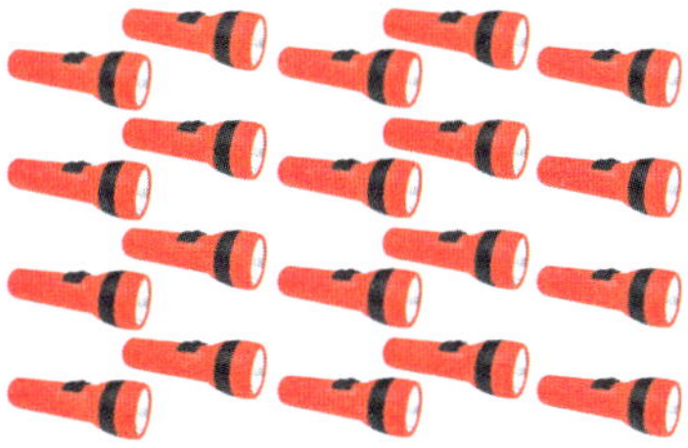

f 2 shares ______

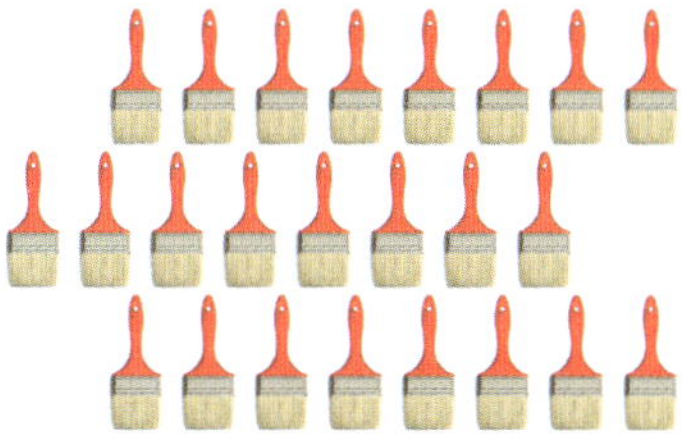

g 4 shares ______

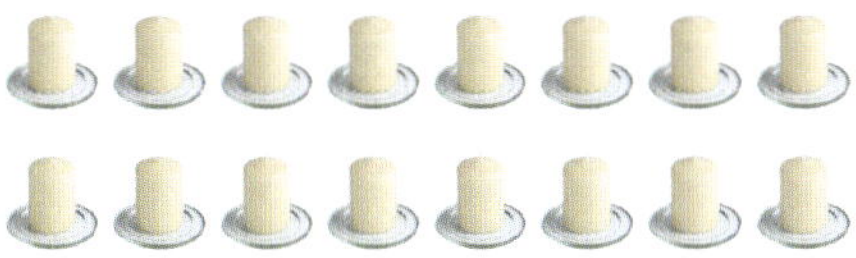

h 3 shares ______

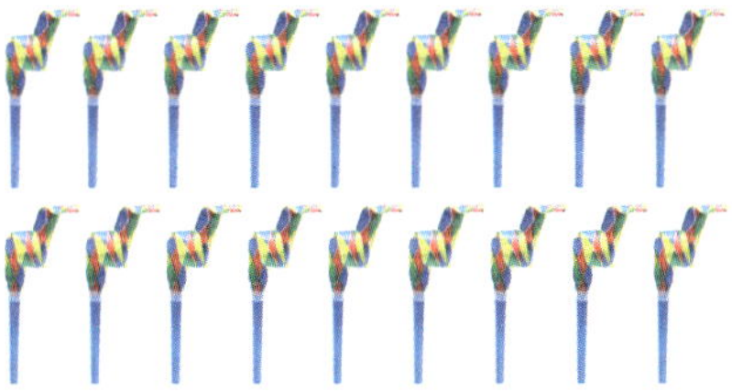

i 4 shares ______

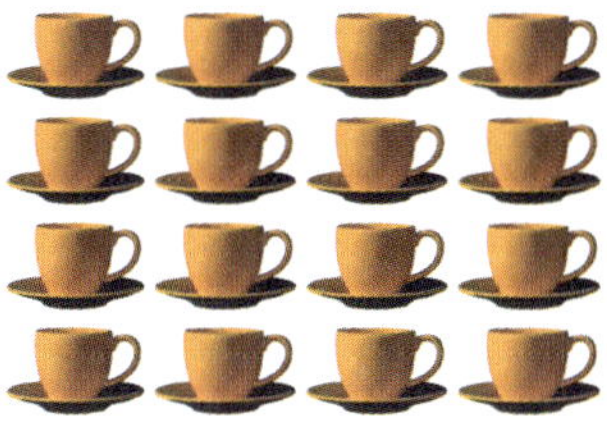

4 a Share 20 lollies into 5 packets. How many lollies in each packet? ______

b Share 15 apples onto 5 plates. How many apples on each plate? ______

c Place 10 children into 2 equal groups. How many children in each group? ______

d Place 50 crayons equally into 10 boxes. How many crayons in each box? ______

e Share 27 coins among 3 girls. How many coins does each girl get? ______

Unit 22 Equal groups

1 a Circle groups of 5 pots.

How many pots? ______

How many groups? ______

b Circle groups of 5 hats.

How many hats? ______

How many groups? ______

c Circle groups of 3 eggs.

How many eggs? ______

How many groups? ______

2 a Circle groups of 3 hearts.

How many groups? ______

How many hearts? ______

b Circle groups of 4 hearts.

How many groups? ______

How many hearts? ______

c Circle groups of 2 hearts.

How many groups? ______

How many hearts? ______

3 There are 24 rockets.

a Circle 3 equal groups.

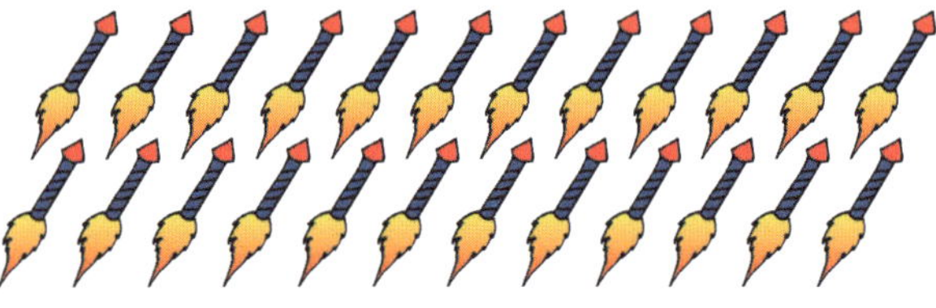

How many in each group? ______

b Circle 6 equal groups.

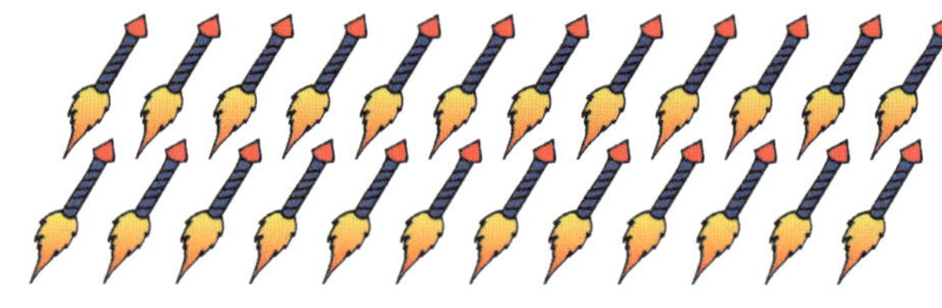

How many in each group? ______

c Circle 2 equal groups.

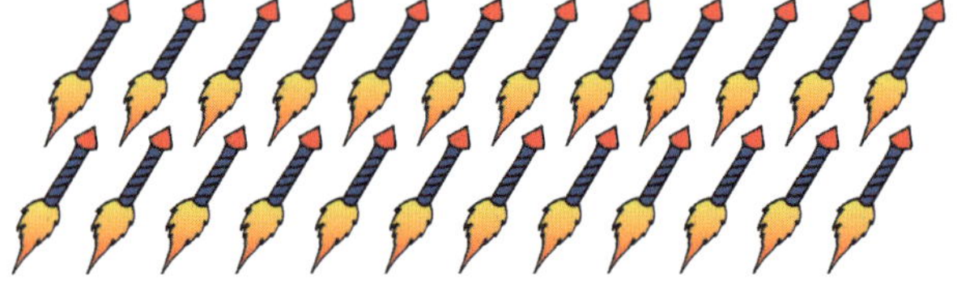

How many in each group? ______

d Circle 8 equal groups.

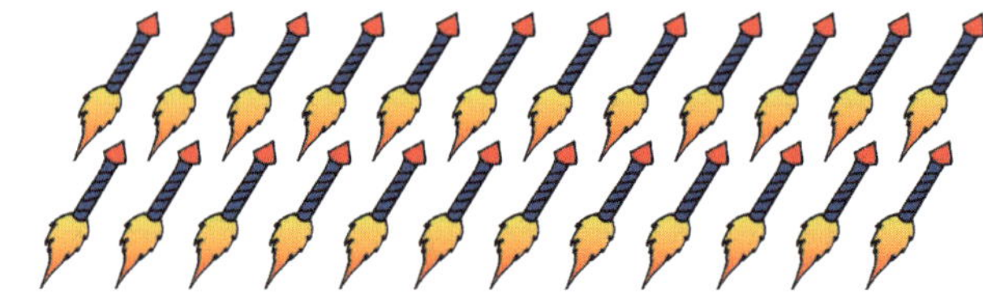

How many in each group? ______

Mastery Checklist I can:
- ☐ work out fair shares
- ☐ work out fractions of a group
- ☐ make equal groups.

Problem solving

Grandpa's treat

Grandpa has 36 fifty-cent coins. He says that he could share them evenly among his grandchildren even if he had 2, 3, 4, 5, 6, 7, 8 or 9 grandchildren. Is he right? Show your working.

Yes, he can share between 2 grandchildren. **36 ÷ 2 = 18 2 × 18 = 36**

I can solve problems by:

- ☐ dividing and related multiplication
- ☐ writing algorithms.

Unit 23 Equivalent fractions

$\frac{1}{2}$	$\frac{1}{2}$									halves
$\frac{1}{3}$	$\frac{1}{3}$	$\frac{1}{3}$								thirds
$\frac{1}{4}$	$\frac{1}{4}$	$\frac{1}{4}$	$\frac{1}{4}$							quarters
$\frac{1}{5}$	$\frac{1}{5}$	$\frac{1}{5}$	$\frac{1}{5}$	$\frac{1}{5}$						fifths
$\frac{1}{10}$	$\frac{1}{10}$	$\frac{1}{10}$	$\frac{1}{10}$	$\frac{1}{10}$	$\frac{1}{10}$	$\frac{1}{10}$	$\frac{1}{10}$	$\frac{1}{10}$	$\frac{1}{10}$	tenths

1 How many in 1 whole?

a halves _____ b fifths _____ c thirds _____ d tenths _____ e quarters _____

2 How many:

a quarters make $\frac{1}{2}$? _____ b tenths make $\frac{1}{2}$? _____

c eighths make $\frac{1}{2}$? _____ d eighths make $\frac{1}{4}$? _____

3 Circle the larger fraction.

a $\frac{1}{5}$ $\frac{1}{10}$ b $\frac{1}{3}$ $\frac{1}{2}$ c $\frac{1}{4}$ $\frac{1}{5}$ d $\frac{1}{3}$ $\frac{2}{5}$ e $\frac{3}{5}$ $\frac{1}{2}$

4 True (T) or false (F)? The larger the denominator the smaller the fraction. _____

How do you know? _____

5 Write three fractions that are smaller than $\frac{1}{2}$. _____ _____ _____

What do you notice about their denominators? _____

Number AC9M3N02 recognise and represent unit fractions and their multiples in different ways; combine fractions with the same denominator to complete the whole

Unit 23 Fraction names

Working with fractions

1 Match.

$\frac{2}{10}$	2 out of 3 equal parts	four-fifths
$\frac{2}{3}$	2 out of 10 equal parts	two-thirds
$\frac{4}{5}$	3 out of 4 equal parts	two-tenths
$\frac{3}{4}$	4 out of 5 equal parts	three-quarters

$\frac{2}{5}$ 2 = numerator, 5 = denominator

This means 2 equal parts out of 5.

2 Write the fraction coloured.

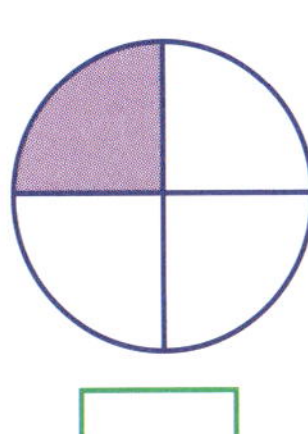

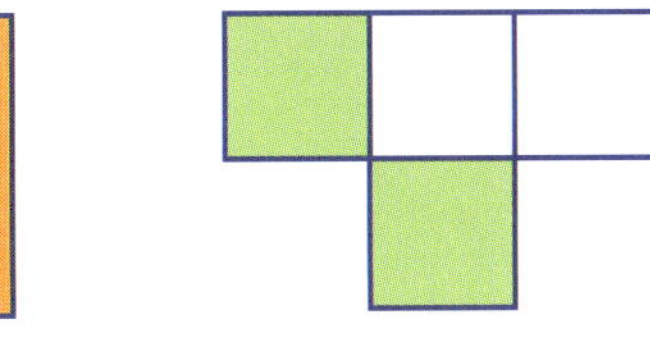

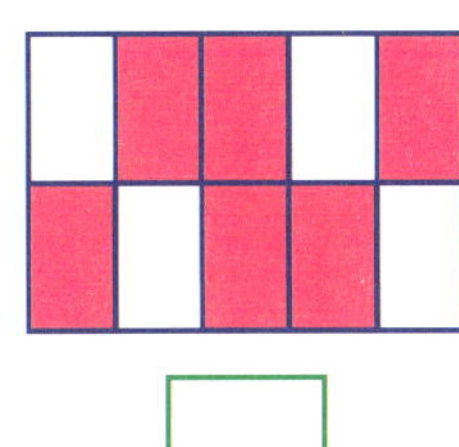

3 Colour to match the fraction.

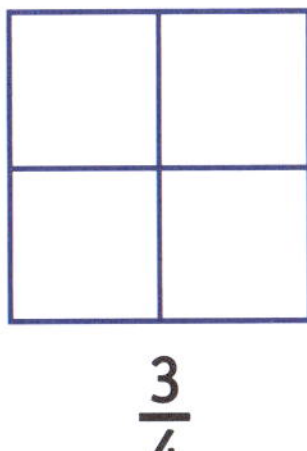

$\frac{3}{4}$

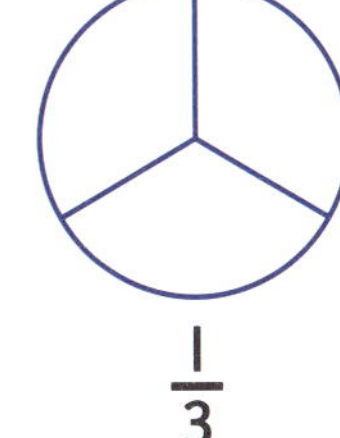

$\frac{1}{3}$

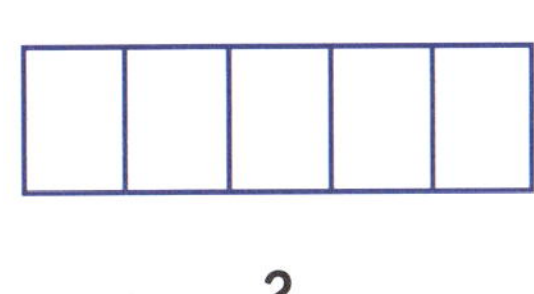

$\frac{2}{5}$

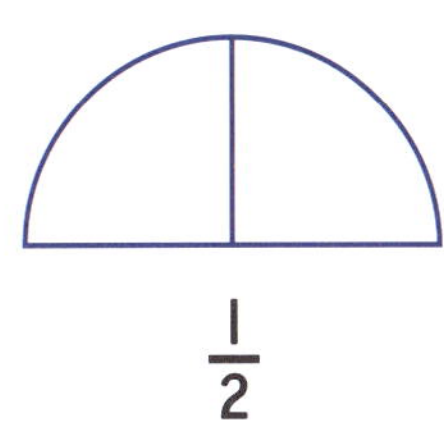

$\frac{1}{2}$

4 Look at page 112. Write another name for:

a one-quarter ________________

b one-half ________________

c one-fifth ________________

d five-tenths ________________

5 Draw a diagram to show:

$\frac{4}{5}$

$\frac{3}{10}$

Unit 23 Parts of a group

1 What is one-half of:

a 10 pears? _____

b 14 tomatoes? _____

c 16 onions? _____

2 What is one-quarter of:

a 8 mangoes? _____

b 12 peas? _____

c 16 mushrooms? _____

3 What is one-fifth of:

a 5 chillies? _____

b 10 oranges? _____

c 15 pumpkins? _____

4 Draw.

a $\frac{1}{5}$ of 10 bananas

b $\frac{1}{4}$ of 24 cherries

c $\frac{3}{4}$ of 8 apples

5 **a** $\frac{1}{2}$ of a bunch of grapes = 10. 1 whole bunch of grapes = _________

b $\frac{1}{2}$ of a dozen eggs = 6. 1 whole dozen eggs = _________

c $\frac{1}{4}$ of a bag of sweets = 3. 1 whole bag of sweets = _________

d $\frac{1}{5}$ of a box of plums = 6. 1 whole box of plums = _________

e $\frac{1}{10}$ of a packet of biscuits = 5. 1 whole packet of biscuits = _________

Mastery Checklist I can:
- ☐ work out how many fractions in one whole
- ☐ work out equivalent fractions
- ☐ recognise fraction names
- ☐ colour to show a fraction
- ☐ work out fractions of a group.

Number AC9M3N02 recognise and represent unit fractions and their multiples in different ways; combine fractions with the same denominator to complete the whole
AC9M3N06 use mathematical modelling to solve practical problems

Problem solving

Fractions at the party

1 There are 20 party hats to give out.

$\frac{1}{2}$ of them are red. $\frac{1}{4}$ of them are blue.

$\frac{1}{5}$ of them are green. The rest are pink.

Colour the hats correctly. Circle and label the groups with their fractions.

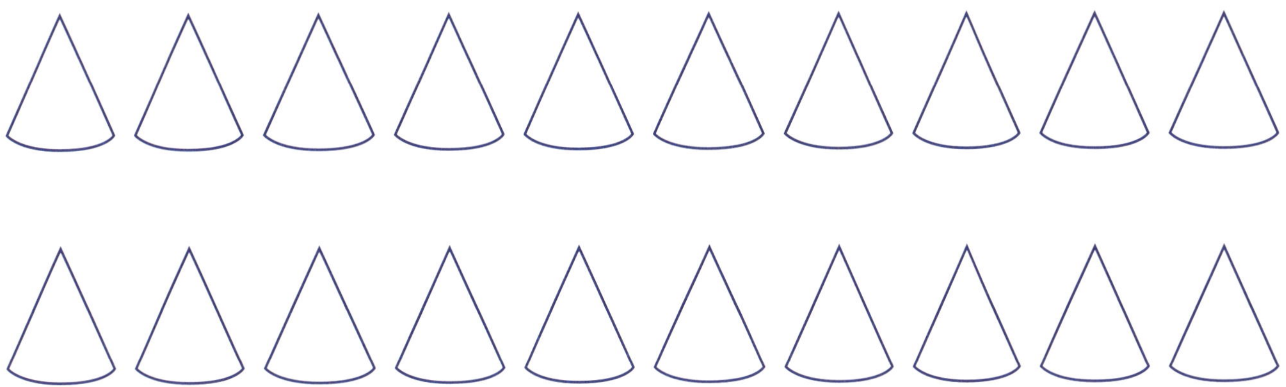

2 Answer true or false.

a $\frac{1}{2}$ of 20 hats is more than $\frac{1}{5}$ of 20 hats. ____________

b $\frac{1}{5}$ of 20 hats is more than $\frac{1}{4}$ of 20 hats. ____________

c $\frac{1}{4}$ of 20 hats is half as much as $\frac{1}{2}$ of 20 hats. ____________

d $\frac{1}{2}$ is the same as $\frac{1}{5}$ of the hats and $\frac{1}{4}$ of the hats together. ____________

How do you know? ____________

e $\frac{1}{2}$ of the hats plus $\frac{1}{4}$ of the hats is all the hats. ____________

How do you know? ____________

3 Write two of your own statements about the fractions of the hats.

____

____

____

____

____

I can solve problems by:

☐ understanding fractions of an amount ☐ using diagrams.

Holidays!

Investigation 3

survey the class

It's time for a holiday!
You need to plan everything.

Decide where you will go — camping, the snow, a city or the beach.

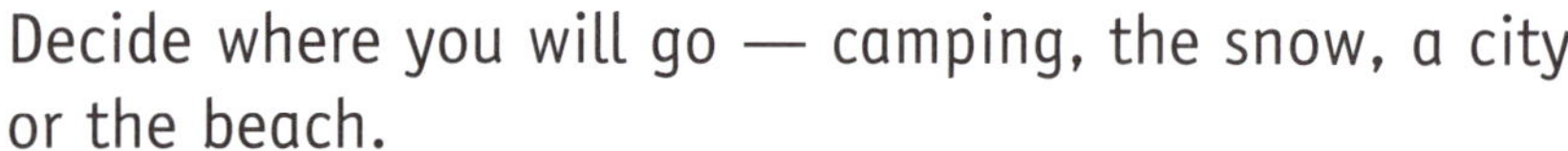

1 Survey your class to find the best place.

Tally

1 Camping ____________________

2 Snow ____________________

3 City ____________________

4 Beach ____________________

2 Display your results here.

3 Choose what holiday you want to go on.

____

4 Choose the month you will be away. Fill in the calendar.
Colour the 7 days you plan to be on holiday.

Month ____________________

Sun	Mon	Tues	Wed	Thurs	Fri	Sat

Leaving home: ____________________ Arriving back: ____________________

Statistics AC9M3ST01 & AC9M3ST02 & AC9M3ST03 acquire data for categorical and discrete numerical variables; record the data using appropriate methods • create and compare different graphical representations of data sets; interpret the data in terms of the context • conduct guided statistical investigations

Holidays!

Investigation 3

5 What will you do on your holiday? Plan the days.

6 You can only take 3 shirts and 2 pairs of jeans or 2 skirts. Draw your clothes and the different outfits. How many different outfits can you wear? _______

To carry out these tasks I need to:

- ☐ ask survey questions
- ☐ make a tally
- ☐ make a horizontal column graph
- ☐ read a calendar and record days on it
- ☐ explain choice of time
- ☐ calculate time and cost for activities
- ☐ draw diagrams to show choices of clothing.

I enjoyed this task!

☆☆☆☆☆

Revision

Write your answer in the box.

1

$5.90	$4.10	$2.40	$1.40	$6.80
koala	windmill	paints	wand	top

Su-Yin bought two toys and spent $7.30. Which two toys did she buy?

[ ] and [ ]

Shade one bubble.

2 What is the total value of these notes and coins?

$73.50 ◯ $68.50 ◯ $23.50 ◯ $73.00 ◯

3 Josef bought a drink for $1.50 and a sandwich for $2.20.
How much change did he get from $5?

$2.20

$1.50

$1.30 ◯ $3.70 ◯ $2.30 ◯ $0.70 ◯

4 4 out of 10 squares are coloured pink. What is another name for $\frac{4}{10}$?

$\frac{4}{4}$ ◯ $\frac{2}{4}$ ◯ $\frac{1}{2}$ ◯ $\frac{2}{5}$ ◯

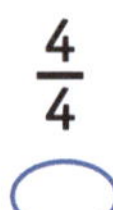

Write your answer in the box.

5 Complete.

a

37	63
?	

? = ______

b

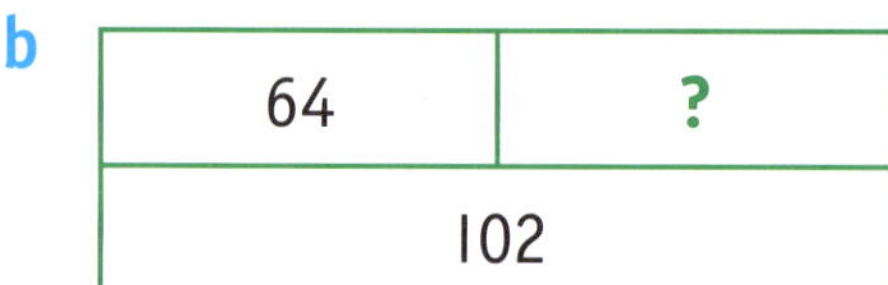

64	?
102	

? = ______

Revision

6 Joh started his bushwalk at . He walked for two hours.

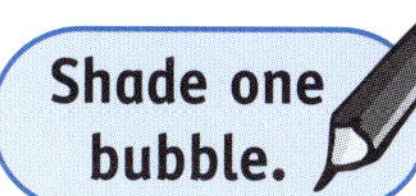

Which clock shows his finishing time?

7 Ahmed had to make 5 fair shares from these cupcakes.

How many in each share? 3 4 5 6

8 This graph shows how many glasses of water these children drank on Monday.

How many glasses did Murphy and Ari drink altogether?

10 5 8 9

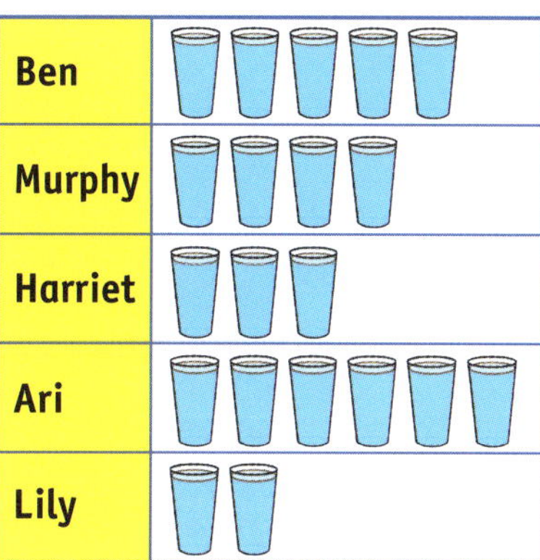

9 Which child made correct estimations of the capacity of these containers?

	Tamsie	Jacque	Hiram	Lottie
Tea cup	Less than $\frac{1}{2}$ L	About 1 L	About $\frac{1}{2}$ L	About $\frac{1}{2}$ L
Juice carton	About 2 L	About 2 L	About 1 L	Less than $\frac{1}{2}$ L
Yoghurt carton	About $\frac{1}{2}$ L	About $\frac{1}{2}$ L	Less than $\frac{1}{2}$ L	About 1 L
Milk jug	About 1 L	Less than $\frac{1}{2}$ L	About 2 L	About 2 L

10 How many angles in this shape?

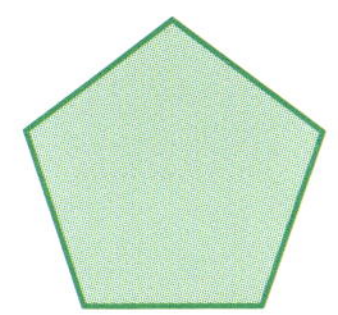

10 7 5 3

11 Which shape is a pyramid?

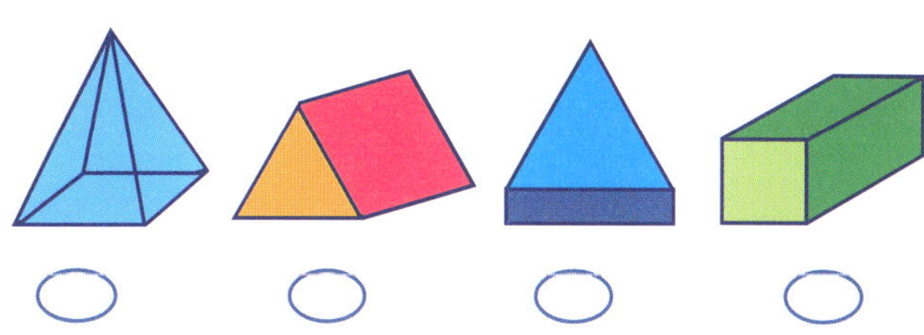

Unit 24 Missing terms

Patterns 

2 18 25 3

28

35 10 36 14

30

45 32

4 21 5

8

The young bears are lost. Match the mothers with their children. Give your reasons why.

2 ______ ______ ______

Reason ____

3 ______ ______ ______

Reason ____

4 ______ ______ ______

Reason ____

5 ______ ______ ______

Reason ____

HINT! Each mother can only have 3 children.

Unit 24 Describing patterns

1 Write the missing term, then write a reason for your answer.

a $\frac{1}{2}$, $\frac{1}{4}$, $\frac{1}{8}$, ______

Reason ______

b $1.80, $1.70, ______, $1.50, $1.40, $1.30

Reason ______

c 2, 7, 12, ______, ______, 27

Reason ______

d 25, 40, ______, 70, ______, ______

Reason ______

e 36, 45, 54, 63, ______, 81

Reason ______

f 10, 120, 230, ______, ______, 560

Reason ______

2

9 × 6	5 × 3
3 × 4	double 27
8 + 7	4 × 4
36 − 4	1 dozen
9 + 3 + 4	9 × 5
100 − 55	8 × 4

3 Use a calculator.

a Press AC b Press 5 c Press + + d Press =

e What does your calculator show? ______ f Press = again.

g Keep pressing = and write the answers. ______ ______ ______ ______

h What is the pattern? ______

Unit 24 Number patterns

Patterns 

1 Complete these patterns.

a 2, 4, 6, ______, ______, ______, 14, 16, ______, ______, ______

b 15, 18, ______, ______, ______, 30, 33, ______, ______, ______

c 10, 20, ______, ______, ______, ______, 70, ______, ______, 100

d 62, 57, ______, ______, 42, ______, ______, ______, 22, ______

e 15, 20, ______, ______, ______, ______, 45, ______, ______, 60

2 Use the rule in each square to fill in the missing numbers.

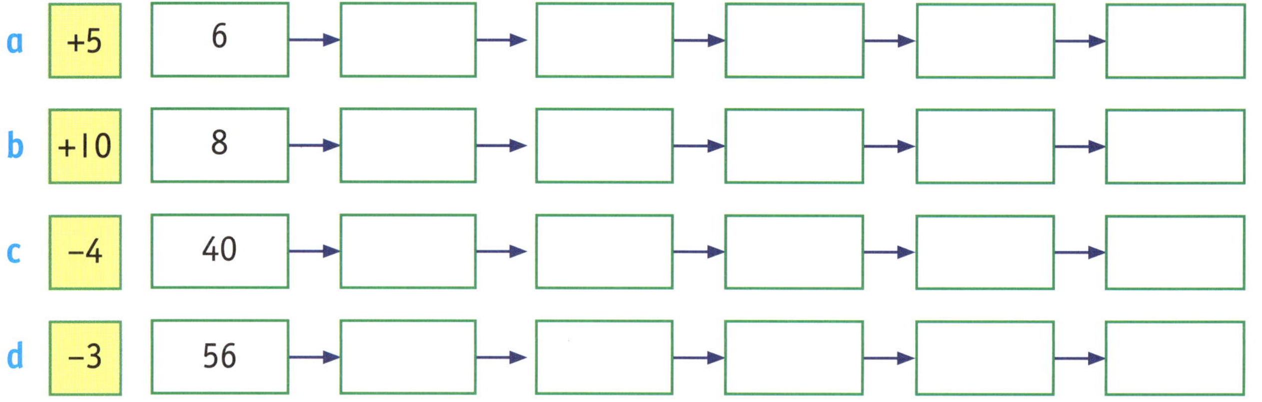

3 **a** Colour the 3s pattern red. Continue to 100.

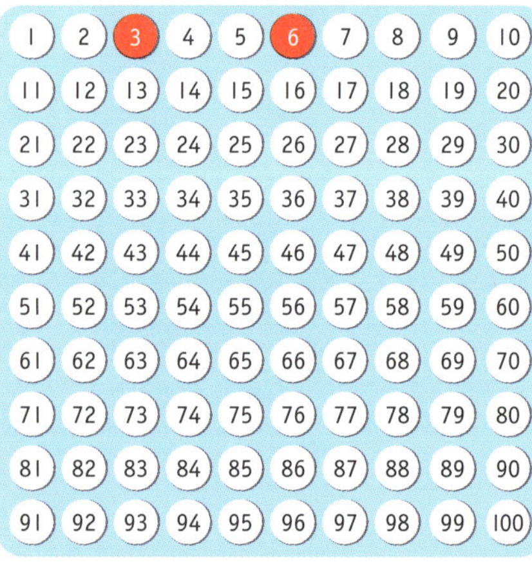

1	2	3	4	5	6	7	8	9	10
11	12	13	14	15	16	17	18	19	20
21	22	23	24	25	26	27	28	29	30
31	32	33	34	35	36	37	38	39	40
41	42	43	44	45	46	47	48	49	50
51	52	53	54	55	56	57	58	59	60
61	62	63	64	65	66	67	68	69	70
71	72	73	74	75	76	77	78	79	80
81	82	83	84	85	86	87	88	89	90
91	92	93	94	95	96	97	98	99	100

b Colour the 4s pattern green. Continue to 100.

1	2	3	4	5	6	7	8	9	10
11	12	13	14	15	16	17	18	19	20
21	22	23	24	25	26	27	28	29	30
31	32	33	34	35	36	37	38	39	40
41	42	43	44	45	46	47	48	49	50
51	52	53	54	55	56	57	58	59	60
61	62	63	64	65	66	67	68	69	70
71	72	73	74	75	76	77	78	79	80
81	82	83	84	85	86	87	88	89	90
91	92	93	94	95	96	97	98	99	100

c Colour the 5s pattern yellow. Continue to 100.

1	2	3	4	5	6	7	8	9	10
11	12	13	14	15	16	17	18	19	20
21	22	23	24	25	26	27	28	29	30
31	32	33	34	35	36	37	38	39	40
41	42	43	44	45	46	47	48	49	50
51	52	53	54	55	56	57	58	59	60
61	62	63	64	65	66	67	68	69	70
71	72	73	74	75	76	77	78	79	80
81	82	83	84	85	86	87	88	89	90
91	92	93	94	95	96	97	98	99	100

d Which numbers are coloured on all three grids? ______________________

Challenge!

Complete these patterns.

215, 224, 233 ☐ ☐ ☐ ☐ ☐

528, 519, 510 ☐ ☐ ☐ ☐ ☐

Number AC9M3N07 follow and create algorithms involving a sequence of steps and decisions to investigate numbers; describe any emerging patterns

Unit 24 Table patterns

1 Write the pattern for adding 6 in this table.

Order of term	1	2	3								
Term	6	12									

2 Write the pattern for adding 7 in this table.

Order of term	1	2	3								
Term	7	14									

3 Complete these addition and subtraction patterns.

a 18 + 9 = ______
______ − 9 = 18

b 36 + 9 = ______
______ − 9 = 36

c 36 − 9 = ______
______ + 9 = 36

d ______ − 6 = 54
54 + 6 = ______

e 72 − 8 = ______
______ + 8 = 72

f 81 − 7 = ______
______ + 7 = ______

4 a Write your own pattern using addition or subtraction.

_____ _____ _____ _____ _____ _____ _____ _____

b Write the rule. ______________________________

c Make a table for adding 9.

Order of term	1	2	3								
Term	9	18									

5 Colour each path across the river.

Mastery Checklist I can:
- ☐ find patterns in numbers
- ☐ write the missing term in a pattern
- ☐ use a calculator to make number patterns
- ☐ follow a rule to make a number pattern
- ☐ complete addition and subtraction patterns.

Number AC9M3N07 follow and create algorithms involving a sequence of steps and decisions to investigate numbers; describe any emerging patterns
Algebra AC9M3A01 recognise and explain the connection between addition and subtraction as inverse operations, apply to partition numbers and find unknown values in number sentences

Unit 25 Position

1 Draw the cake they choose.

Mandy	Mitch	Milly	Min	Mark
top row, on the left	bottom row, 2nd from the right	middle row, on the right	bottom row, on the left	top row, in the middle

2 Write the position of:

a the cupcake with the cherry on top. ______

b the meringue snowman. ______

c the cream frog. ______

d the apricot cheesecake. ______

e the strawberry slice. ______

3 Write the names and positions of the three cakes you like best.

a ______

b ______

c ______

Space AC9M3SP02 interpret and create two-dimensional representations of familiar environments, locating key landmarks and objects relative to each other

Unit 25 Rows and columns

Position

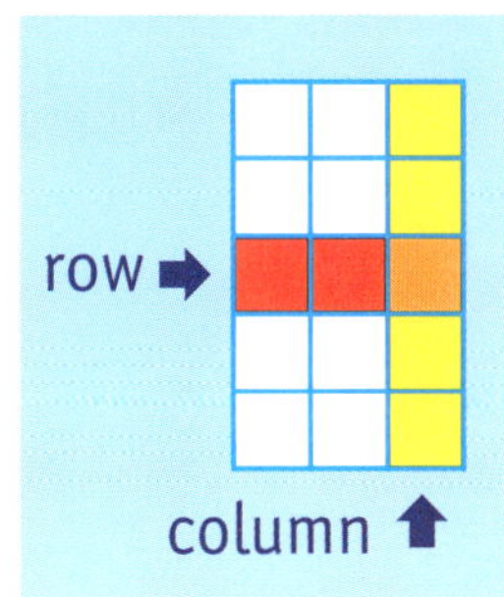

1 Which letter is:

a third column, top row? _____

b last column, bottom row? _____

c fifth column, second row? _____

d second last column, third row from the bottom? _____

e third column from the right, fourth row from the top? _____

f These letters spell a word. What is the word? __________

U	P	G	A	D	C
D	S	K	V	E	B
F	B	Y	O	A	N
G	R	O	T	E	F
H	I	L	N	M	R

2 Here is the map of 3B's classroom.

Tim	Simon		Kirsty	Zoe		Samad		
Lionel	Bob		Adam			Chloe	Gill	Lenny
	Chris		Brian	Amy		Samir	Lilly	Gopal
Lucy	Sam		Jim	Judith		Joe	Ajit	Leah

Miss Brown

a How many children are in Miss Brown's class? _______

b Who is sitting next to Brian? __________

c Who is sitting in front of the teacher? __________ __________

d Who is sitting behind Lionel? __________

e How many children are in Chloe's row? _______

f Rodger wants to sit in the third row. Who will he sit next to? __________

g Joe was talking. He was sent to sit behind Kirsty. Mark his new seat on the map.

h Draw in red how Joe would get to his new seat.

i Lucy wanted to borrow a pencil. She walked across the front of the room and down the aisle between Ajit and Leah. She asked the person in the third row on her left.

Who did she ask? __________

j Write directions for the path Adam would take to sit next to Samad.

____

Unit 25 Street map

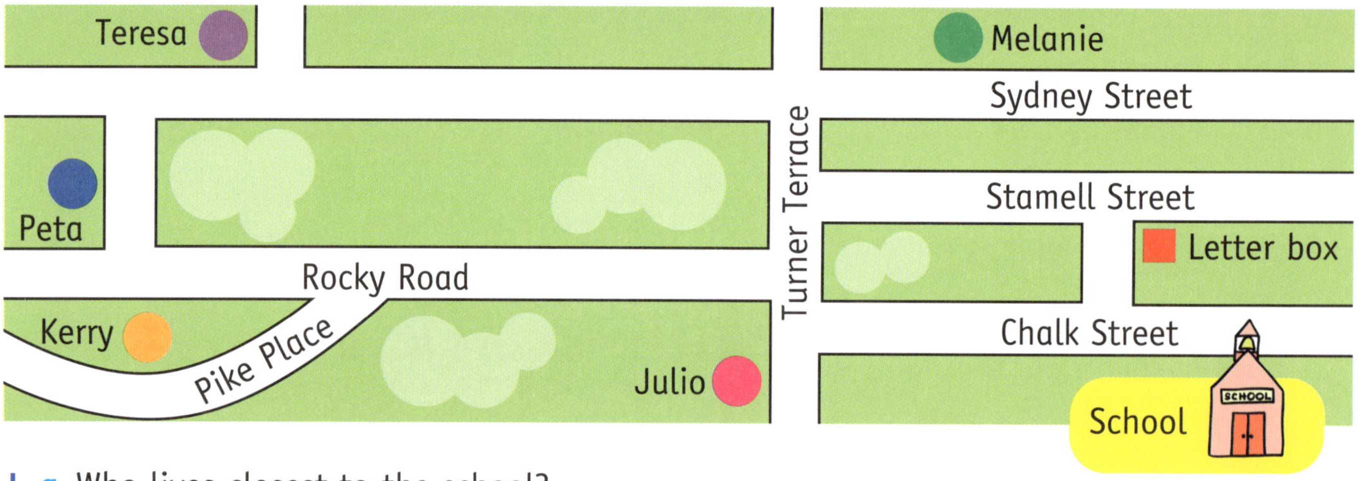

Teresa
Melanie
Sydney Street
Peta
Turner Terrace
Stamell Street
Letter box
Rocky Road
Kerry
Pike Place
Chalk Street
Julio
School

1 a Who lives closest to the school? ______________________

b On which street does Melanie live? ______________________

c Who lives at the corner of two streets? ______________________

d Peta went to visit her friend. She walked out her front gate, turned left, then turned right. She walked past Turner Terrace, and entered a house on her left.

Who did she visit? ____________

e Draw the path she followed in red.

f Who lives furthest from Julio? ____________

2 Teresa's mum asked her to post a letter on her way to school. In green, draw her path to school.

3 Write directions to tell how Kerry walks home from school.

____

____

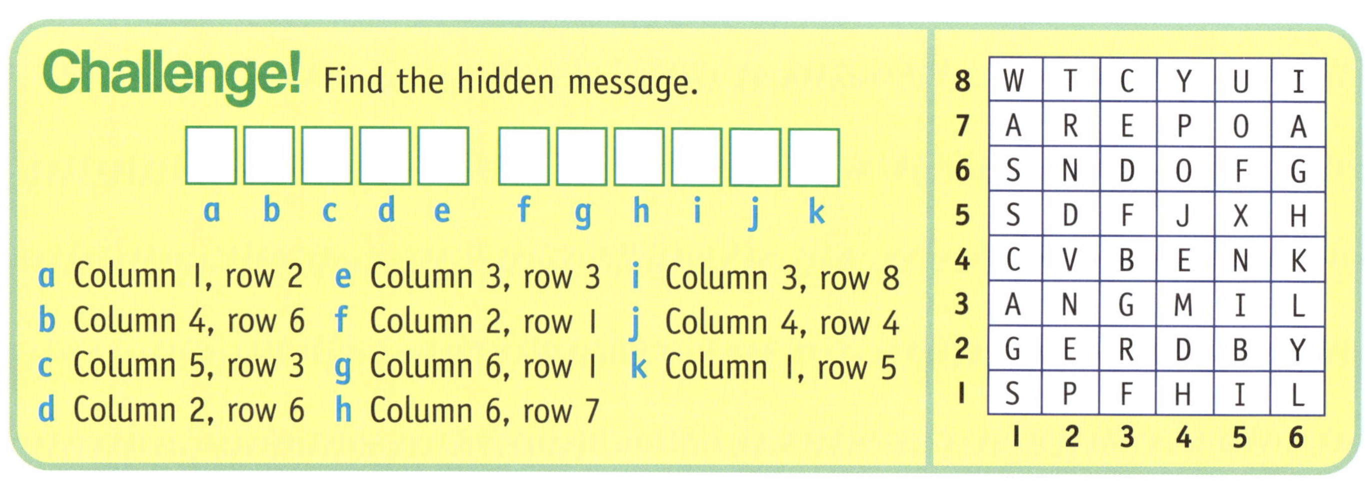

Challenge! Find the hidden message.

☐☐☐☐☐ ☐☐☐☐☐☐

a b c d e f g h i j k

a Column 1, row 2
b Column 4, row 6
c Column 5, row 3
d Column 2, row 6
e Column 3, row 3
f Column 2, row 1
g Column 6, row 1
h Column 6, row 7
i Column 3, row 8
j Column 4, row 4
k Column 1, row 5

8	W	T	C	Y	U	I
7	A	R	E	P	O	A
6	S	N	D	O	F	G
5	S	D	F	J	X	H
4	C	V	B	E	N	K
3	A	N	G	M	I	L
2	G	E	R	D	B	Y
1	S	P	F	H	I	L
	1	2	3	4	5	6

Mastery Checklist I can:
- ☐ describe the position of an object in a group
- ☐ use columns and rows to identify a position
- ☐ understand directions on a street map.

Space AC9M3SP02 interpret and create two-dimensional representations of familiar environments, locating key landmarks and objects relative to each other

Problem solving

Lost gold adventure

You are on a quest to find a hidden treasure!

Rules:
- Start at 🟡.
- You cannot travel through the forest, river or swamp.
- ❌ marks the spot where you will find the treasure.

1 Follow each person's instructions to find out who made it to the treasure.

Kylie	Syd	Dalla	
Down 5	Right 2	Down 4	Right 1
Right 3	Down 1	Right 3	Down 1
Up 2	Right 1	Up 2	Right 1
Right 3	Down 5	Right 1	Down 1
Down 3	Right 3	Down 2	

Who wrote the correct instructions?

____

2 Write a different set of directions to get from 🟡 to ❌.

____

____

____

____

____

____

I can solve problems by:

☐ understanding position ☐ drawing paths.

Unit 26 Mass

measure and compare mass

Find three small boxes. Label them **A**, **B** and **C**. Fill each box with sand.

1 a Feel the weight of each box.

  b Write the boxes in order from lightest to heaviest.

  lightest _____ _____ _____ heaviest

2 Use balance scales to order the boxes.

  lightest _____ _____ _____ heaviest

3 a Empty the boxes and fill them with something different, eg marbles or blocks.

  b Order the boxes from lightest to heaviest.

  lightest _____ _____ _____ heaviest

4 Is the order the same each time? ________

5 How could you weigh this book using sand or marbles?

____

6 Do you know a better method to weigh this book?

____

Unit 26 Introducing the kilogram

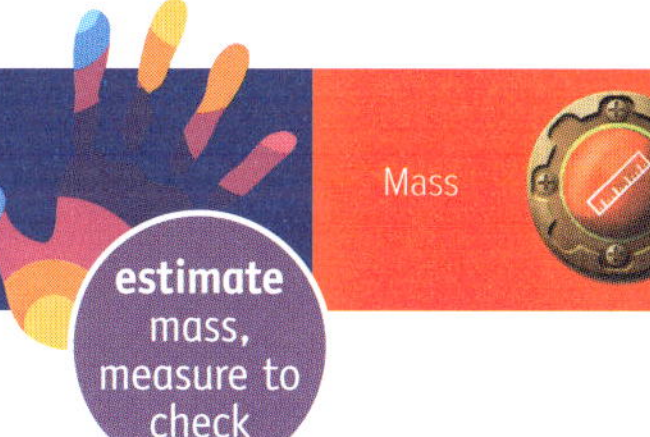

1 Hold a one kilogram weight. Feel how heavy it is.

Estimate whether these items are heavier or lighter than 1 kg. Use balance scales to check.

Objects are weighed in kilograms.
kg is the short way to write kilograms.

Item	Estimate	Balance scales
a 2 maths books		
b a pencil case		
c a book box		
d a full lunch box		
e 1 brick		
f a bottle of water		
g a football		
h a backpack		
i a whiteboard marker		
j 20 pencils		

2 a

The pumpkin weighs _______ than 1 kg.

b

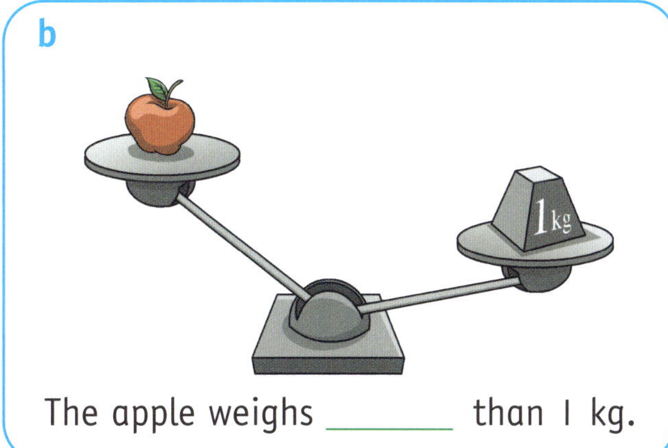

The apple weighs _______ than 1 kg.

c

The sugar ___________________

____

d

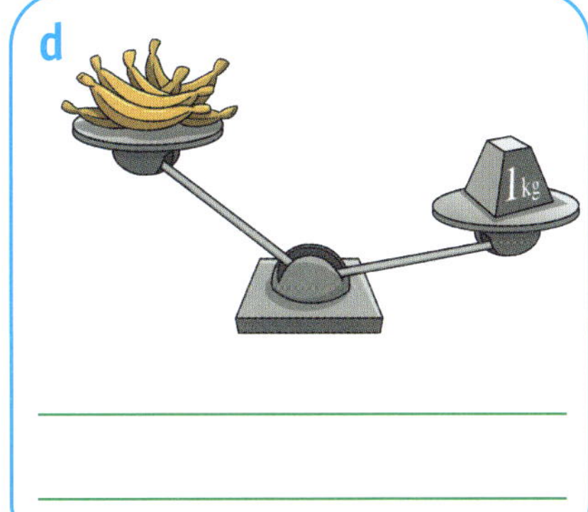

____

____

e

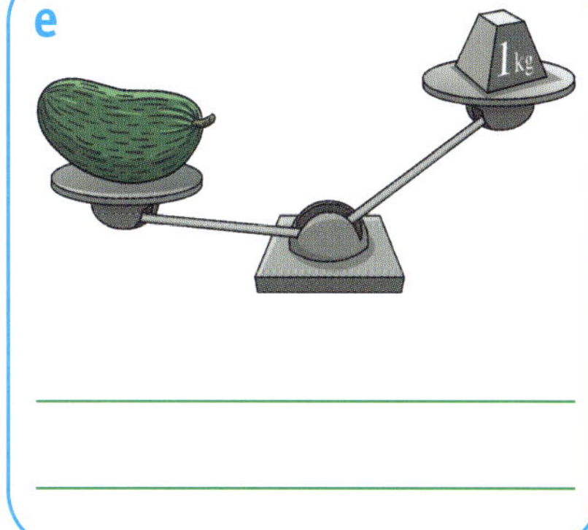

____

____

3 Write five items that are weighed in kilograms, eg sugar.

__________ __________ __________ __________ __________

4 How many kilograms do you weigh? _______

Unit 26 Weighing in kilograms

1 What is the mass for each box?

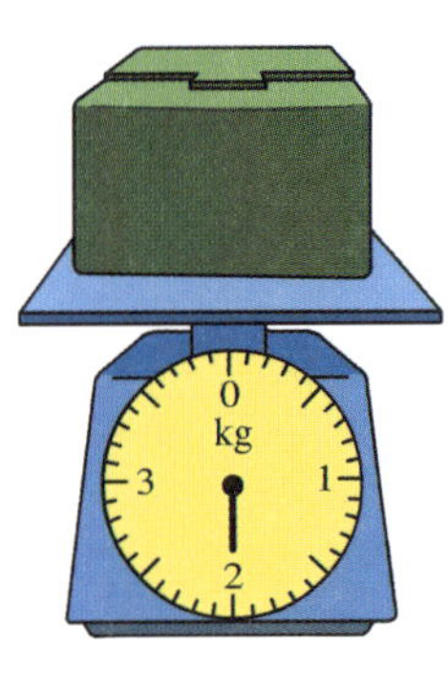
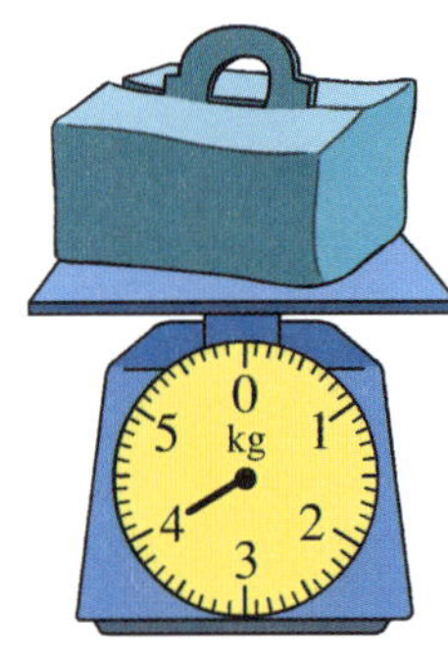
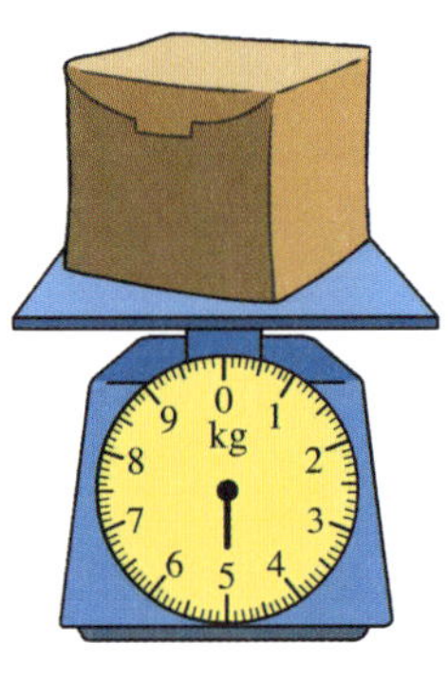

a ______ kg b ______ kg c ______ kg d ______ kg

e What is the total mass of the four boxes? ______

2 What is the mass for each object?

a ______ kg b ______ kg c ______ kg d ______ kg

e Order the objects from lightest to heaviest.

______ ______ ______ ______

3 Use balance scales to find:

a two things that weigh about 1 kg. ______ ______

b two things that weigh about 2 kg. ______ ______

c two things that weigh about $\frac{1}{2}$ kg. ______ ______

d two things that are exactly the same weight. ______ ______

How heavy are they? ______

measure mass with balance scales

Mastery Checklist I can:

- ☐ compare the masses of real-life objects
- ☐ compare masses to 1 kilogram
- ☐ read scales in kilograms
- ☐ use balance scales.

Measurement AC9M3M01 identify which metric units are used to measure everyday items; use measurements of familiar items and known units to make estimates
AC9M3M02 measure and compare objects using familiar metric units of length, mass and capacity, and instruments with labelled markings

Problem solving

Heavy duty

1 You can carry 7 kg and your little sister can carry 5 kg.

How many ways can you carry all these bags between you?

Solutions: ______________________________

____

____

____

2 How can you find the heaviest of three similar objects with only a balance scale and no weights?

Solution: ______________________________

____

____

____

3 How can you weigh your dog when he won't stand still on the scales?

Hint: *Use these.*

____

____

____

____

I can solve problems by:

☐ understanding mass ☐ measuring and comparing masses.

Unit 27 Passing time

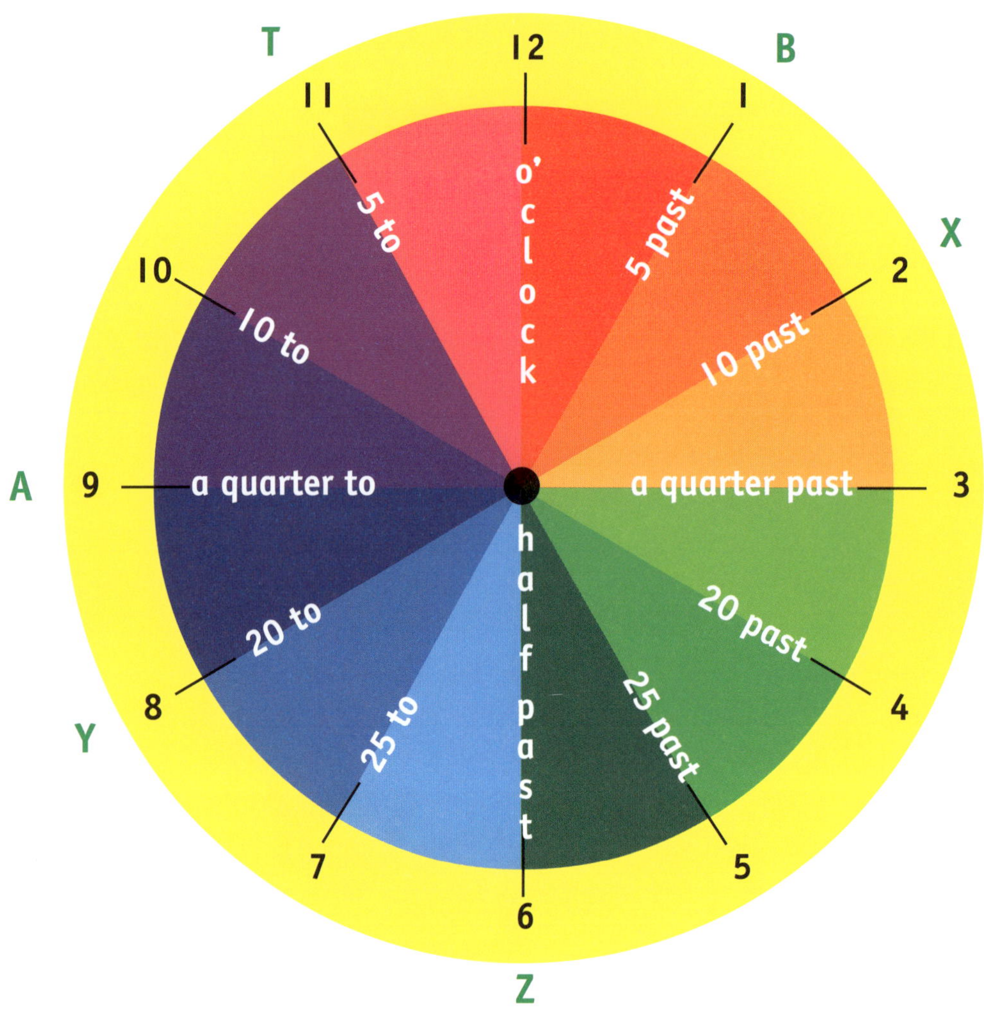

1 Study the analogue clock and count the minutes between the letters, counting clockwise.

a A and B ______ b X and Y ______ c T and Z ______

2 Write the analogue time 5 minutes after:

a 10 past 5 ______ b 20 past 4 ______

c 5 past 3 ______ d a quarter past 7 ______

3 Write the analogue time 10 minutes before:

a 20 past 2 ______ b a quarter past 6 ______

c 10 past 8 ______ d half past 9 ______

4 Write the analogue time 15 minutes after:

a 25 past 4 ______ b twenty to 11 ______

c half past 7 ______ d ten to 5 ______

5 Write the analogue time 5 minutes before:

a twenty to 3 ______ b ten to 12 ______

Measurement AC9M3M04 describe the relationship between the hours and minutes on analogue and digital clocks, and read the time to the nearest minute

Unit 27 Time and action

1 How many hours have passed:

a between 1 pm and 4 pm? ________

b between 11 am and 1 pm? ________

c between 6 pm and 12 midnight? ______

d between 10 am and 9 pm? ________

2 Write a reasonable activity that takes about this much time.

a 15 minutes ____________________

b 25 minutes ____________________

c 2 hours ____________________

d 1 hour 5 minutes ____________________

3 How many minutes have passed? What might you do in this time?

a between 3:45 pm and 4:15 pm

____

____

b between 5:10 am and 5:24 am

____

____

c between 12 noon and 12:32 pm

____

____

d between 11:26 am and 11:38 am

____

____

4 Show the two times on the clocks and answer the question.

a Cam started to clean the car at 9:10 am. He finished at 9:45 am.

How long did it take him to clean the car?

____

b Joan's appointment was at 3:20 pm but she arrived at 3:50.

How late was she?

____

Challenge!

Mum says, "Meet me here at four o'clock." As time passes, you look at your watch 4 times. How long do you have each time?

2:45 [ ] 3:05  3:25  3:50 [ ]

Mastery Checklist I can:
- ☐ tell time to the nearest 5 minutes
- ☐ work out times before and after
- ☐ work out how long activities take
- ☐ show time on a clock.

Unit 28 Reading a table

Tallies and graphs

SSL Table — Central Districts

	Games	Won	Lost	Drawn	Points
Giants	8	6	1	1	26
Bradies	8	6	2	0	24
Dragons	8	5	3	0	20
Furies	8	4	3	1	18
Brongoes	7	4	3	0	16
Tigers	8	4	4	0	16
Meteors	7	2	5	0	8
Wallabies	8	2	6	0	8

Here is the Schools Soccer League results table for this year.

1 What are the points for the:

a Wallabies? ________ b Giants? ________

c Dragons? ________ d Meteors? ________

2 a How many points do the teams score for a win? ________

b How many points do they get for a draw? ________

3 How many rounds have been played by most teams? ________

4 Who has yet to play their eighth game? ________

5 Which two teams had a draw? ________

6 If the Brongoes win their 8th round match, what will the top 4 teams be?

____

7 Could the Furies become the league leaders after playing two more games? ________

How? ________

8 If the Tigers win the next 4 games, will they be leaders? ________

Why? ________

Challenge! Update the table using these results:

Round 8 Brongoes 4 Meteors 2

Round 9 Giants 3 Wallabies 1 Bradies 2 Dragons 1

Meteors 4 Furies 3 Brongoes 2 Tigers 2

Who is top of the table now? ________

Statistics AC9M3ST01 acquire data for categorical and discrete numerical variables to address a question of interest or purpose by observing, collecting and accessing data sets; record the data using appropriate methods including frequency tables and spreadsheets

Unit 28 Graphs

Data

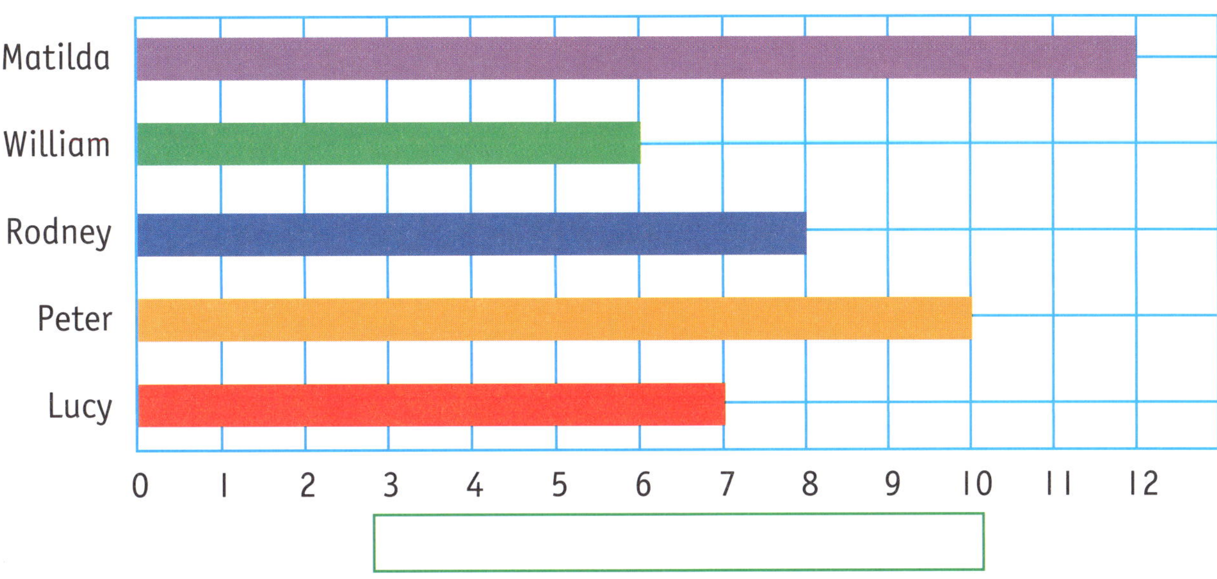

1 **a** How many students compared homework? ________

b Write the label for the bottom numbers.

c Who did the most homework? ________________

d Who did the least homework? ________________

e Who did 8 hours of homework? ________________

f Name three students who did more homework than Lucy.

________________ ________________ ________________

2 Draw a picture graph to show the same information. Use one clock to show one hour. Label your graph clearly.

Unit 28 Collecting data

Tally marks are in groups of 5

𝍸 || = 7

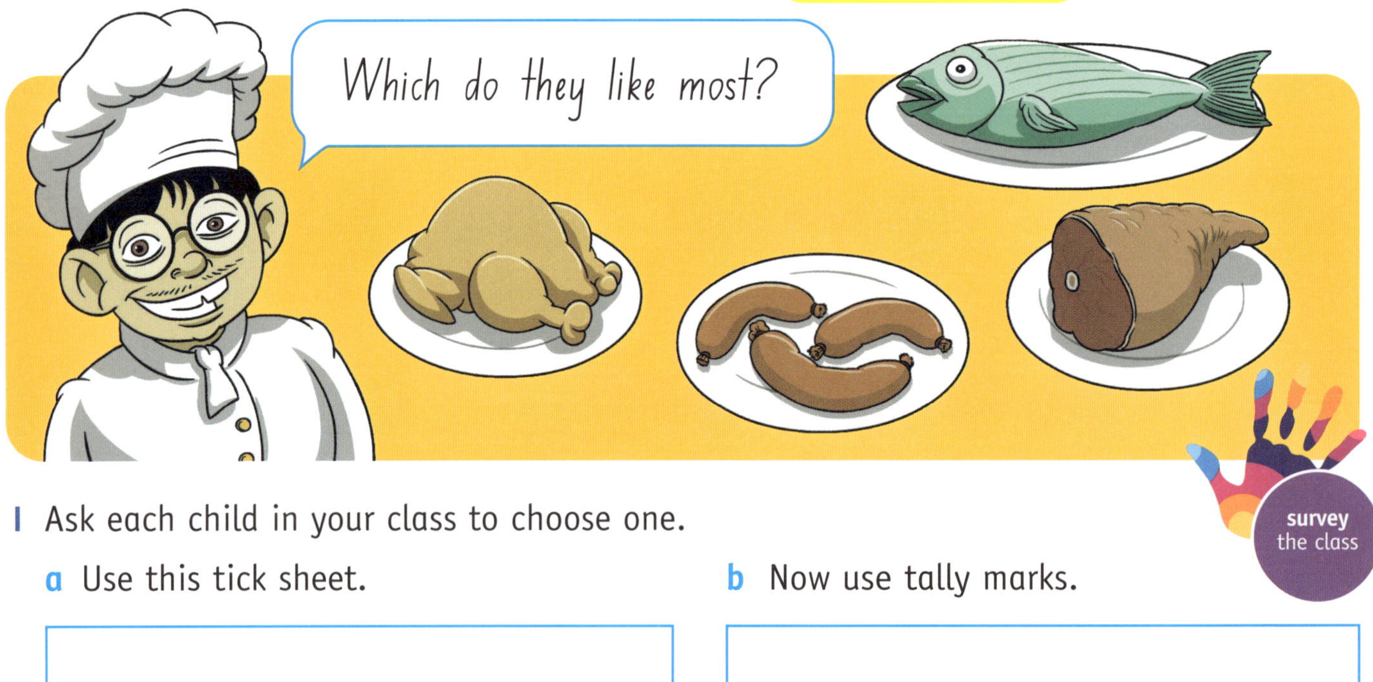

survey the class

1 Ask each child in your class to choose one.

a Use this tick sheet.

b Now use tally marks.

2 Make a column graph to show these choices. Remember all the labels.

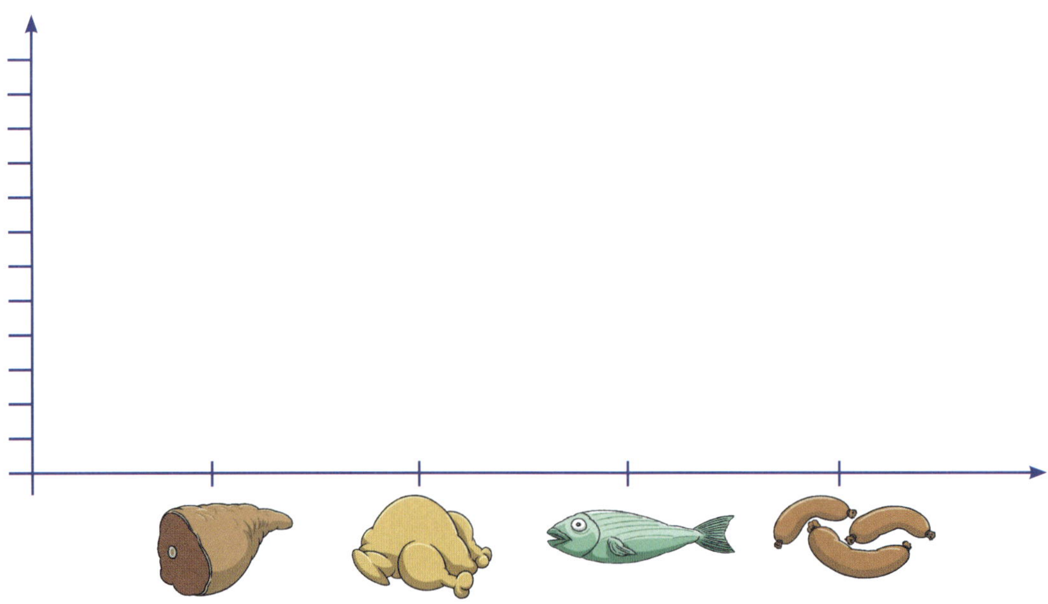

Statistics AC9M3ST01 & AC9M3ST02 & AC9M3ST03 acquire data for categorical and discrete numerical variables; record the data using appropriate methods • create and compare different graphical representations of data sets; interpret the data in terms of the context • conduct guided statistical investigations

Unit 28 Chance

1 What is the likelihood of each happening? Use one of these words.

certain   likely   unlikely   impossible

a You will eat a boiled egg for breakfast tomorrow.

____

b Your teacher will have purple hair next week.

____

c It will rain next Wednesday.

____

d My mother is older than me.

____

e You will eat food tomorrow.

____

f Next month is September.

____

2 From this bag, which colour:

a is most likely to be drawn out? ______________________

Why? ______________________

b is least likely to be drawn out? ______________________

Why? ______________________

c will never be drawn out? ______________________

Why? ______________________

d Which colours have the same chance? ______________________

Why? ______________________

Challenge!

Write down:

- 3 things you think are FAIR and
- 3 things you think are UNFAIR.

FAIR	UNFAIR

Mastery Checklist I can:

- ☐ answer questions about a table
- ☐ answer questions about a column graph
- ☐ make a picture graph
- ☐ collect data and use tally marks
- ☐ make a column graph
- ☐ understand certain, likely, unlikely and impossible.

Revision Term 3

1 Sam had \$5. He bought one chocolate for \$3.20 and one lollipop for 60c. p 96

a How much did he spend? ______

b How much change did he get? ______

2 p 97

a $\begin{array}{r} 174 \\ +\ 13 \\ \hline \end{array}$ b $\begin{array}{r} 383 \\ +\ 15 \\ \hline \end{array}$ c $\begin{array}{r} 460 \\ +\ 37 \\ \hline \end{array}$

3 Fill in the boxes. p 97

a $\begin{array}{r} 2\square \\ +\ 54 \\ \hline \square 9 \\ \hline \end{array}$ b $\begin{array}{r} \square 2 \\ +\ 34 \\ \hline 7\square \\ \hline \end{array}$ c $\begin{array}{r} 64 \\ +\ \square\square \\ \hline 78 \\ \hline \end{array}$

4 p 101

a $9 \times 5 =$ ______ b $9 \times 0 =$ ______

c $3 \times 9 =$ ______ d $9 \times 4 =$ ______

5 Use colours to match. p 102

9 + 9 + 9	six fours
7 × 5	27
6 groups of 4	6 × 3
10 × 0	7 + 7 + 7 + 7 + 7
3+3+3+3+3+3	0

6 Each chapter in a book has 8 pages. How many pages has Liam read if he's read 4 chapters? p 103

______

7 p 105

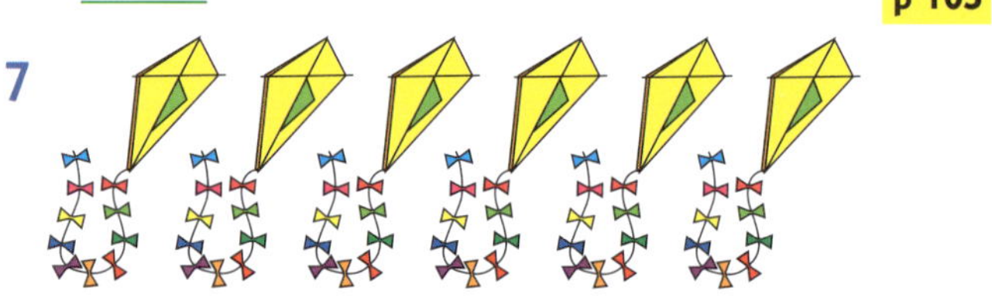

a How many kites? ______

b How many bows on each kite? ______

c How many bows altogether? ______

d ______ × ______ = ______

8 p 106

a $\begin{array}{r} 4 \\ \times\ 1 \\ \hline \end{array}$ b $\begin{array}{r} 5 \\ \times\ 3 \\ \hline \end{array}$ c $\begin{array}{r} 4 \\ \times\ 9 \\ \hline \end{array}$ d $\begin{array}{r} 10 \\ \times\ 6 \\ \hline \end{array}$

9 Make fair shares. p 108

7 shares. 1 share = ______

10 a Draw 24 balls. p 110

b How many groups of 4? ______

c How many groups of 3? ______

d How many groups of 12? ______

11 Circle the larger fraction. $\frac{1}{2}$, $\frac{1}{5}$ p 112

12 True or false? p 112

a $\frac{1}{2}$ is the same as $\frac{2}{4}$ ______

b $\frac{1}{2}$ is more than $\frac{2}{5}$ ______

13 Colour the fraction to match. p 113

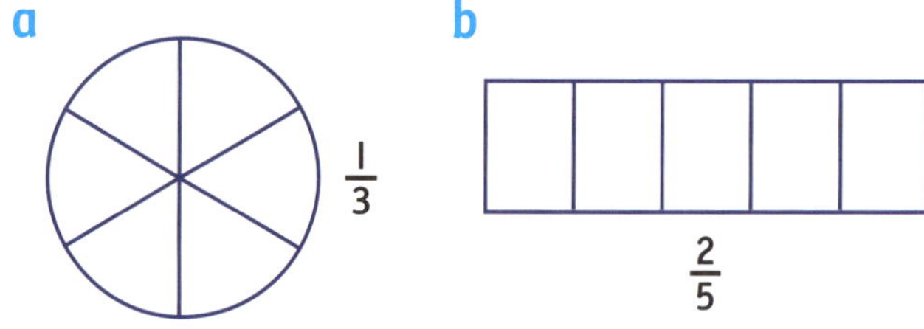

14 What is: p 114

a $\frac{1}{4}$ of 12 oranges? ______

b $\frac{1}{3}$ of 15 beans? ______

Revision Term 3

15 Write the missing terms. p 121

a $1.80, $1.60, ____, $1.20, ____

b 25, 33, 41, ______, ______, 65

16 Write the pattern for adding 6 in this table. p 123

Order of the term	1	2	3			
Term	6					

17 p 124

What is:

a on the top row in the middle?

____

b in the middle row on the left?

____

Write the position of:

c the jacket. ______________________

____

d the sunglasses. ______________________

____

18 Name something that is: p 129

a heavier than 1 kg.

____

b lighter than 1 kg.

____

19 How much does it weigh? p 130

a

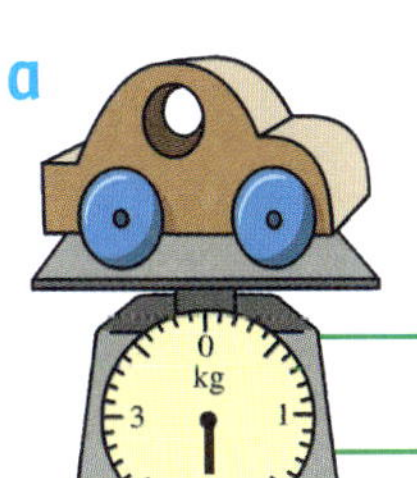

b

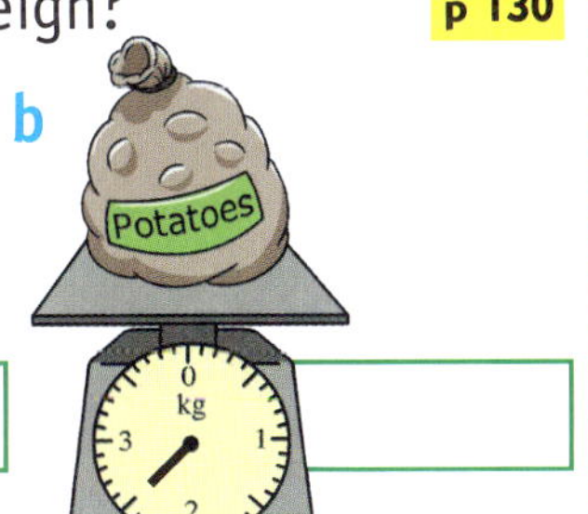

20 Draw both times on the clocks. p 132

The writing lesson started at 11:40 am and went for 35 minutes. Write the time it finished in words.

____

21 What is the likelihood of: p 137

a the school holidays being 3 months long? ______________

b it raining next week? ______________

22 Give an example that matches each description. p 137

a certain ______________________

____

b impossible ______________________

____

c likely ______________________

____

d unlikely ______________________

____

23 Look at the bag of cubes. p 137

a Which colour is least likely to be drawn out? __________

b Which two colours have the same chance? __________ and __________

c Which colour will never be drawn out? Circle it.

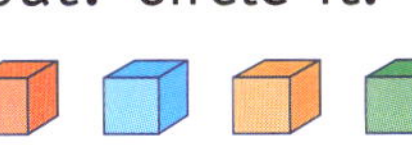

Unit 29 Writing four-digit numbers

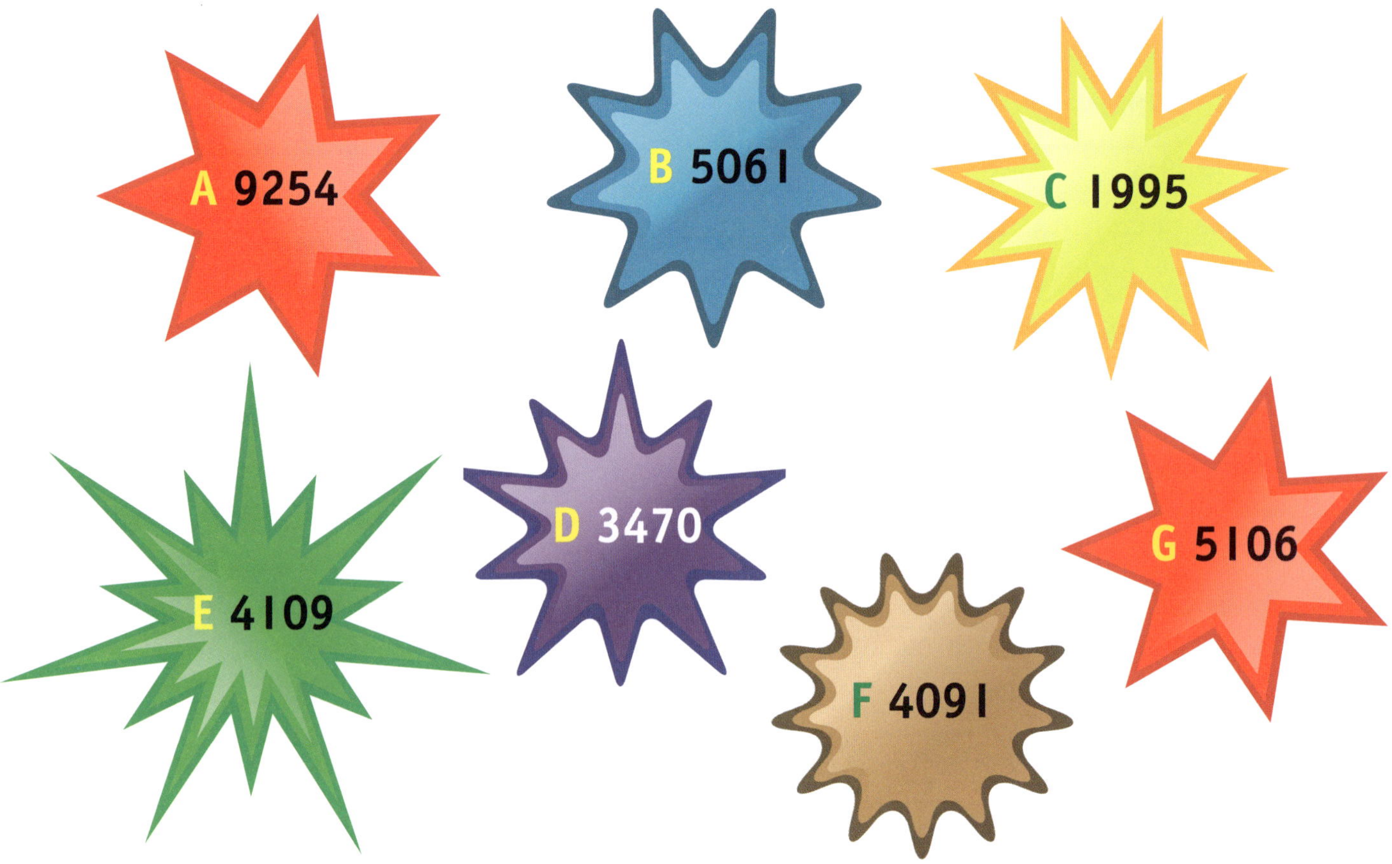

Number words 

A 9254

B 5061

C 1995

D 3470

E 4109

F 4091

G 5106

1 Write each number in words.

A ______

B ______

C ______

D ______

E ______

F ______

G ______

2 Write the numbers in ascending order.

3 Which number is:

a closest to 4000? ______

b closest to 6000? ______

4 Which number comes:

a after 1995? ______

b before 4091? ______

c before 5061? ______

d after 4109? ______

Number AC9M3N01 recognise, represent and order natural numbers using naming and writing conventions for numerals beyond 10 000

Unit 29 Rounding numbers

1 Round to the nearest ten.

a 74 ________ b 81 ________
c 25 ________ d 67 ________
e 12 ________ f 40 ________
g 89 ________ h 36 ________
i 93 ________ j 58 ________

2 Round to the nearest hundred.

a 654 ________ b 463 ________
c 871 ________ d 202 ________
e 108 ________ f 961 ________
g 235 ________ h 579 ________
i 96 ________ j 310 ________

3 Round to the nearest thousand.

a 7398 ________ b 5650 ________
c 1427 ________ d 1901 ________
e 5006 ________ f 9433 ________
g 2192 ________ h 3198 ________
i 945 ________ j 8072 ________

Remember:

1, 2, 3, 4 go down
5, 6, 7, 8, 9 go up.

To round to the nearest ten, look at the ones place.

82 → 80

To round to the nearest hundred, look at the tens place.

168 → 200

To round to the nearest thousand, look at the hundreds place.

3248 → 3000

4 6105 5160 5016 5601 6510

Write the number:

a with thousands digit 5 and ones digit 1. ☐
b with hundreds digit 1 and ones digit 5. ☐
c with hundreds digit 5 and ones digit 0. ☐
d with thousands digit 5 and ones digit 6. ☐

Work backwards

What number am I?
My thousands digit is 2 more than my tens digit.
My tens digit is 3 less than my hundreds digit.
My hundreds digit is 4 more than my ones digit which is 2. ☐

Unit 29 Round and add

1 Round each number to the nearest 10 and then add to estimate.

	Round to the nearest 10	Add the rounded numbers
a 24 + 38	20 + 40	60
b 63 + 19	____ + ____	____
c 86 + 227		
d 192 + 23		
e 51 + 314		

2 Round each number to the nearest 100 and then add to estimate.

	Round to the nearest 100	Add the rounded numbers
a 123 + 456	100 + 500	600
b 462 + 321		
c 841 + 753		
d 3936 + 2297		
e 6843 + 1987		

3 Round each number to the nearest 1000 and then add to estimate.

	Round to the nearest 1000	Add the rounded numbers
a 1342 + 3453	1000 + 3000	4000
b 6431 + 6956		
c 7360 + 4493		
d 8255 + 2873		
e 1046 + 3097		

 Number AC9M3N05 estimate the quantity of objects in collections and make estimates when solving problems to determine the reasonableness of calculations

Unit 29 Four-digit numbers

1 Write 'is more than' or 'is less than' to make the statements true.

a 764 ______________________ 674 b 991 ______________________ 919

c 538 ______________________ 583 d 1465 ______________________ 1456

e 2091 ______________________ 2109 f 8691 ______________________ 8961

2 Choose numbers from page 140 to fill in the blanks.

a ________ is less than ________ b ________ is less than ________

c ________ is less than ________ d ________ is more than ________

e ________ is more than ________ f ________ is more than ________

3 Write the value of the 9 in:

a 9254 ________ b 1975 ________ c 4109 ________ d 4091 ________

4 Write the value of the 4 in:

a 9254 ________ b 3470 ________ c 4109 ________ d 4091 ________

5 a 9254 = 9000 + 200 + _____ + _____ b 1995 = _____ + _____ + _____ + _____

c 3470 = _____ + _____ + _____ d 5106 = _____ + _____ + _____

e 5061 = _____ + _____ + _____ f 4091 = _____ + _____ + _____

6 True or false?

a There were about 9000 people at the cinema. ________

b There are about 5000 children in our school. ________

c In our class there are less than 2000 toes. ________

d There are 1000 cents in $10. ________

e A large bottle can hold 2000 mL. ________

f There are 6914 birds sitting on the window sill. ________

g Grandma read 3011 books last week. ________

h There are more than 2000 words in this book. ________

Challenge!

If you turn a calculator upside down, some numbers look like letters, eg 1 = i, 7 = L, 4 = h etc. 7714 = hill

What numbers make these words?

sell	lose	shoe	goes	legs

Unit 29 Using numeral expanders

1 Write these numbers.

a 7 Thousands 6 Hundreds 2 Tens 9 Ones ______

b 9 Thousands 4 Hundreds 5 Tens 2 Ones ______

c 4 Thousands 7 Hundreds 0 Tens 3 Ones ______

d 1 Thousands 0 Hundreds 8 Tens 6 Ones ______

e 6 Thousands 3 Hundreds 5 Tens 0 Ones ______

These are expanded numbers.

2 Complete these numeral expanders.

a 5218

☐ Thousands ☐ Hundreds ☐ Tens ☐ Ones

☐ ☐ Hundreds ☐ Tens ☐ Ones

☐ ☐ ☐ Tens ☐ Ones

☐ ☐ ☐ ☐ Ones

b 3964

☐ Thousands ☐ Hundreds ☐ Tens ☐ Ones

☐ ☐ Hundreds ☐ Tens ☐ Ones

☐ ☐ ☐ Tens ☐ Ones

☐ ☐ ☐ ☐ Ones

3 Use the numeral expanders above to express:

a 5218 as ______ thousands, ______ tens, ______ ones

b 5218 as ______ hundreds, ______ tens, ______ ones

c 5218 as ______ tens, ______ ones

4 How many hundreds in:

a 7450? ______ b 6307? ______ c 2094? ______ d 8813? ______

5 How many tens in:

a 1638? ______ b 5920? ______ c 4107? ______ d 9022? ______

6 How many ones in:

a 7004? ______ b 2500? ______ c 1234? ______ d 9990? ______

Mastery Checklist I can:
- ☐ write 4-digit numbers in different ways
- ☐ round numbers
- ☐ round and add to estimate
- ☐ understand place value to thousands.

Number AC9M3N01 recognise, represent and order natural numbers using naming and writing conventions for numerals beyond 10 000

Unit 30 Number facts 3×

Here are 10 groups of 3 children.

1 How many children in:

a 3 groups? ______ b 6 groups? ______ c 4 groups? ______ d 2 groups? ______

e 10 groups? ______ f 8 groups? ______ g 5 groups? ______ h 7 groups? ______

i 9 groups? ______ j 0 groups? ______ k 11 groups? ______ l 12 groups? ______

2 Complete.

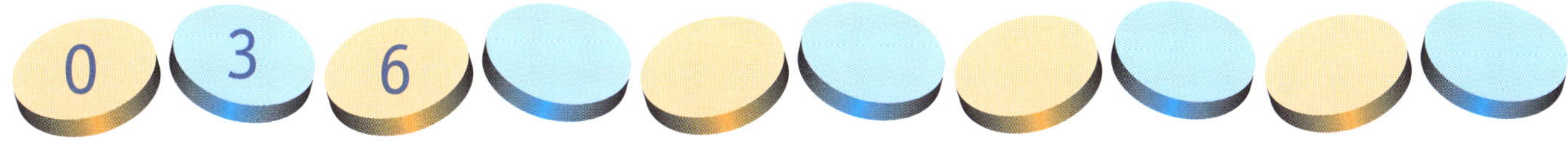

3

×	6	10	2	8	4	0	7	3	9	1	5
3											

4 It takes 3 minutes to walk around the oval. How long will it take to walk around the oval 8 times?

______

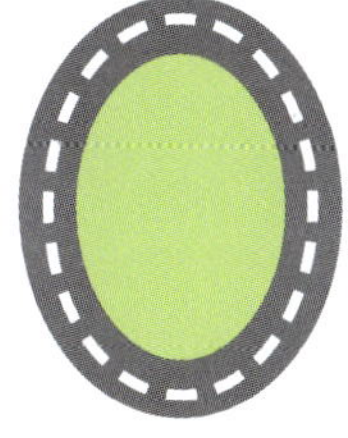

5 1 toy costs $3. How much will 5 toys cost?

______

6 There are 3 flowers on each plant. How many flowers are there on 7 plants?

______

7 Make up your own '3' story.

______

______

______

Unit 30 Number facts 4×

1 How many paws on:

a 1 cat? ______ b 6 cats? ______ c 4 cats? ______ d 9 cats? ______

e 2 cats? ______ f 10 cats? ______ g 3 cats? ______ h 8 cats? ______

i 7 cats? ______ j 5 cats? ______ k 0 cats? ______ l 11 cats? ______

2 Join.

10 × 4 2 × 4 5 × 4

7 × 4 8 × 4

16 12 28 8 20 0

3 × 4 0 × 4

40 36 24 4 32

9 × 4 1 × 4

4 × 4 6 × 4

3 Complete these as quickly as you can.

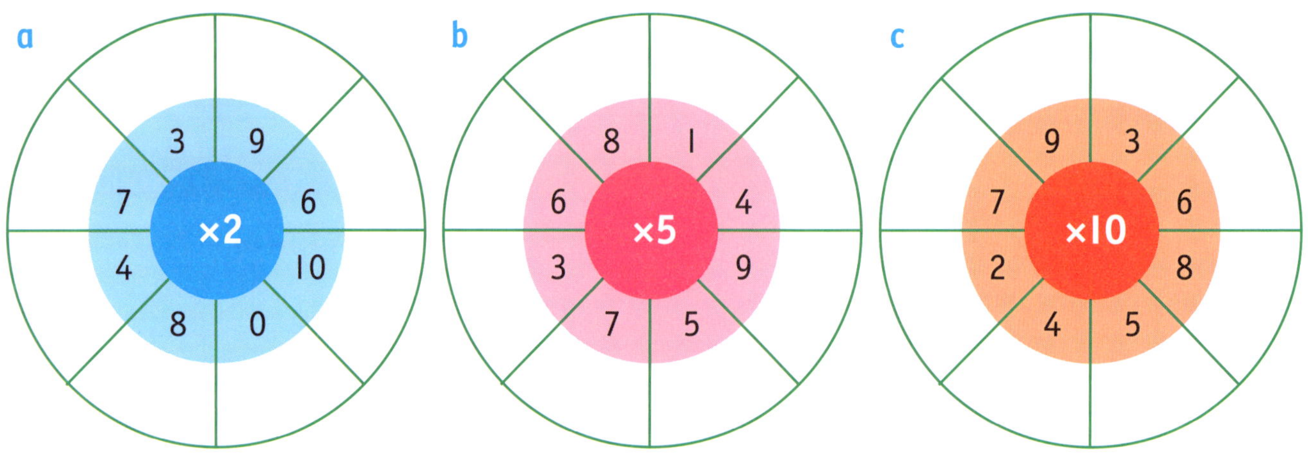

 Number AC9M3N06 use mathematical modelling to solve practical problems involving additive and multiplicative situations including financial contexts; formulate problems using number sentences and choose calculation strategies **Algebra AC9M3A03** recall and demonstrate proficiency with multiplication facts for 3, 4, 5 and 10

Unit 30 Number facts 10×

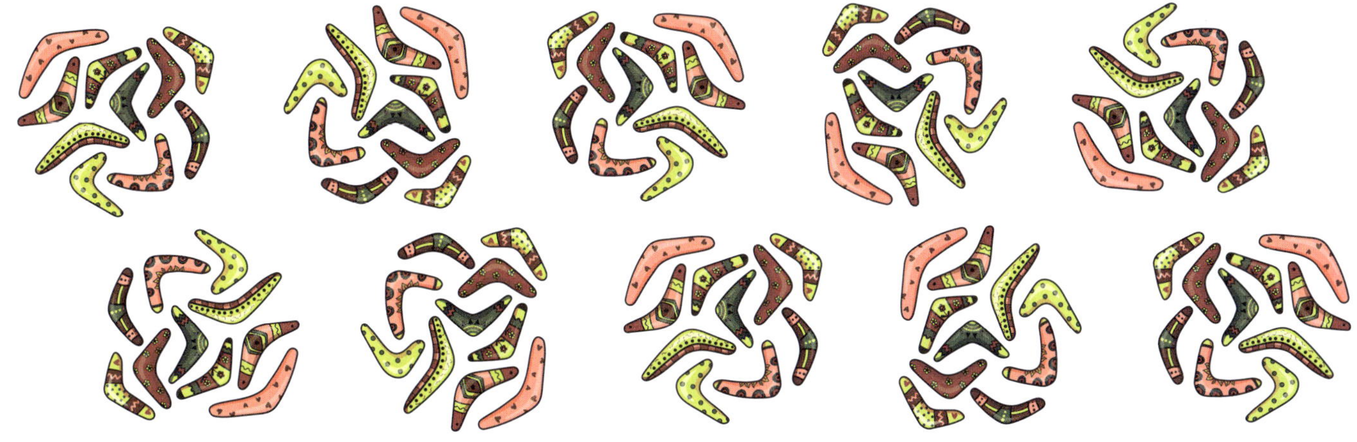

1 How many boomerangs in each group? ______

2 How many groups? ______

3 How many boomerangs?

a in 1 group ______ b in 5 groups ______ c in 3 groups ______

d in 8 groups ______ e in 6 groups ______ f in 10 groups ______

g in 12 groups ______ h in 4 groups ______ i in 11 groups ______

j in 2 groups ______ k in 7 groups ______ l in 9 groups ______

4 Match the number sentence to the answer.

a 10 × 7
b 10 × 0
c 10 × 11
d 10 × 6
e 10 × 12
f 10 × 8
g 10 × 10

70 0 100 110 80 60 90 30 50 120 10 40 20

h 10 × 9
i 10 × 3
j 10 × 4
k 10 × 1
l 10 × 2
m 10 × 5

5 Complete from memory.

×	3	1	6	8	12	4	7	0	11	9	5	10	2
10													

Unit 30 Multiplication facts

A

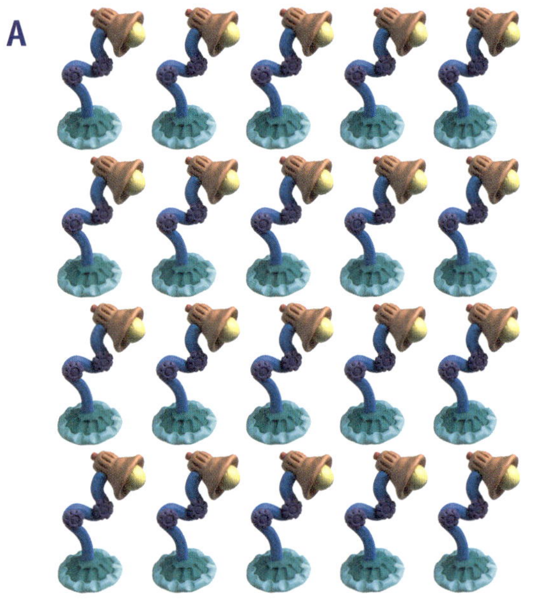

B

C

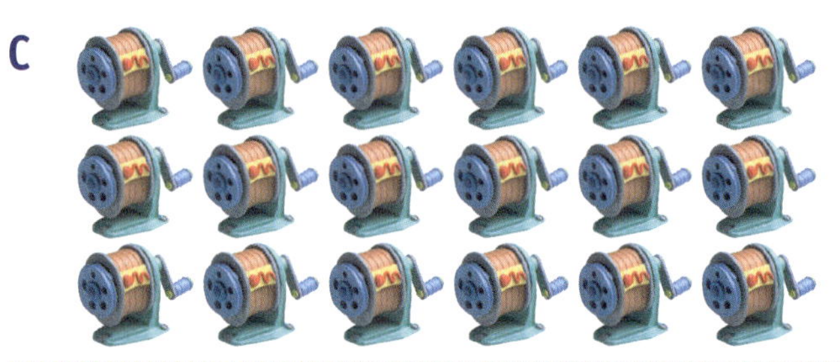

D

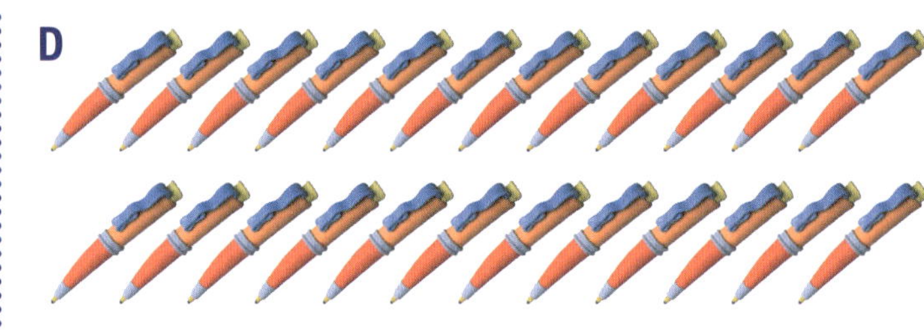

E

F

Write as many multiplication facts as you can for each group.

A	B	C

D	E	F

 Number AC9M3N04 multiply and divide one- and two-digit numbers, representing problems using number sentences, diagrams and arrays, and using a variety of calculation strategies
Algebra AC9M3A03 recall and demonstrate proficiency with multiplication facts for 3, 4, 5 and 10

Unit 30 Products

Product is the answer when numbers are multiplied.

Match the number sentence to its answer.
Then write the letter in the secret message.

9 a 8×5 ____ b 9×3 ____ c 10×0 ____ d 7×10 ____ e 5×7 ____ f 4×8 ____

10 Write the product of:

a 6 and 4 ____ b 3 and 6 ____ c 10 and 2 ____ d 2 and 5 ____

e 4 and 3 ____ f 7 and 4 ____ g 6 and 3 ____ h 8 and 3 ____

11 Fill in the missing facts.

eg	(array of 24 dots)	4 groups of 6	6×4 (vertical)	6 × 4	24
a		3 groups of 5			
b			5×5 (vertical)		
c					16

Unit 30 Multiples

3, 4, 5, 10 tables

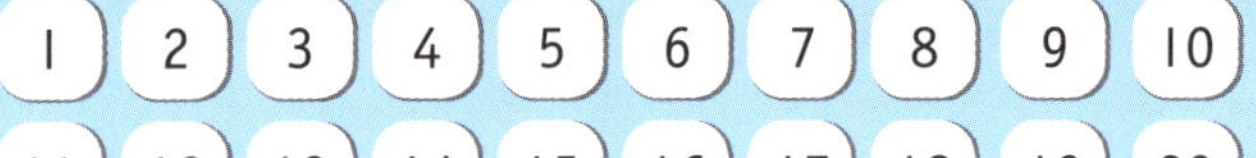

1	2	3	4	5	6	7	8	9	10
11	12	13	14	15	16	17	18	19	20
21	22	23	24	25	26	27	28	29	30
31	32	33	34	35	36	37	38	39	40
41	42	43	44	45	46	47	48	49	50
51	52	53	54	55	56	57	58	59	60
61	62	63	64	65	66	67	68	69	70
71	72	73	74	75	76	77	78	79	80
81	82	83	84	85	86	87	88	89	90
91	92	93	94	95	96	97	98	99	100

1 a Colour the multiples of 3 yellow.
  b Colour the multiples of 4 red.
  c Colour the multiples of 5 green.
  d Colour the multiples of 10 blue.
  e Which numbers have been coloured more than once?

  ____

  f Why? ______________________________

  ____

  ____

  ____

2 Colour the multiples of the middle number.

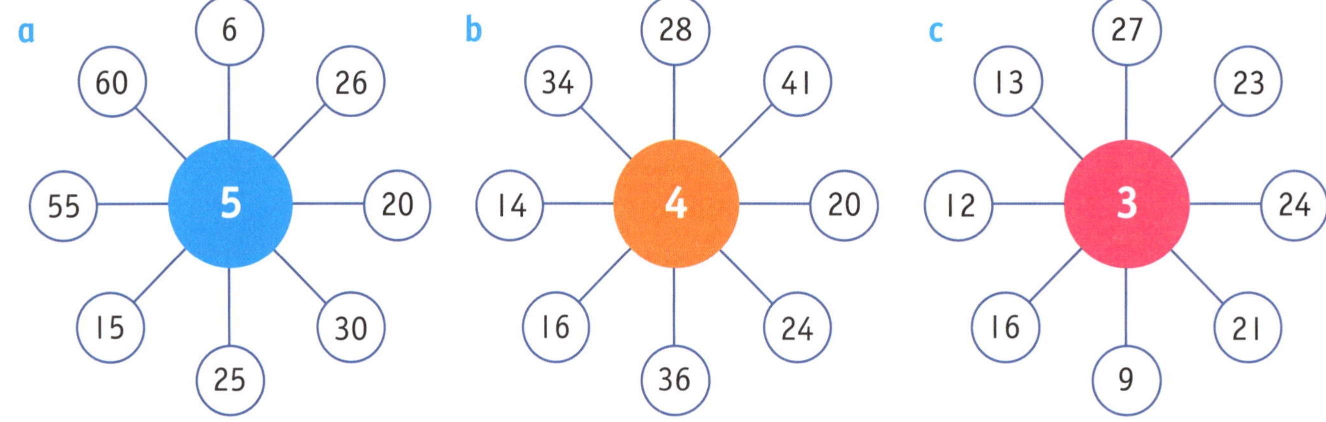

3 What is the value of each pile?

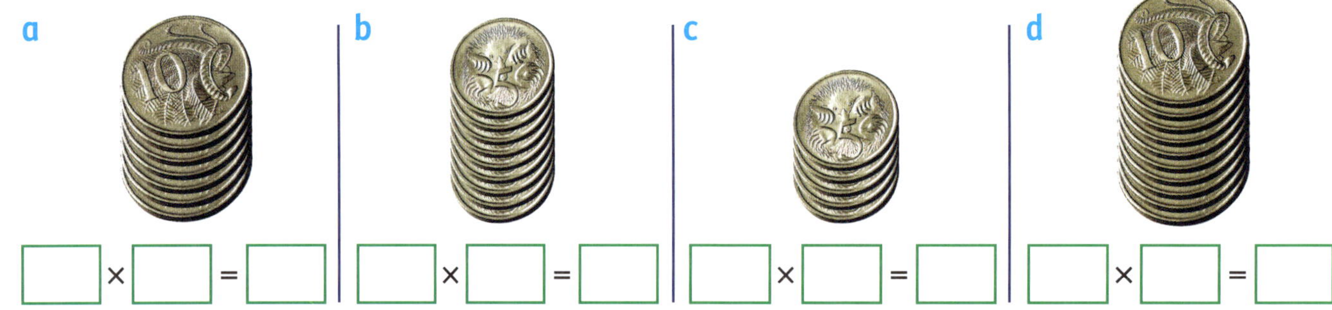

a ☐ × ☐ = ☐

b ☐ × ☐ = ☐

c ☐ × ☐ = ☐

d ☐ × ☐ = ☐

Mastery Checklist I can:
- ☐ remember the 3× and 4× tables
- ☐ remember the 5× and 10× tables
- ☐ write different multiplciation facts for a picture array
- ☐ find the product
- ☐ show multiples on a 100 square
- ☐ identify multiples of 3, 4, 5 and 10.

Number AC9M3N07 follow and create algorithms involving a sequence of steps and decisions to investigate numbers; describe any emerging patterns
Algebra AC9M3A03 recall and demonstrate proficiency with multiplication facts for 3, 4, 5 and 10; extend and apply facts to develop the related division facts

Problem solving

Operations

1 John has 8 pairs of socks. How many socks altogether?

8 × 2 = ☐

Answer ☐ socks

2 Sammy bought 7 apples for 10 cents each. How much did he spend?

☐ × ☐ = ☐

Answer ☐

3 Mrs Tiredout has 5 children. Each child has 4 T-shirts. How many T-shirts altogether?

☐ × ☐ = ☐

Answer ☐ T-shirts

4 Jack gathers 4 eggs every day. How many eggs in 1 week?

☐ × ☐ = ☐

Answer ☐ eggs

You write the questions.

5 ______

☐ × ☐ = ☐ Answer 30 bananas

6 ______

☐ × ☐ = ☐ Answer 48 monsters

7 Use a calculator.

Farmer Joe had 14 paddocks. There were 25 cows in each of 4 paddocks and 34 sheep in each of 3 paddocks.

a How many cows? ☐ × ☐ = ☐

b How many sheep? ☐ × ☐ = ☐

c How many animals altogether?

______

I can solve problems by:

☐ using multiplication ☐ writing questions and algorithms.

Unit 31 Division

÷ 5, ÷ 10

These are stamps used in the country of Weirdo.

1 Wrod only ever bought 5c stamps. How many could he buy for:

a 40c? ______ b 30c? ______ c 15c? ______ d 5c? ______ e 50c? ______

2 Wred only bought 10c stamps. How many could she buy for:

a 60c? ______ b 90c? ______ c 20c? ______ d 50c? ______ e 70c? ______

3 Weid only bought $2 stamps. How many could he buy for?

a $14? ______ b $8? ______ c $18? ______ d $6? ______ e $12? ______

4 Wido had $13. Could she buy eight $2 stamps? ________

Why? ______________________________

5 How much for: a seven 5c stamps? __________ b five $5 stamps? __________

6 Wodi has 85c. How many 10c stamps can she buy? __________

7 a How much to buy 1 of each stamp? __________

b How much change from $10? __________

Challenge! Make a list

Werd has a package to send. List the ways she can make $3.10 using 5 or less stamps.

Number AC9M3N04 & AC9M3N06 multiply and divide one- and two-digit numbers, representing problems using number sentences, diagrams and arrays, and using a variety of calculation strategies • use mathematical modelling to solve practical problems

Unit 31 The division sign

1 Divide 20 cars into 4 equal groups.

20 ÷ 4 = ______

There are ______ cars in each group.

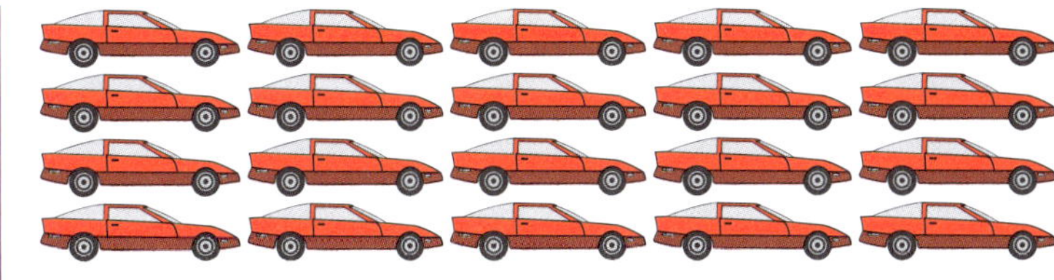

2 Divide 12 leaves into 3 equal groups.

12 ÷ 3 = ______

There are ______ leaves in each group.

3 Divide 24 stars into 4 equal groups.

24 ÷ 4 = ______

There are ______ stars in each group.

4 Divide 18 cats into 3 equal groups.

18 ÷ 3 = ______

There are ______ cats in each group.

5 Divide 30 dice into 10 groups.

30 ÷ 10 = ______

There are ______ dice in each group.

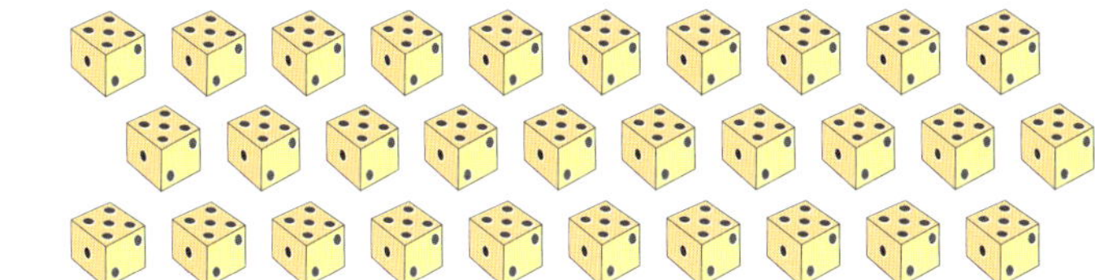

6 Divide 24 foxes into groups of 4.

24 ÷ 4 = ______

There are ______ groups of foxes.

7 Divide 15 girls into groups of 3.

15 ÷ 3 = ______

There are ______ groups of girls.

8 Divide 20 bugs into groups of 5.

20 ÷ 5 = ______

There are ______ groups of bugs.

9 Divide 22 fish into groups of 2.

22 ÷ 2 = ______

There are ______ groups of fish.

Unit 31 Using the division sign

12 ÷ 3 = 4
12 ÷ 4 = 3
3 × 4 = 12
4 × 3 = 12

1 Use this group of 24 ice-creams to help you to divide.

a 24 ÷ 8 = ______ b 24 ÷ 6 = ______
c 24 ÷ 3 = ______ d 24 ÷ 24 = ______
e 24 ÷ 4 = ______ f 24 ÷ 1 = ______

2 Use this group of 30 bears to help you to divide.

a 30 ÷ 10 = ______
b 30 ÷ 6 = ______
c 30 ÷ 3 = ______
d 30 ÷ 5 = ______
e 30 ÷ 30 = ______
f 30 ÷ 1 = ______

3 Complete these number sentences.

a	b	c	d
5 × 6 = ______	3 × 6 = ______	4 × 8 = ______	10 × 9 = ______
30 ÷ 5 = ______	18 ÷ 3 = ______	32 ÷ 4 = ______	90 ÷ 10 = ______
30 ÷ 6 = ______	18 ÷ 6 = ______	32 ÷ 8 = ______	90 ÷ 9 = ______

4 a 42 ÷ 7 = ______ b 10 ÷ 5 = ______ c 20 ÷ 10 = ______ d 40 ÷ 10 = ______
e 27 ÷ 9 = ______ f 48 ÷ 8 = ______ g 49 ÷ 7 = ______ h 36 ÷ 6 = ______
i 54 ÷ 9 = ______ j 35 ÷ 5 = ______ k 9 ÷ 9 = ______ l 100 ÷ 10 = ______

5 a 30 balls are packed into boxes of 6. How many boxes are needed?

☐ ÷ ☐ = ☐

b Mrs Lim is making 50 cupcakes. She puts 10 cupcakes on each tray. How many trays are needed?

☐ ÷ ☐ = ☐

c 5 children share 25 biscuits equally. How many biscuits each?

☐ ÷ ☐ = ☐

d Mr Baker has 60 apples. He puts 6 apples in each bag. How many bags?

☐ ÷ ☐ = ☐

Mastery Checklist I can:
- ☐ solve money division problems
- ☐ recognise ÷ 
- ☐ divide into equal groups to solve problems
- ☐ connect division to multiplication
- ☐ solve division word problems.

Number AC9M3N04 & AC9M3N06 multiply and divide one- and two-digit numbers, representing problems using number sentences, diagrams and arrays, and using a variety of calculation strategies • use mathematical modelling to solve practical problems

Problem solving

Bags to pack

Jerry, Sam and Tye bought 48 grocery items. They wanted to find how many ways they could pack them equally into bags. Jerry found the most ways. Sam thought of 3 ways, 1 less than Tye. Tye thought of 4 less than Jerry. How many ways did Jerry find?

____

____

____

What might be the ways that Jerry thought of, apart from this way?

I can solve problems by:

☐ using multiplication and division ☐ writing algorithms.

Unit 32 Denominators

equivalent – having the same value, equal to

$\frac{1}{1} = 1$

The denominator 1 divides one whole into 1 part.

$\frac{1}{2}$	$\frac{1}{2}$

The denominator 2 divides one whole into two equal parts.

$\frac{1}{4}$	$\frac{1}{4}$	$\frac{1}{4}$	$\frac{1}{4}$

The denominator 4 divides one whole into 4 equal parts.

$\frac{1}{8}$	$\frac{1}{8}$	$\frac{1}{8}$	$\frac{1}{8}$	$\frac{1}{8}$	$\frac{1}{8}$	$\frac{1}{8}$	$\frac{1}{8}$

The denominator 8 divides one whole into 8 equal parts.

1 $\frac{1}{4}$ is one of four parts.

a $\frac{2}{4}$ is __________ of four parts.

b $\frac{3}{4}$ is __________ of four parts.

c $\frac{4}{4}$ is __________ of four parts.

d Are all four parts the same size? __________ Why? ______________________________

e Which fraction is the largest? __________

What is another name for this? ______________________________

2 a Colour the fractions.

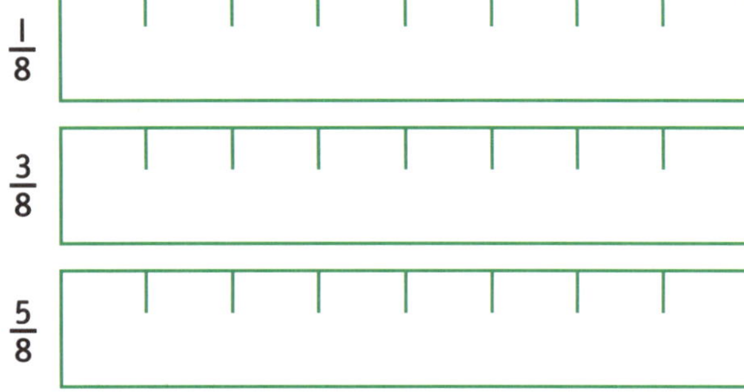

$\frac{1}{8}$ $\frac{3}{8}$ $\frac{5}{8}$ $\frac{7}{8}$

$\frac{2}{8}$ $\frac{4}{8}$ $\frac{6}{8}$ $\frac{8}{8}$

b Find the fraction which is equivalent to $\frac{1}{4}$. ______________ $= \frac{1}{4}$.

c Find the fraction which is equivalent to $\frac{3}{4}$. ______________ $= \frac{3}{4}$.

Number AC9M3N02 recognise and represent unit fractions and their multiples in different ways; combine fractions with the same denominator to complete the whole

Unit 32 Fractions

1 Colour and complete.

a Colour one half.

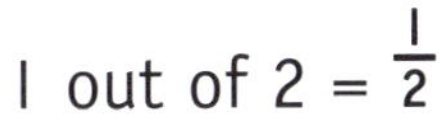

1 out of 2 = $\frac{1}{2}$

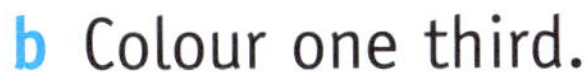

b Colour one third.

1 out of ______ = $\frac{1}{3}$

c Colour one quarter.

1 out of ______ = $\frac{1}{4}$

d Colour one fifth.

______ out of 5 = $\frac{1}{5}$

---

2 Colour the fractions. Then order the fractions from smallest to largest.

a $\frac{1}{4}$

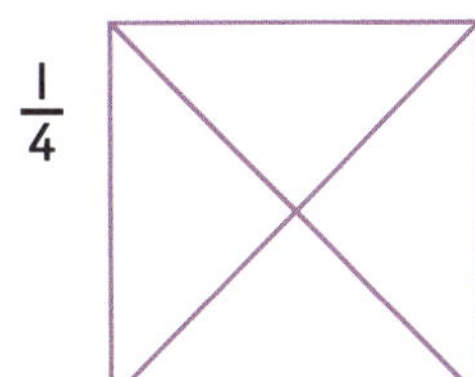

b $\frac{1}{5}$

c $\frac{1}{3}$

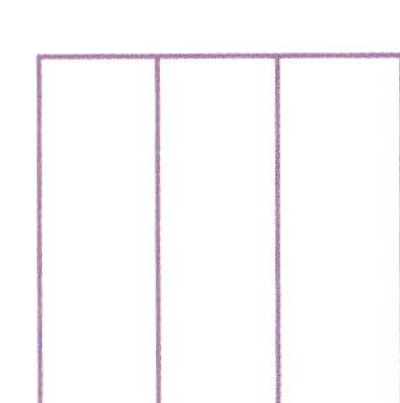

d $\frac{1}{2}$

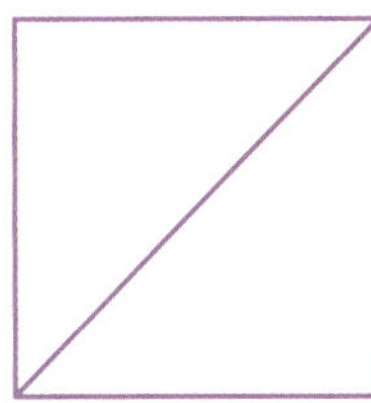

smallest ________ ________ ________ ________ largest

3 Circle the larger fraction in each pair.

a $\frac{1}{2}$ $\frac{1}{3}$

b $\frac{1}{5}$ $\frac{1}{4}$

c $\frac{1}{4}$ $\frac{1}{3}$

d $\frac{1}{5}$ $\frac{1}{4}$

4 a Colour the correct fractions.

$\frac{1}{3}$

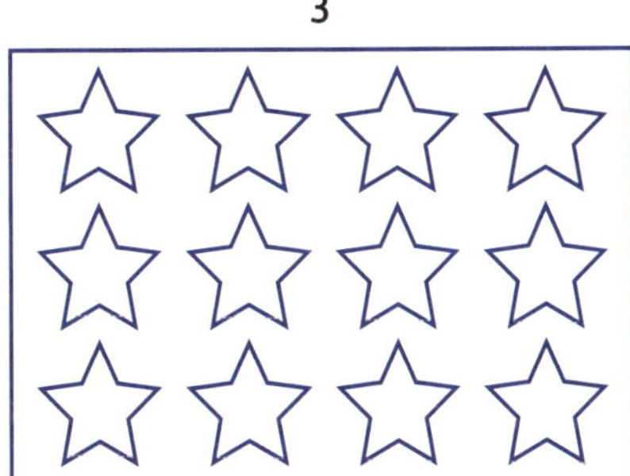

$\frac{1}{4}$

$\frac{1}{2}$

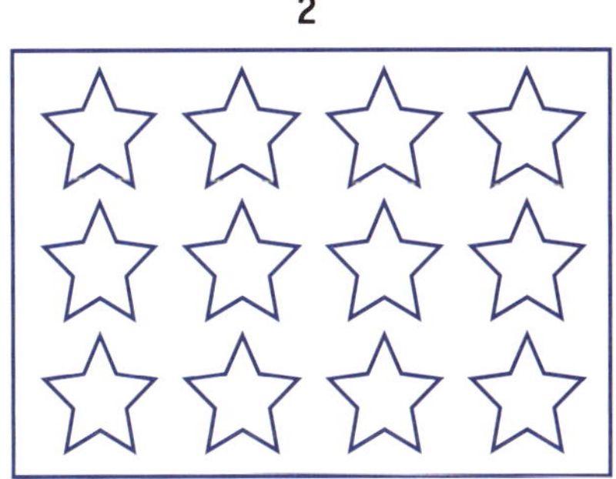

b Order the fractions of the group of 12 stars from smallest to largest. ______ ______ ______

5 a The denominator of the fraction tells how many ____________________.

b As the denominator gets bigger, the fraction gets ____________________.

Number AC9M3N02 recognise and represent unit fractions and their multiples in different ways; combine fractions with the same denominator to complete the whole

Unit 32 More denominators

1 a $\frac{1}{3}$ means one of ________ parts.

b Write all the thirds in order. ________ ________ ________

c If you cut one into three equal parts, what is each piece called? ________________

d Cut each shape into thirds.

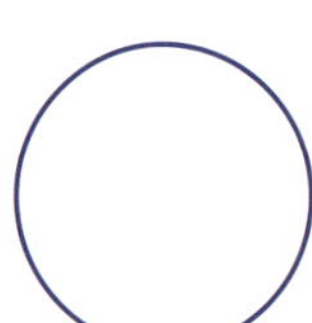

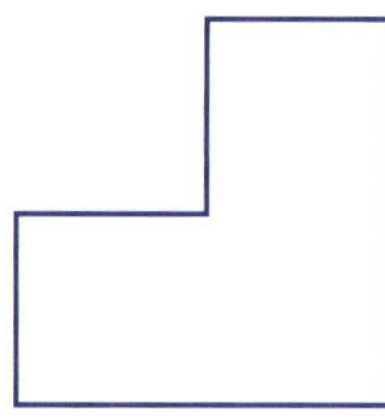

2 a $\frac{1}{5}$ means one of ________ parts.

b Write all the fifths in order. ________ ________ ________ ________ ________

c Write $\frac{3}{5}$ in other ways. Use words. ________________________

Use numbers. ________________________

d Make each number sentence equal 1 whole.

________ + $\frac{1}{5}$ = 1 whole ________ + $\frac{2}{5}$ = 1 whole

________ + $\frac{3}{5}$ = 1 whole ________ + $\frac{4}{5}$ = 1 whole

3 Colour one fifth ($\frac{1}{5}$) and two tenths ($\frac{2}{10}$) to show they are equivalent.

4 Answer true or false.

a $\frac{4}{10}$ equals $\frac{1}{5}$ ________ b $\frac{3}{10}$ is less than $\frac{1}{5}$ ________

c $\frac{7}{10}$ is more than $\frac{3}{5}$ ________ d $\frac{9}{10}$ is more than $\frac{4}{5}$ ________

5 Place these on the number line.

$\frac{1}{2}$, $\frac{3}{5}$, $\frac{7}{10}$, $\frac{2}{5}$, $\frac{2}{10}$

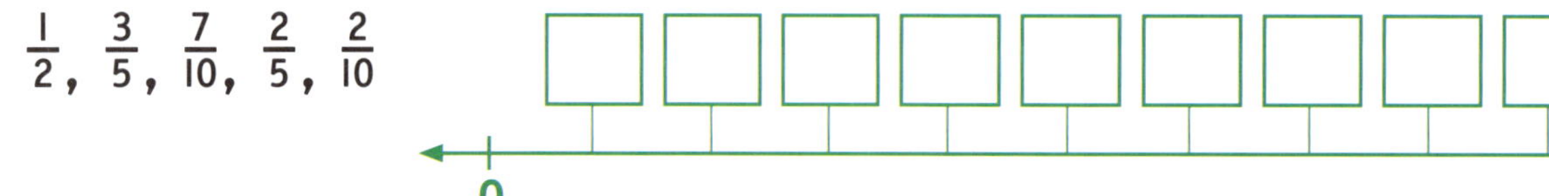

Mastery Checklist I can:
- ☐ connect denominators to one whole
- ☐ colour to show fractions
- ☐ order fractions from smallest to largest
- ☐ show fractions of groups
- ☐ locate fractions on a number line.

 Number AC9M3N02 recognise and represent unit fractions and their multiples in different ways; combine fractions with the same denominator to complete the whole

Unit 33 Centimetres and millimetres

estimate and measure cm

1 a Is a millimetre smaller than a centimetre? ______

b How many millimetres in one centimetre? ______

2 Measure in centimetres:

a the width of the house. ______

b the height of the window. ______

c the short side of the chimney. ______

d the height of the house wall. ______

e the height of a fence paling. ______

f the width of a tree branch. ______

3 Without measuring, name three things that are about 2 cm.

a ______ b ______ c ______

4 Measure the three things to see how close you are.

a ______ b ______ c ______

5 Draw a line that is: a 4 cm 6 mm long.

b 3 cm 2 mm long.

Unit 33 Millimetres

m is metre
cm is centimetre
mm is millimetre
10 mm = 1 cm
100 cm = 1 m

1 How many centimetres in:

a 2 m? _____ b 5 m? _____ c 3 m? _____ d $4\frac{1}{2}$ m? _____ e $1\frac{1}{2}$ m? _____

2 How many millimetres in:

a 3 cm? _____ b 7 cm? _____ c 10 cm? _____ d 1 cm? _____ e 9 cm? _____

3 Change these to metres.

a 100 cm _____ b 700 cm _____ c 900 cm _____ d 350 cm _____ e 550 cm _____

4 Change these to centimetres.

a 50 mm _____ b 10 mm _____ c 40 mm _____ d 20 mm _____ e 70 mm _____

5 Name three things you might measure in millimetres.

a _____________ b _____________ c _____________

6 Draw these straight lines and label them.

A 10 mm B 40 mm C 55 mm D 25 mm E 38 mm F 73 mm

7 Give each alien a name then measure its height.

Name __________
Height __________

Name __________
Height __________

Name __________
Height __________

Name __________
Height __________

Challenge! Measure your height in: centimetres. 

millimetres.

Measurement AC9M3M02 measure and compare objects using familiar metric units of length, mass and capacity, and instruments with labelled markings

Unit 33 Metres

Length

There are 100 centimetres in 1 metre.

100 cm = 1 m

1 If 1 centimetre on this page = 1 metre on the ground, how long is each line?

a ________ m

b ________ m

c ________ m

d ________ m

2 Convert the lengths.

a 3 m = ________ cm

b 7 m = ________ cm

c 2.5 m = ________ cm

d 1.5 m = ________ cm

e 10 m = ________ cm

f 5 m = ________ cm

g 9.5 m = ________ cm

h 9 m = ________ cm

i 4.5 m = ________ cm

j 12 m = ________ cm

k 15 m = ________ cm

l 18.5 m = ________ cm

3 m

3.5 m

4.5 m

4.8 m

3 What is the difference in length between:

a the pink ribbon and the red ribbon? ________

b the longest ribbon and the shortest ribbon? ________

c the yellow ribbon and the red ribbon? ________

Unit 33 Comparing lengths

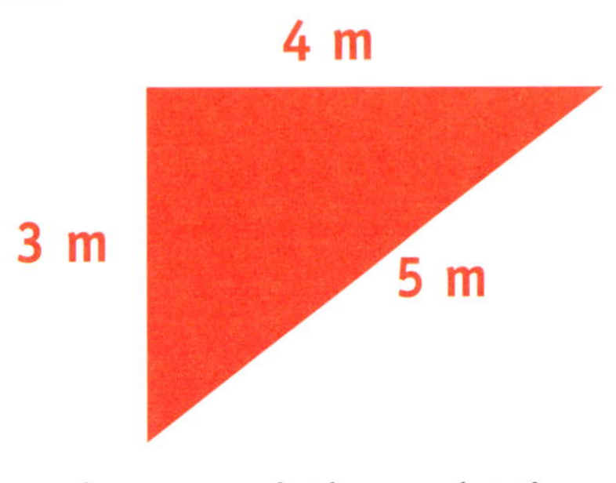

The length around the red triangle is 3 m + 4 m + 5 m = 12 m

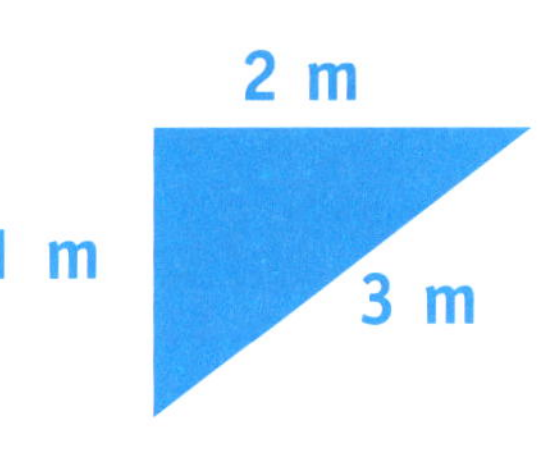

The length around the blue triangle is 1 m + 2 m + 3 m = 6 m

The difference in the lengths around the triangles is 12 m – 6 m = 6 m

---

1 Add the lengths around each rectangle and write the total.

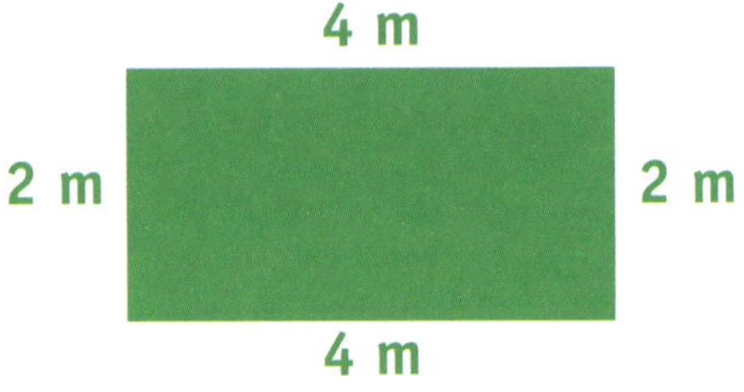

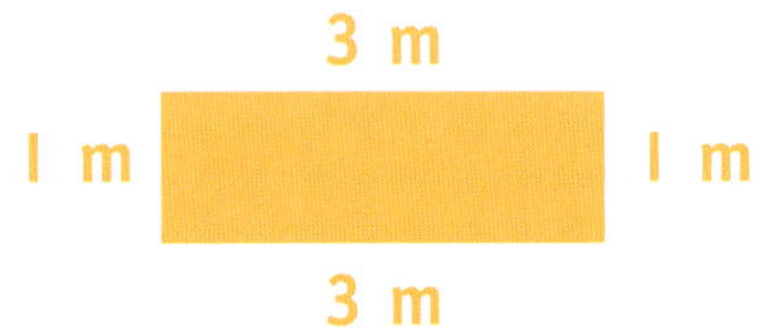

a Length around = ________ m

b Length around = ________ m

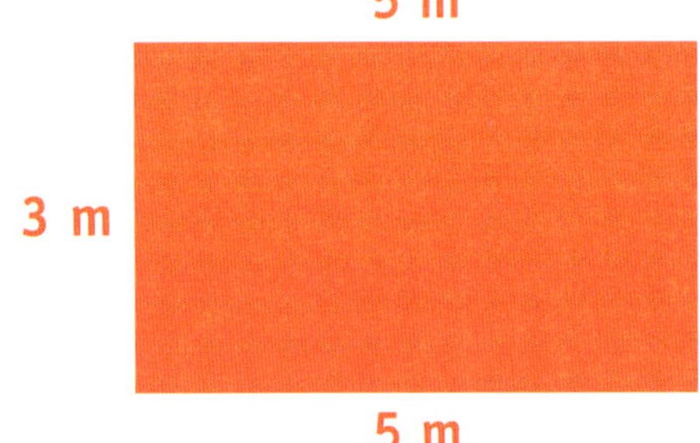

c Length around = ________ m

---

2 Fill in the gaps.

a The ________ rectangle has the longest length around the outside.

b The ________ rectangle has the shortest length around the outside.

c The difference in the lengths around the ouside of the green rectangle and the yellow rectangle is ________ m.

d The difference in the lengths around the outside of the orange rectangle and the green rectangle is ________ m.

Mastery Checklist I can:
- ☐ compare centimetres to millimetres
- ☐ measure in cm and mm
- ☐ compare centimetres to metres
- ☐ add lengths around a shape.

Measurement AC9M3M02 measure and compare objects using familiar metric units of length, mass and capacity, and instruments with labelled markings

Problem solving

Flag heights

Three flagpoles are being put up.

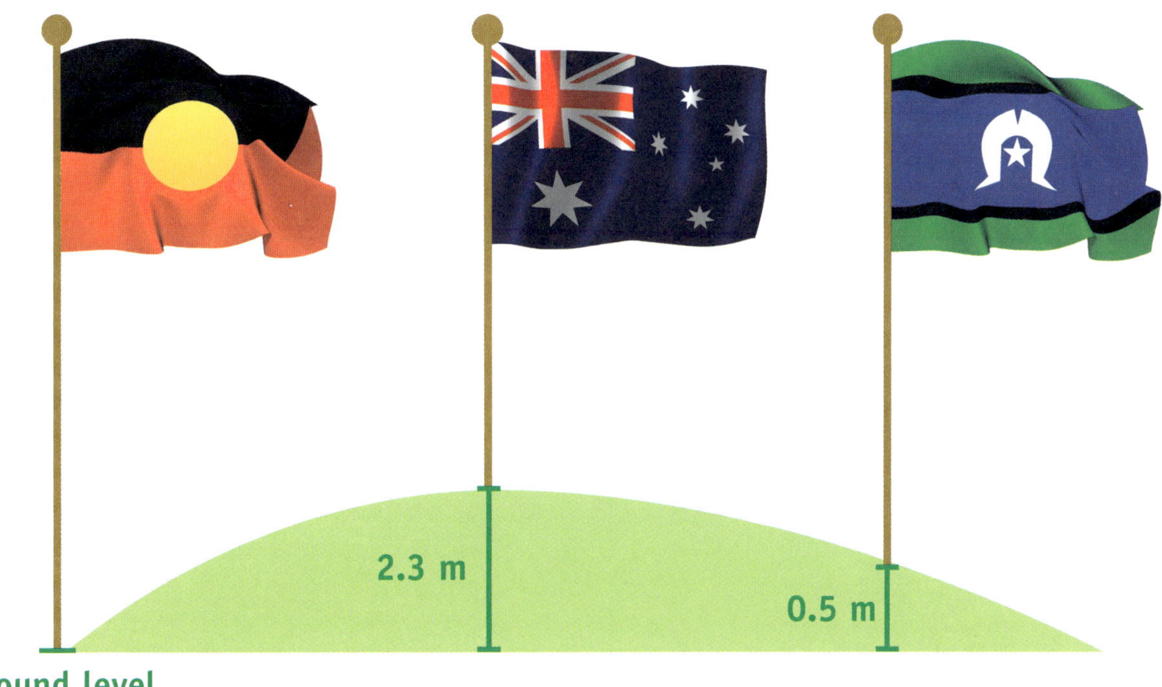

The tops of the flagpoles have to be at equal heights. The Aboriginal flagpole is 3.7 metres tall.

1 What will be the height of the Australian flagpole? ______________

2 What will be the height of the Torres Strait flagpole? ______________

If each flagpole has an extra 1.2 m of pole underground to hold it steady, what is the total height of each flagpole?

3 Aboriginal flagpole ______________

4 Australian flagpole ______________

5 Torres Strait flagpole ______________

I can solve problems by:

☐ understanding length ☐ comparing the lengths of different objects.

Paper planes

Investigation 4

make paper planes

1 Construct three different paper planes.

2 Draw your paper planes:

Paper plane A
Paper plane B
Paper plane C

3 Conduct three throws with each paper plane. Record in metres how far the plane travelled. Then add to get the total distance for each plane.

	First throw	Second throw	Third throw	Total distance
Paper plane A				
Paper plane B				
Paper plane C				

Paper planes

Investigation 4

4 Which plane flew the greatest distance? ____________________

5 Which plane flew the smallest distance? ____________________

6 Draw a column graph to show the total distance travelled by each plane.

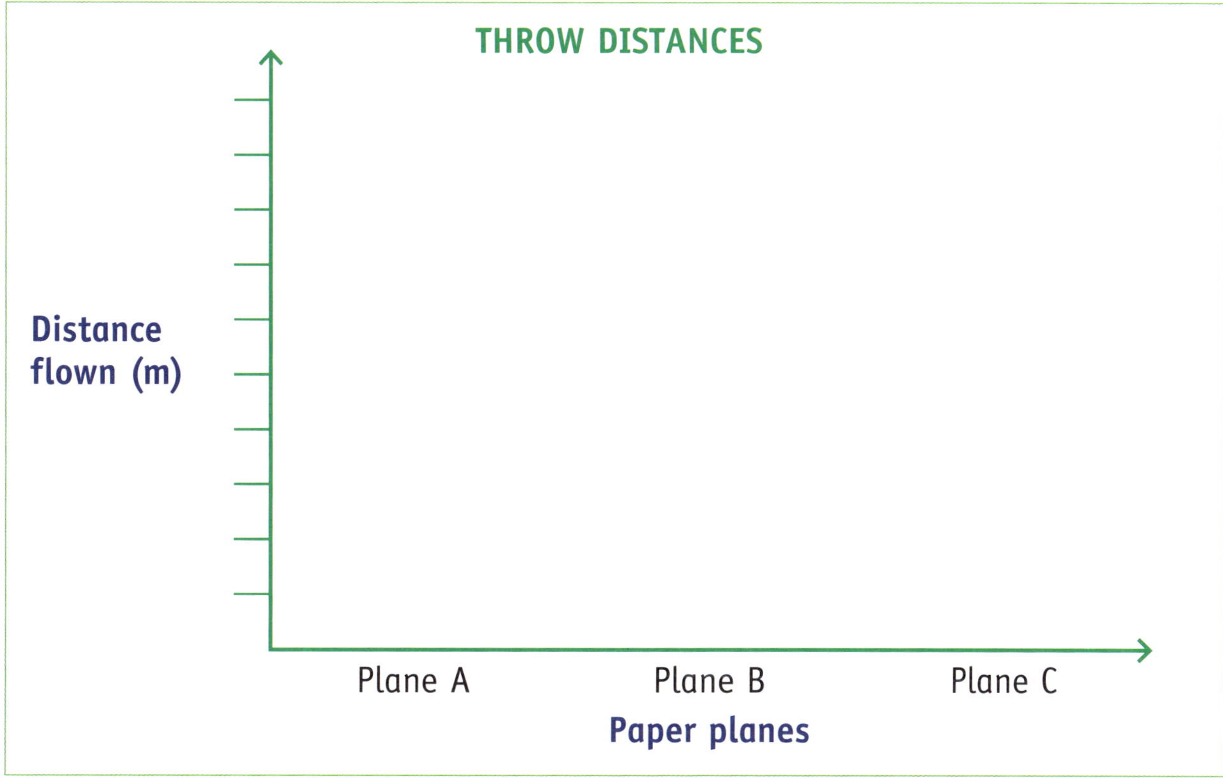

7 How could you improve your paper plane designs? Draw and label your ideas.

To carry out these tasks I need to:

- ☐ construct 3 different paper planes
- ☐ throw the planes and measure and record the distances
- ☐ graph the results
- ☐ think of ways to improve my paper plane designs.

Revision

1 Which operation shows these shells divided into 6 equal groups?

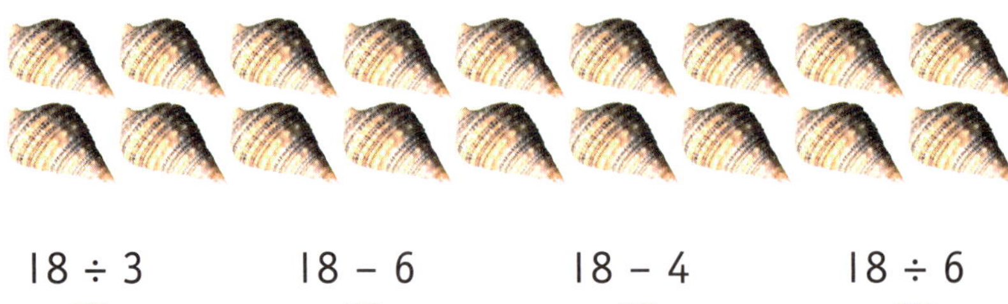

18 ÷ 3 ◯ 18 − 6 ◯ 18 − 4 ◯ 18 ÷ 6 ◯

2 Which statement is true?

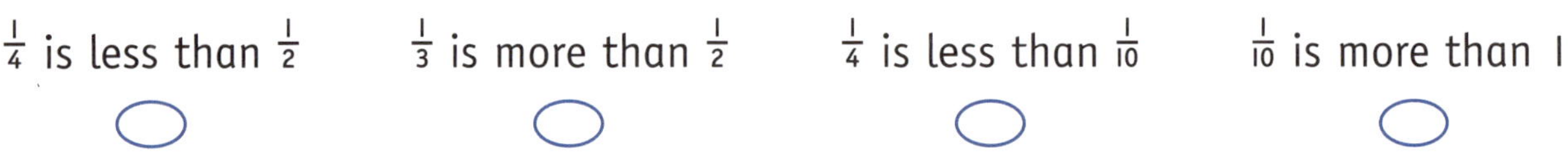

$\frac{1}{4}$ is less than $\frac{1}{2}$ ◯ $\frac{1}{3}$ is more than $\frac{1}{2}$ ◯ $\frac{1}{4}$ is less than $\frac{1}{10}$ ◯ $\frac{1}{10}$ is more than 1 ◯

3 Mum cut some oranges into quarters.

How many whole oranges did she cut?

16 ◯ 4 ◯ 8 ◯ 6 ◯

4 This fruit was placed in a bag.
Jay closed his eyes to pick one piece.
What is the chance he picked a banana?

certain ◯ impossible ◯ likely ◯ unlikely ◯

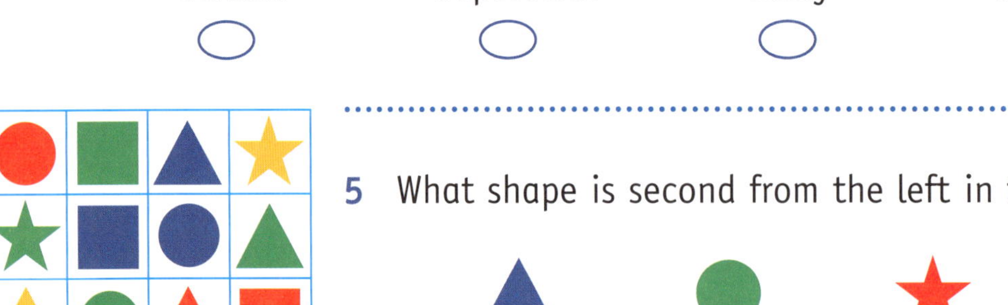

5 What shape is second from the left in the top row?

Revision

6 Which number is 356 written to the closest ten?

Write your answer.

7 Multiply.

a 5 × 8 = ______	f 10 × 11 = ______	k 4 × 4 = ______
b 3 × 5 = ______	g 4 × 9 = ______	l 5 × 10 = ______
c 5 × 7 = ______	h 3 × 6 = ______	m 4 × 3 = ______
d 10 × 0 = ______	i 3 × 1 = ______	n 5 × 2 = ______
e 3 × 12 = ______	j 10 × 10 = ______	o 4 × 11 = ______

8 What is the height of this alien?

Shade one bubble.

4 cm 4 mm 4 m 40 cm

9 Fifi thought of a number. She then doubled it and added 3. The answer was 19. What number did she first think of?

5 6 7 8

10 Which star shows a number that is not a multiple of 4?

Unit 34 Changing numbers

Sequences 

In this amazing machine, numbers are changed into a pattern of four more numbers.

1 What comes out if these numbers are put into A?

a 10 ______ ______ ______ ______ b 35 ______ ______ ______ ______

c 24 ______ ______ ______ ______ d 9 ______ ______ ______ ______

2 What comes out if these numbers are put into F?

a 3 ______ ______ ______ ______ b 25 ______ ______ ______ ______

c 12 ______ ______ ______ ______ d 38 ______ ______ ______ ______

3 What comes out if these numbers are put into D?

a 7 ______ ______ ______ ______ b 9 ______ ______ ______ ______

c 4 ______ ______ ______ ______ d 11 ______ ______ ______ ______

4 What comes out if these numbers are put into B?

a 24 ______ ______ ______ ______ b 19 ______ ______ ______ ______

c 16 ______ ______ ______ ______ d 27 ______ ______ ______ ______

5 What comes out if these numbers are put into E?

a 3 ______ ______ ______ ______ b 15 ______ ______ ______ ______

c 30 ______ ______ ______ ______ d 41 ______ ______ ______ ______

Number AC9M3N03 add and subtract two- and three-digit numbers using place value to partition, rearrange and regroup numbers to assist in calculations without a calculator
Number AC9M3N07 follow and create algorithms involving a sequence of steps and decisions to investigate numbers; describe any emerging patterns

Unit 34 Matching answers

1 True (T) or false (F)?

a $6 + 4 = 4 + 6$ ____ b $8 + 5 = 5 + 8$ ____ c $1 + 7 = 7 + 1$ ____ d $3 + 9 = 9 + 3$ ____

e $5 + 8 = 8 + 5$ ____ f $7 + 6 = 6 + 7$ ____ g $3 + 7 = 7 + 3$ ____ h $4 + 5 = 5 + 4$ ____

i What rule can you make? ____________________

____

2 True (T) or false (F)?

a $3 \times 9 = 9 \times 3$ ____ b $7 \times 4 = 4 \times 7$ ____ c $8 \times 5 = 5 \times 8$ ____ d $5 \times 9 = 9 \times 5$ ____

e $3 \times 5 = 5 \times 3$ ____ f $6 \times 5 = 5 \times 6$ ____ g $9 \times 4 = 4 \times 9$ ____ h $10 \times 8 = 8 \times 10$ ____

i What rule can you make? ____________________

____

3 Are the rules the same? ____________________

4 True (T) or false (F)?

a $6 - 2 = 2 - 6$ ____ b $9 - 5 = 5 - 9$ ____ c $8 - 3 = 3 - 8$ ____ d $7 - 4 = 4 - 7$ ____

e Can you make a rule? ____________________

5 True (T) or false (F)?

a $18 \div 3 = 3 \div 18$ ____ b $25 \div 5 = 5 \div 25$ ____

c $40 \div 4 = 4 \div 40$ ____ d $9 \div 3 = 3 \div 9$ ____

e Can you make a rule? ____________________

6 True (T) or false (F)?

a $9 + 7 = 7 + 9$ ____ b $21 \div 3 = 3 \div 21$ ____

c $14 - 6 = 6 - 14$ ____ d $9 \times 3 = 9 + 3$ ____

e $8 + 11 = 11 + 8$ ____ f $6 + 8 = 8 - 6$ ____

g $90 \div 10 = 10 \div 90$ ____ h $26 + 42 = 42 + 26$ ____

i $68 \times 97 = 97 \times 68$ ____ j $42 - 36 = 42 + 36$ ____

7 What happens to all numbers if they are multiplied by 1?

____

Challenge!

3 7 4

a Add these numbers together in four different ways. Are the answers always the same? [ ]

b Use a calculator to multiply the numbers together in four different ways. Are the answers always the same? [ ]

Unit 34 Making patterns

Mary used matches to make some shapes. Draw the next shape in the box, then complete the table. Look for patterns.

1 a

b

Number of shapes	1	2	3	4	5	6	7	8
Number of matches	4	7	10					

2 a

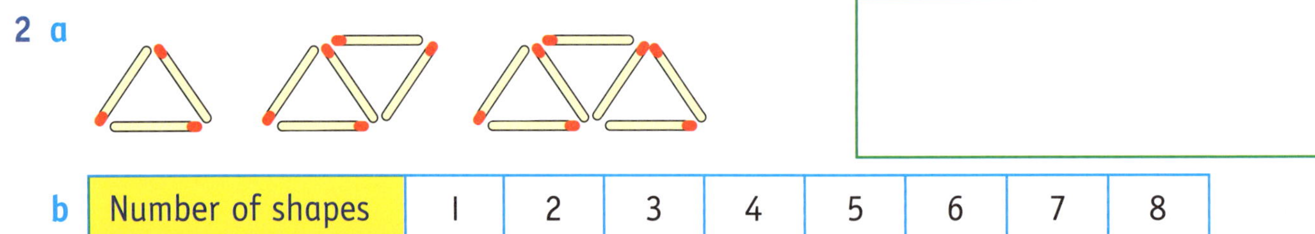

b

Number of shapes	1	2	3	4	5	6	7	8
Number of matches								

3 a

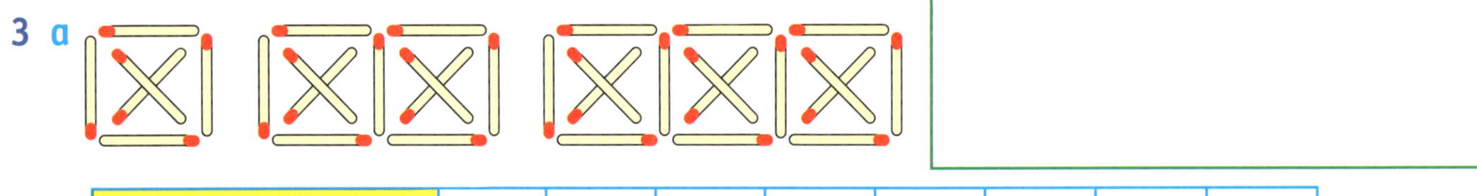

b

Number of shapes	1	2	3	4	5	6	7	8
Number of matches								

4 a

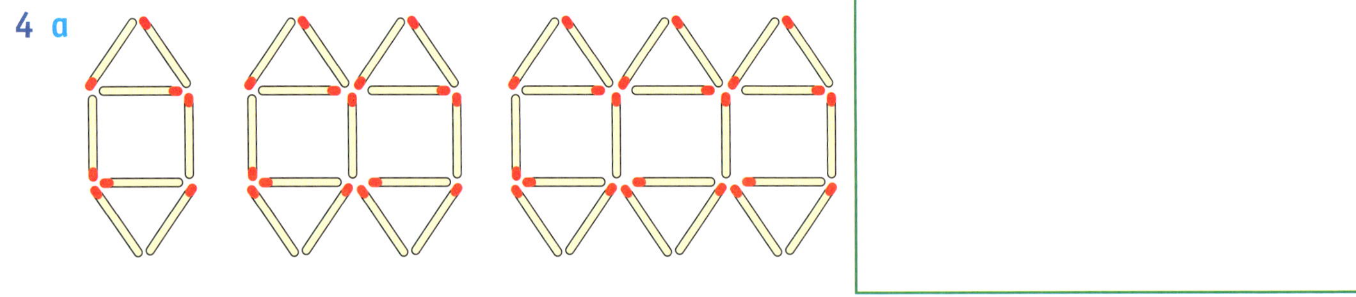

b

Number of shapes	1	2	3	4	5	6	7	8
Number of matches								

Mastery Checklist I can:
- ☐ follow algorithms to make a pattern
- ☐ investigate patterns with +, −, ×, ÷
- ☐ investigate shape patterns with matches.

Number AC9M3N07 follow and create algorithms involving a sequence of steps and decisions to investigate numbers; describe any emerging patterns

Unit 35 Angle search

When two straight lines meet, they make an angle.
eg 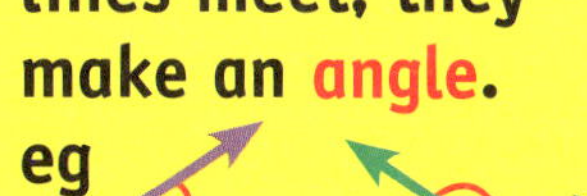

1 a What shape is the aquarium? ______________________
  b What type of angles are at the corners? ______________________

2 How many angles can you see inside:
  a the red fish? ______ b the purple fish? ______
  c the green fish? ______ d the yellow fish? ______

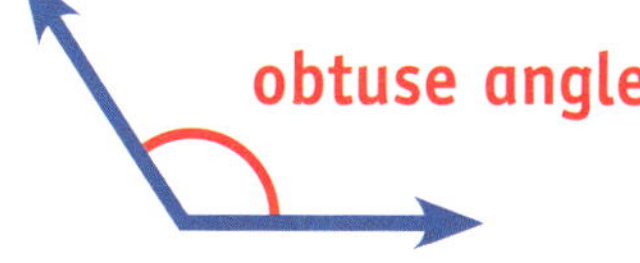

3 How many right angles can you see inside:
  a the red fish? ______ b the purple fish? ______
  c the green fish? ______ d the yellow fish? ______

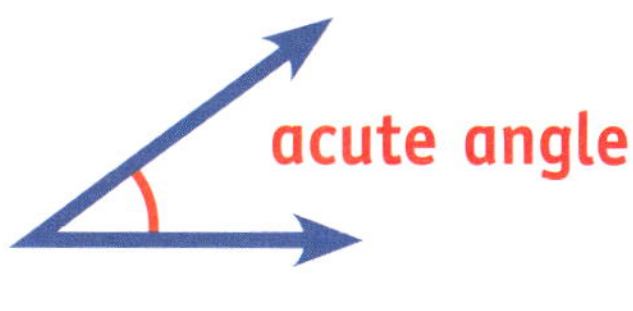

4 How many obtuse angles can you see inside:
  a the red fish? ______ b the yellow fish? ______

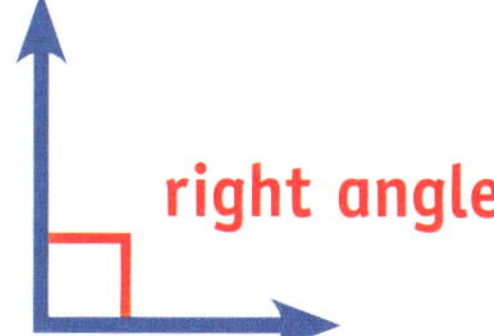

5 How many acute angles can you see inside:
  a the green fish? ______ b the purple fish? ______

6 Draw another angle fish.

Unit 35 Angle size

1

A Here are 4 angles.	B Copy the angle.	C Draw a larger angle.	D Draw a smaller angle.
a	b	c	d
e	f	g	h
i	j	k	l
m	n	o	p

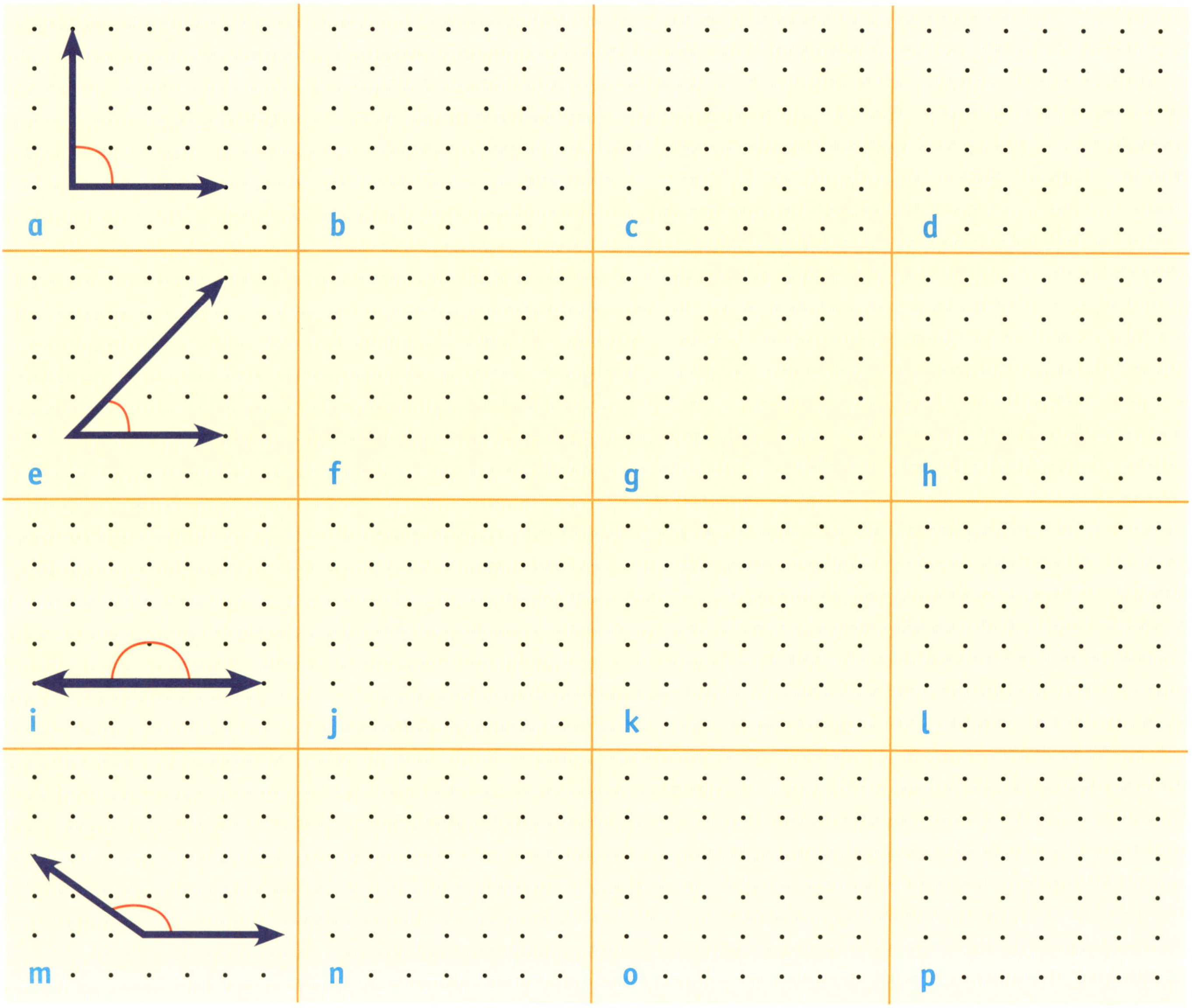

2 Which angle is the largest in:

a column A? _____ b column B? _____ c column C? _____ d column D? _____

3 Which angle is the smallest in:

a column A? _____ b column B? _____ c column C? _____ d column D? _____

4 Look around the classroom and write 3 places where you can see right angles.

_____ _____ _____

Draw a diagram

Draw a house. Colour the right angles blue, colour the acute angles pink, colour the obtuse angles orange.

Unit 35 Comparing angles

The corners of this page are square corners.
A square corner is called a right angle.

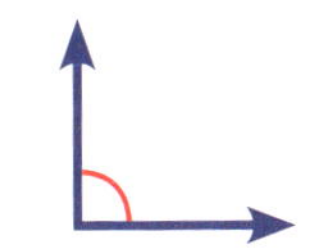

Acute angles are smaller than right angles.
Obtuse angles are larger than right angles.

1 Colour the right angles red; the angles bigger than a right angle green; the angles smaller than a right angle yellow.

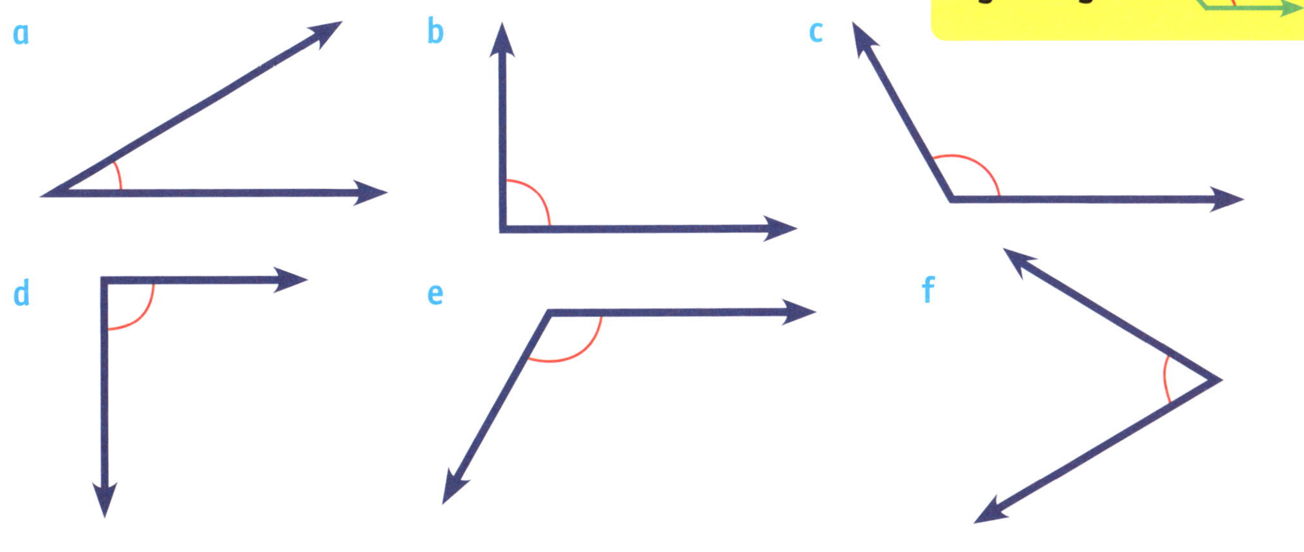

2 a Draw a right angle.

b Draw an acute angle.

c Draw an obtuse angle.

3

Make a movable angle with 2 strips of cardboard and a fastener.

Use your movable angle to find and circle angles the same as A.

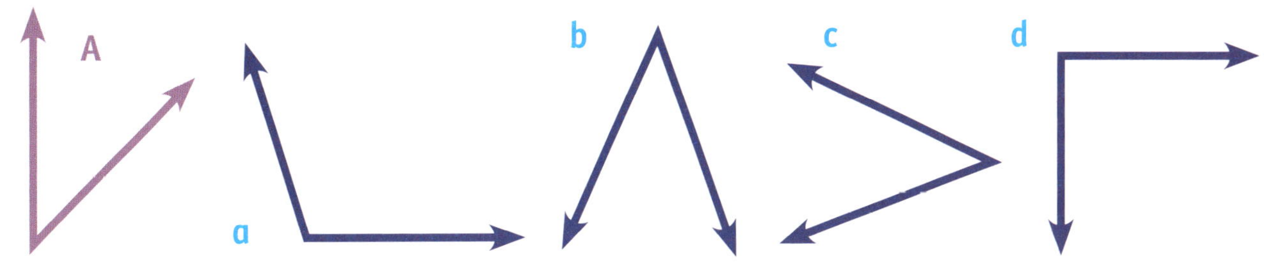

Unit 35 Reading a timetable

This is Tim's school day.

A		B	
7:15	Wake up	12:30	Lunch break
7:20	Shower and clean teeth	1:10	Back to class
7:30	Get dressed	3:10	School finishes
7:45	Have breakfast		Arrive home and have a snack
8:00	Feed dog, cat and rabbit	4:00	Begin homework
8:20	Walk to school	5:00	Finish homework
8:45	Arrive at school	5:05	Play
9:00	Start school	6:15	Dinner
10:55	Morning recess	7:00	Watch TV
11:10	Back to class	8:30	Bed

1 Which column shows pm time? ________

2 When does Tim begin his shower? ________

3 How long does it take for him to get dressed? ________ minutes

4 Does Tim have any pets? ________ How do you know? ____________________

5 a How long does it take for Tim to walk to school? ________ minutes

b It takes him the same time to walk home from school.
Complete the timetable by writing the time Tim arrives home.

6 How long is school lunchtime? ________ minutes

7 How many minutes does Tim spend on his homework? ________ minutes

8 How long in hours and minutes does Tim spend watching TV? _____ hours _____ minutes

9 Tim watches the same amount of TV each night from Monday to Friday.
How much TV is this for the 5 days? ________ hours _____ minutes

Mastery Checklist I can:
- ☐ identify obtuse, acute and right angles
- ☐ draw larger and smaller angles
- ☐ compare angles
- ☐ answer questions about a timetable.

Measurement AC9M3M03 & AC9M3M04 recognise and use the relationship between formal units of time including days, hours, minutes and seconds to estimate and compare the duration of events • describe the relationship between the hours and minutes on analogue and digital clocks, and read the time to the nearest minute

Unit 36 Design a classroom

Here is an aerial view of a classroom you have been asked to design.

First, think about what you like about your own classroom. What could be improved?

Here are the things you must include:

- seats for 28 children
- 1 teacher's desk
- 1 computer desk
- 2 bookshelves
- 2 storage cupboards

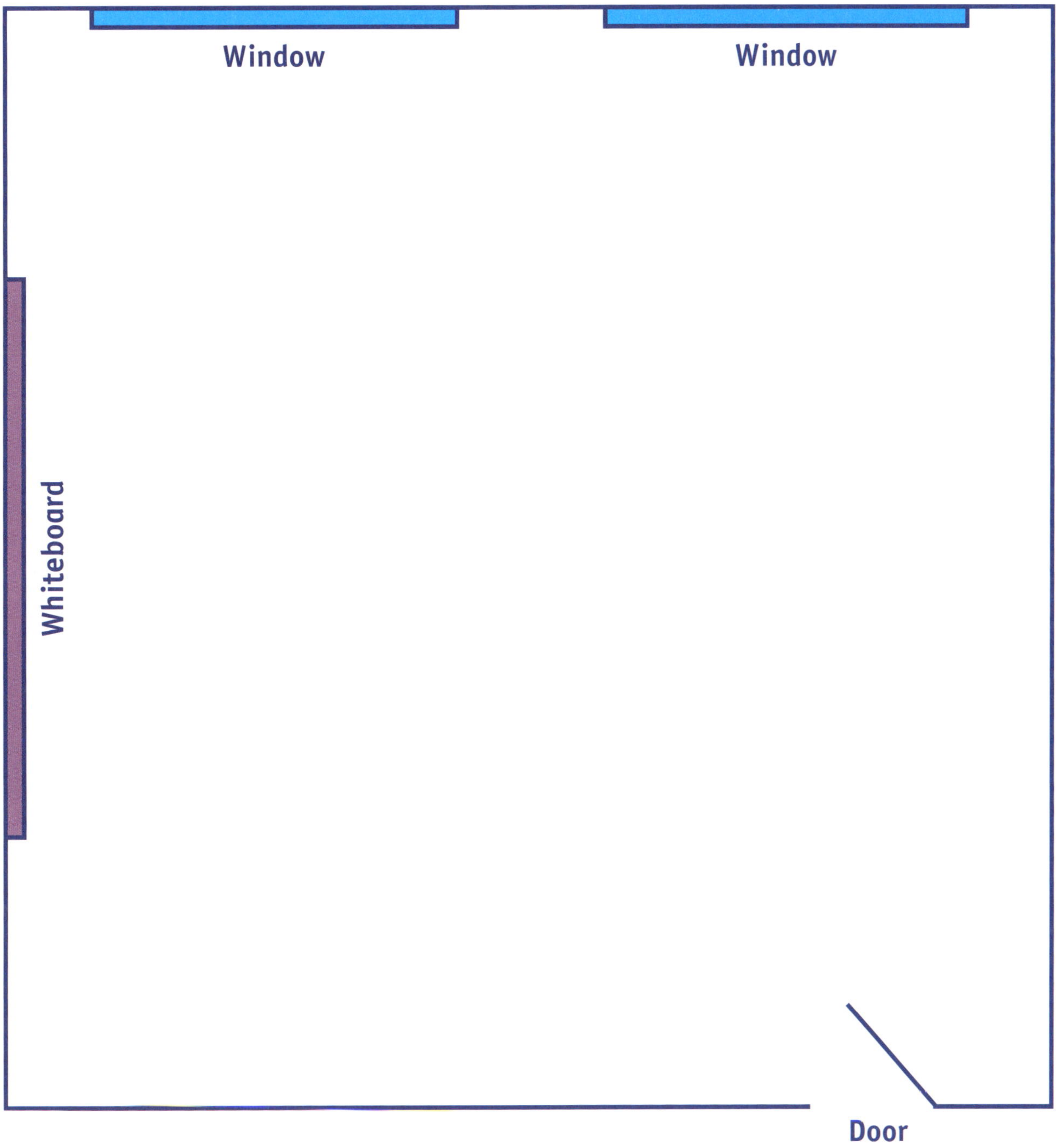

Window

Window

Whiteboard

Door

Unit 36 Position

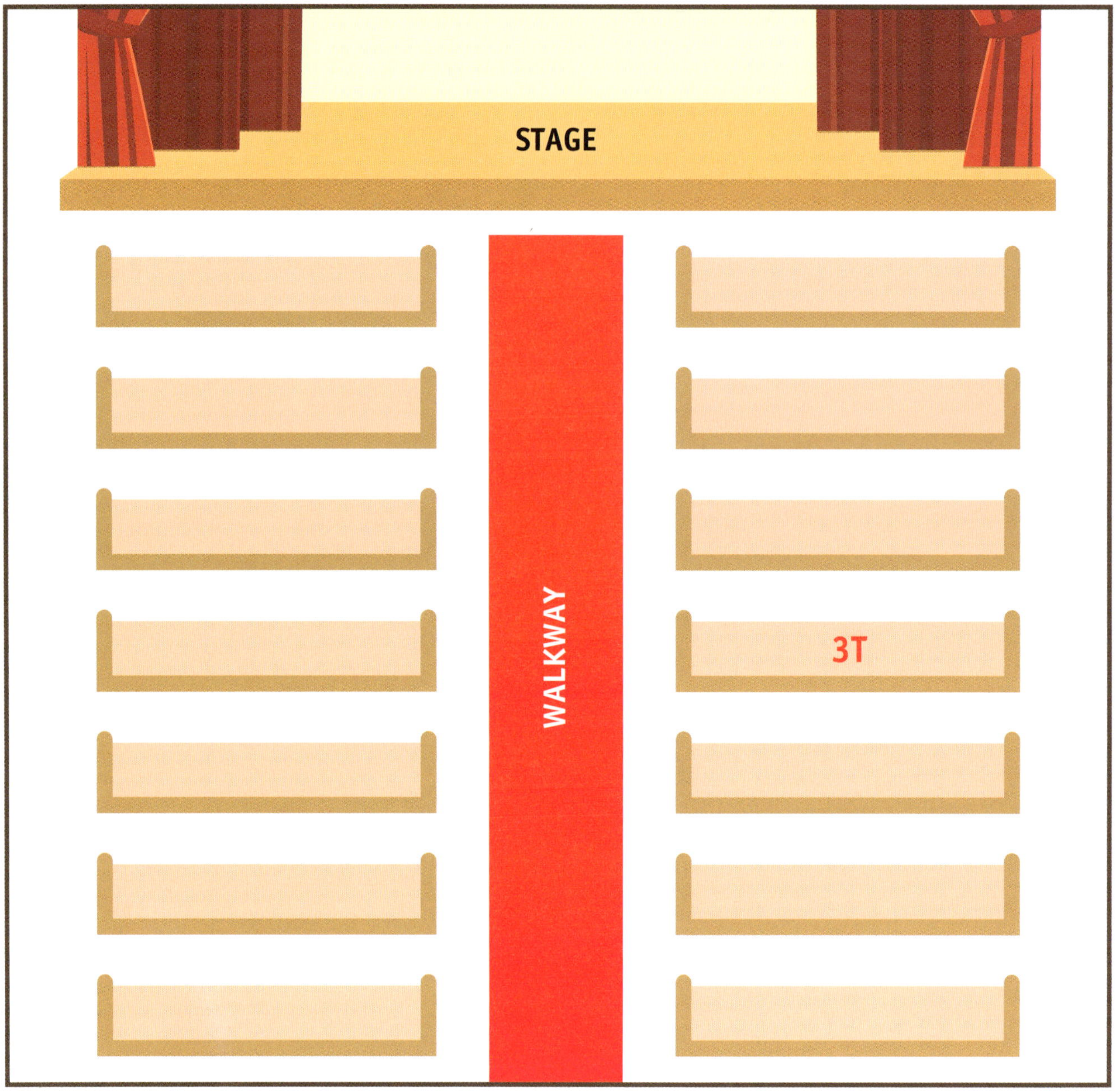

STAGE

WALKWAY

3T

At Boorloo Primary, there is an assembly every Friday. You are in class **3T**.

Use the clues below to label the assembly class chart.

- KG is at the front of the assembly on the left side.
- KJ is three classes in front of 3T.
- 4C is seated behind 3T.
- 5Z is seated behind 4C.
- 6A is seated behind 5Z.
- 1D is seated behind KJ.
- 3F is seated in front of 4B.
- 1N is seated behind KG.
- 2P is seated in front of 3T.
- 5M is seated to the left of 5Z.
- 4B is seated three classes behind 1N.
- 2C is seated to the left of 2P.
- 6G is seated behind 5M.

Space AC9M3SP02 interpret and create two-dimensional representations of familiar environments, locating key landmarks and objects relative to each other

Unit 36 Following directions

1 Write the moves made on the grid. Start at *.

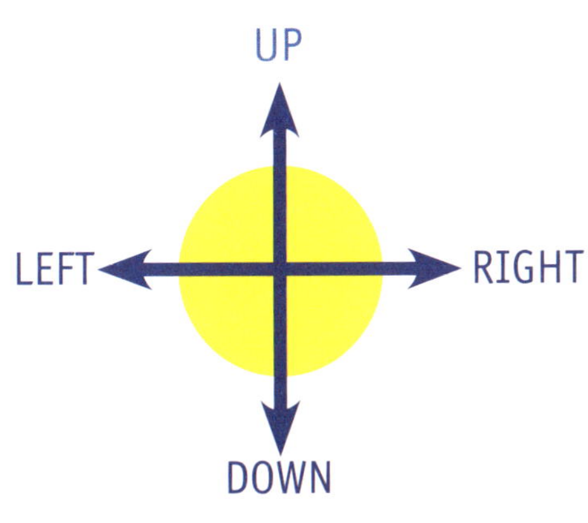

4 left
4

2 Start at * and follow the directions.

The first two moves have been done.

a 1 right   b 2 down   c 1 right
d 1 down   e 2 right   f 1 up
g 1 right   h 2 up   i 1 left
j 1 up   k 3 left   l 2 up
m 1 right   n 1 up   o 3 right
p 1 down

q What number have you drawn? ______

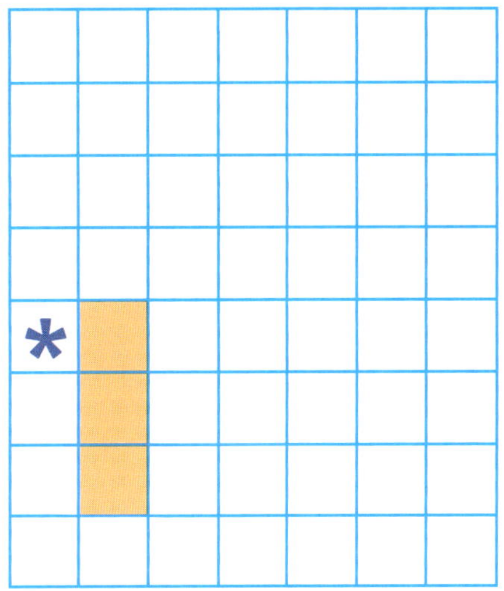

3 Ari has made a path for Caleb to follow. There is a mistake in the directions. Correct the mistake.

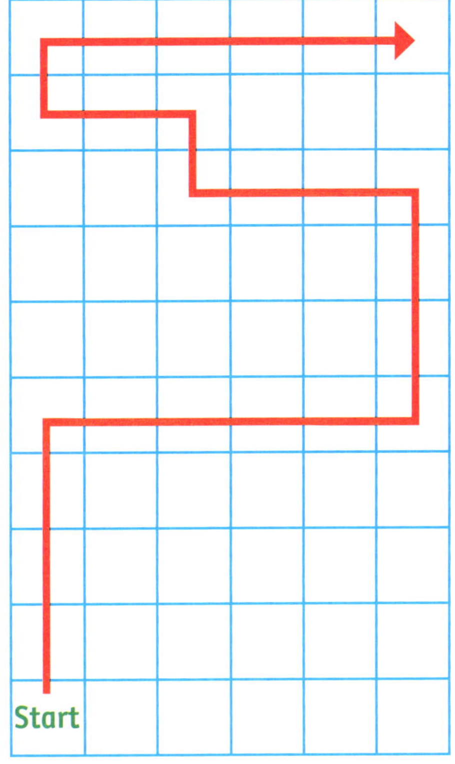

Start
Go up 4
Right 5
Up 3
Left 3
Down 1
Left 2
Up 1
Right 5

Problem solving

Zoo directions

1 Pia is lost at the zoo. The guide has these instructions to find her, starting from the entrance: Right 3, Down 4, Right 3, Up 3, Right 1.

Where is Pia? ____________

2 Start at the entrance. Write instructions to find each animal. Use the words: up, down, left, right.

a Elephant ______________________________

____

b Emu ______________________________

____

c Bat ______________________________

____

d Penguin ______________________________

____

I can solve problems by:

☐ understanding position ☐ following directions on a grid.

Space AC9M3SP02 interpret and create two-dimensional representations of familiar environments, locating key landmarks and objects relative to each other

Unit 36 Possible paths

Position

Larry's house

Larry

Larry likes to look at different things when he walks home.

1 Colour red his shortest way home.

2 Colour blue a very long way home.

3 Find another 4 ways Larry could walk home. Show each way in a different colour.

4 How many different ways do you think he can walk home? ☐

Mastery Checklist I can:
- ☐ make a floorplan for my classroom
- ☐ use descriptions to work out positions
- ☐ follow directions for a path on a grid
- ☐ draw paths on a map.

Unit 37 Possible outcomes

Main Course

Spaghetti

Fish

Hamburger

Chicken

Dessert

Ice-cream

Cheesecake

Fruit salad

*

1 This is the menu for Claire's Cosy Cafe.

a How many main courses are there? ________

b How many desserts are there? ________

c Hal ordered spaghetti. How many different desserts could he have with it? ________

d Ivy ordered ice-cream. How many different main courses could she have with it? ________

e List all possible combinations of meals.

Main Course	Dessert	Main Course	Dessert

2 Sam painted different shapes on some tiles and put them in a box.

a How many circles? ________

b How many triangles? ________

c How many squares? ________

Without looking, he took one tile out of the box.

d What shape was the most likely? ________________

e What shape was the least likely? ________________

Unit 37 Chance

1 a How many faces on a die? ________

b Which three faces are showing on this die? ______ ______ ______

c Which three faces are not seen? ______ ______ ______

d If the die is tossed, what numbers could be on top?

______ ______ ______ ______ ______ ______

e Is there any chance 7 dots could appear? ________

Why? ____________________

2 Match one of the words in the list with each of these statements.

a I will watch television tonight. ________

b It will snow today. ________

c The sun will rise in the morning. ________

d I will grow taller than my mother. ________

e I will see a horse on the road. ________

impossible
unlikely
likely
certain

3 a How many different outcomes are possible with this spinner? ________

b Do all shapes on this spinner have the same chance of being selected? ________

c Draw the shape that is most likely to be selected.

d Draw the shape that is least likely to be selected.

e True or false?

(cross) is more likely to be selected than (star). ________

(four-pointed star) has more chance of being selected than all the other shapes together. ________

f What is the chance that the arrow will point to (half-circle)? ________

Mastery Checklist I can:
- ☐ work out outcomes and combinations
- ☐ compare the likelihood of events happening
- ☐ understand impossible, unlikely, likely and certain.

Revision Term 4

1 4 7 1 8 p 140

Use the numbers to make:

a the largest number. ______

b the smallest number. ______

2 Round to the nearest hundred. p 141

a 468 ______ b 215 ______

3 Round to the nearest thousand. p 141

a 4695 ______ b 2398 ______

4 Write 'is less than' or 'is more than'. p 143

a 479 ______ 749

b 1280 ______ 1820

c 1005 ______ 1500

d 3600 ______ 3006

5 7426 is the same as: p 144

a ____ tens ____ ones

b ____ hundreds ____ tens ____ ones

c ____ thousands ____ ones

6 Write as many multiplication facts as you can for this group. p 148

______

______

7 What is the product of: p 149

a 3 and 7? ____ b 5 and 10? ____

8 Colour the multiples of 4. p 150

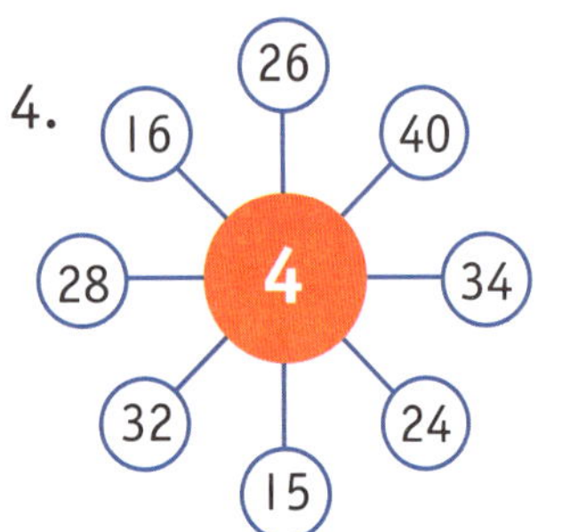

p 152

9 What do seven 5c stamps cost? ______

p 153

10 a $40 \div 10 =$ ____ b $18 \div 2 =$ ____

c $21 \div 3 =$ ____ d $55 \div 5 =$ ____

11

Divide the stars into: p 153

a 2 groups. 1 group = ____ stars

b 3 groups. 1 group = ____ stars

c 9 groups. 1 group = ____ stars

d 6 groups. 1 group = ____ stars

12 Write these from largest to smallest. p 157

$\frac{1}{4}, \frac{1}{8}, \frac{1}{2}, 1, \frac{7}{8}$ ______

13 Colour the fraction. p 157

a $\frac{1}{5}$ b $\frac{1}{2}$

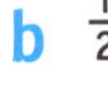

14 Circle the largest fraction in each pair. p 158

a $\frac{3}{5}$ $\frac{3}{10}$ b 1 $\frac{1}{10}$

c $\frac{1}{5}$ $\frac{1}{10}$ d $\frac{5}{5}$ $\frac{8}{10}$

Revision Term 4

15 How many centimetres in: p 160

a 2 m? ______

b $\frac{1}{2}$ m? ______

16 How many millimetres in: p 160

a 5 cm? ______

b 12 cm? ______

17 a Draw a line 38 mm long. p 160

b Measure this line in mm.

____

18 p 162

2 m

4 m

What is the length around the rectangle? ______

19 Draw a shape that has a length around the outside that is 10 cm. p 162

20 This magic machine changes numbers four times to make a sequence. p 168

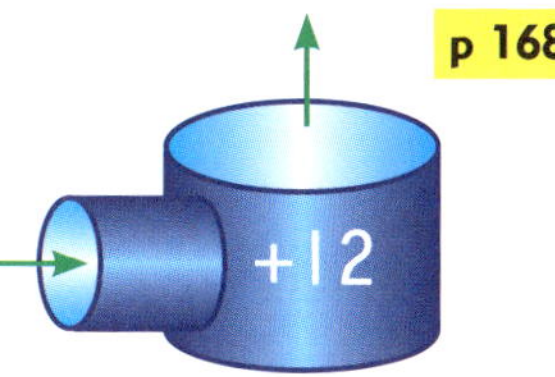

What will these numbers become?

a 7 ______, ______, ______, ______

b 25 ______, ______, ______, ______

These number sequences came out. What number went in?

c 28, 40, 52, 64 ______

d 42, 54, 66, 78 ______

21 True or false? p 169

a $6 \times 8 = 8 \times 6$ ______

b $32 \div 8 = 8 \div 32$ ______

22 p 170

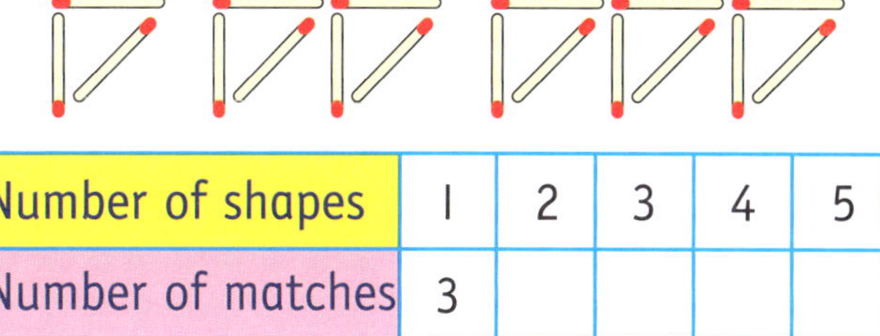

Number of shapes	1	2	3	4	5
Number of matches	3				

23 Draw: p 171

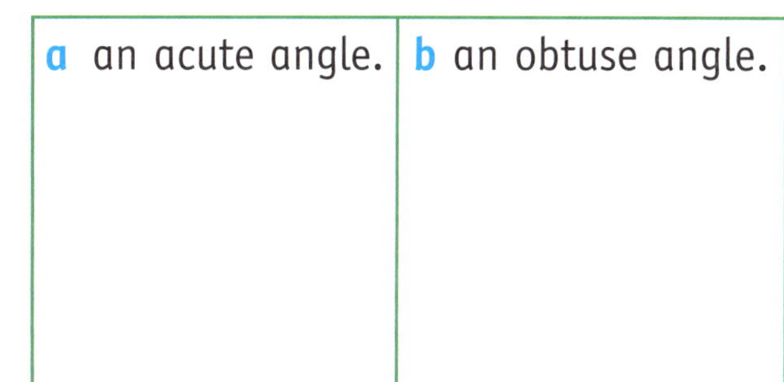

24 Write two places where you can see a right angle. p 172

a ______________________

b ______________________

25 p 173

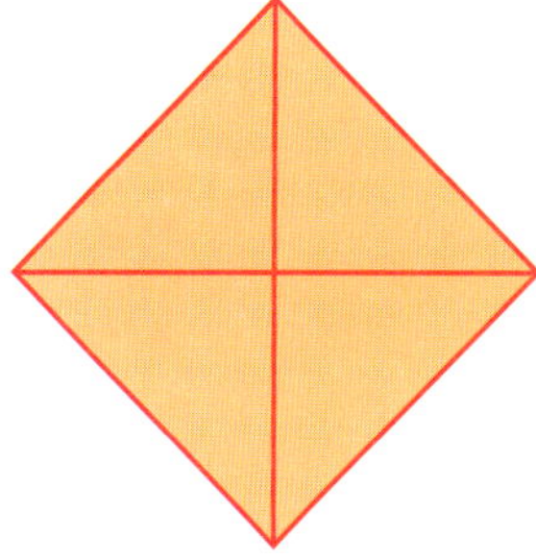

Which statement is true about this diagram? ______

a There are 8 right angles.

b There are 4 right angles and 8 acute angles.

c There are 8 right angles and 8 acute angles.

Revision Term 4

26 p 174

3:30	Finish school
3:45	Afternoon tea
4:00	Play with Jan
5:10	Homework
5:30	Have bath
6:00	Watch TV
6:35	Eat dinner

This is part of Bill's timetable for Monday.

a Is it am or pm? ________

b What did he do at $\frac{1}{4}$ to 4?

____

c How long did he watch TV? ________

d What else did he do between 5:30 and 6:00?

____

e How long was it from finishing school to eating dinner? ________

27 Draw an aerial view of your bedroom. p 175

28 Draw the path by following the directions. Start at * and move: p 177

a 1 up b 3 right

c 2 up d 1 left

e 2 up f 2 left

g 2 up h 2 left

i 2 down

29 Helen has cheese, tomato, ham and lettuce for sandwich making. What are the different two-filling sandwiches she can make? p 180

________ ________

________ ________

________ ________

________ ________

________ ________

________ ________

____

30 Sam wanted ham with one other thing. How many different sandwiches could he have? p 180

____